50
steps
to business
success

50 steps

to business success

ENTREPRENEURIAL LEADERSHIP
IN MANAGEABLE BITES

Peter M. Cleveland

ECW PRESS

Published by ECW PRESS
2120 Queen Street East, Suite 200, Toronto, Ontario, Canada M4E 1E2

NATIONAL LIBRARY OF CANADA CATALOGUING IN PUBLICATION DATA

Cleveland, Peter M.
50 steps to business success: entrepreneurial leadership in manageable bites / Peter M. Cleveland.
ISBN 1-55022-518-9
1. Entrepreneurship 2. Leadership. I. Title. II. Title: Fifty steps to business success
HD57.7.C54 2002   658.4   C2002-902198-7

Acquisition Editor: Emma McKay
Editors: Rob Lutz, Heather Bean
Design and typesetting: Tannice Goddard — Soul Oasis Networking
Production: Heather Bean, Emma McKay
Printing: Transcontinental
Cover design: Lisa Kiss Design

This book is set in Sabon and Zurich

The publication of *50 Steps to Business Success: Entrepreneurial Leadership
in Manageable Bites* has been generously supported by the Canada Council,
the Ontario Arts Council, and the Government of Canada through the
Book Publishing Industry Development Program. Canadä

DISTRIBUTION

CANADA: Jaguar Book Group, 100 Armstrong Avenue,
Georgetown, Ontario L7G 5S4

UNITED STATES: Independent Publishers Group, 814 North Franklin Street,
Chicago, Illinois 60610

EUROPE: Turnaround Publisher Services, Unit 3, Olympia Trading Estate,
Coburg Road, Wood Green, London N2Z 6T2

AUSTRALIA AND NEW ZEALAND: Wakefield Press, 1 The Parade West (Box 2266),
Kent Town, South Australia 5071

PRINTED AND BOUND IN CANADA

ECW PRESS
ecwpress.com

50 Steps to Business Success
*is dedicated to my wife and lifelong partner, Judy,
and to my two boys, Matthew and Adam,
who I hope will follow* 50 Steps to Business Success
*in managing their lives.
I love the three of you dearly.*

Contents

Figures Legend

III   Leading Core Competence

IV   Secrets to Revenue Growth

VIII Change: Evolution or Revolution?

IX Process Improvement: Stimulate or Stagnate

X Check Your Leadership Powertrain

XI The Oxen Are Slow, but the Earth Is Patient

Preface

50 Steps to Business Success: Entrepreneurial Leadership in Manageable Bites offers a systematic approach to leading a successful business. It's designed to bring order to a life that tends naturally toward chaos and, sometimes, even fear. Reaching deep into the experience of leaders of successful companies, it truly captures the heart and soul of every successful business. Each chapter reveals a series of sound business practices, or "manageable bites," each a stepping stone for the next and each dependent upon the other. The bites are proven truisms that guide the planning and leadership of a successful business. When they are applied with patience, discipline, consistency, and ethics, these proven practices pave the way to business success, one step at a time. More than that, they help to eliminate the panic that can be fatal to any business. Patience becomes the guide, manageable bites the discipline, and panic the victim of *50 Steps to Business Success*.

Successful leadership is founded on passionate vision, and that's where this book begins, followed by steps revealing time-tested keys to planning, people, revenue, products, service delivery, and financial stability. Techniques for eliminating barriers to profitable growth, change management, and business process improvement are explained and demonstrated as integral parts of success culture. Through it all, customer satisfaction is the successful leader's primary focus.

All steps lead to annual leadership reviews — the process of planning the leadership necessary for the next level of success. Add a code of ethics, a healthy dose of patience, and very clear communication, and you have *50 Steps to Business Success: Entrepreneurial Leadership in Manageable Bites.*

Peter M. Cleveland

Acknowledgments

This book would not have been possible without the help of many people. I would like to express my deep gratitude to those who were kind enough to take time to provide me with their insights, in particular, Robert Atkinson, retired chairman of GSI Lumonics Inc.; William Knight, past CEO of Credit Union Central of Canada; John Carter, senior partner of Ernst & Young LLP; and Steven Enman, professor of the Fred C. Manning School of Business, Acadia University.

Special thanks to my assistant, June Kemp, who spent many hours patiently sorting my thoughts to make this book possible.

Why This Book?

Throughout my 30 years of working with Ernst & Young clients to achieve their goals, I have met many talented leaders, all with one thing in common — an insatiable appetite for success. Regardless of the revenue size, number of employees, or geographic location of the business, every leader craves success.

Entrepreneurs constantly demand new and more sure-footed trails to success. They search for the simple, yet proven, leadership principles of other successful people. Many books have been written about business theory. Often they are intellectually stimulating but fail to link their abstract thinking with the practical application sought by those seeking success in the real business world. Entrepreneurs and leaders want to know what works. They desire a clear reference between leadership principles and actual practice. *50 Steps to Business Success: Entrepreneurial Leadership in Manageable Bites* provides that reference. The steps in this book are the principles of successful leaders I have met. Each one is articulated through actual cases to demonstrate its practical application. Although the book is written for entrepreneurs and future leaders, it will appeal to all those who feel a need to enhance their leadership skills.

Cases have been carefully selected to appeal to businesses of all sizes —

from small corner stores to large companies and everything in between. Leaders of large companies must be careful not to gloss over convenience-store cases. Likewise, small businesspeople should not rule out examples from larger companies. Size is irrelevant.

So for those striving for real business success, read on. I think you'll find this book a uniquely practical tool. I am proud of it. It is my gift to those entrepreneurs and leaders struggling for success — one step at a time.

How to Use This Book

The reader will find this book easier to digest and derive the greatest benefit if each chapter is viewed as a building block toward total leadership. Figure 1.0 depicts this process as a never-ending leadership assessment through planning, goal achievement, and executing action plans for every area of the business.

Leadership is an ever-strengthening process. From the completion of this annual activity comes knowledge that will strengthen leadership in the next cycle. Actual leadership cases are summarized and interpreted for each manageable bite, and referenced in the Appendix. This book is intended as a reference for your leadership issues as they arise — not as a one-time read.

50 Steps to Business Success
Entrepreneurial Leadership in Manageable Bites

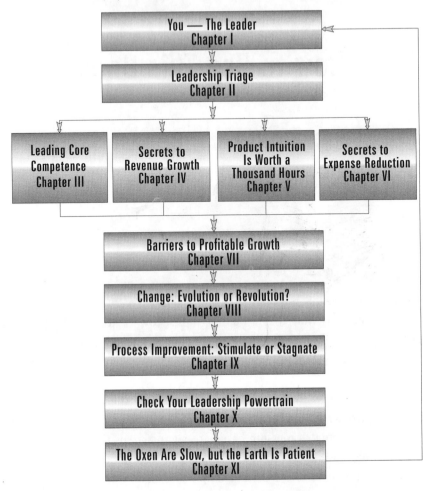

You — The Leader
Chapter I

Leadership Triage
Chapter II

Leading Core Competence
Chapter III

Secrets to Revenue Growth
Chapter IV

Product Intuition Is Worth a Thousand Hours
Chapter V

Secrets to Expense Reduction
Chapter VI

Barriers to Profitable Growth
Chapter VII

Change: Evolution or Revolution?
Chapter VIII

Process Improvement: Stimulate or Stagnate
Chapter IX

Check Your Leadership Powertrain
Chapter X

The Oxen Are Slow, but the Earth Is Patient
Chapter XI

Figure 1.0

1
You —
The Leader

Whether you manage a corner store, an international corporation, or a fishing trawler, you lead a business. As lord and master of your enterprise, you are the lightning rod for its every success and failure. You're the person in whom your bankers, suppliers, employees, and shareholders place their faith, and the one with the lump in the throat when payroll is in doubt. In other words, you attract the heat. Sound familiar? Then you're among those who have chosen the challenge of leadership and all it stands for — the quest for independence, financial security, and personal achievement. Whether you face the leadership challenge alone or flanked by advisors, its reward is always excitement, its penalty anxiety.

Leaders, according to dictionaries, are those who show the way by going first. To show the way, leaders must be capable of developing a vision and articulating it clearly to all stakeholders, both internal and external. They have courage not only to see and believe in the vision themselves, but to articulate it so others believe in it too. They have the passion to live the vision and to persuade others to live it also, in both good and bad times. They are determined to develop and drive business strategies to achieve their goals, and they have the discipline to ensure action plans to accomplish those strategies are implemented. They're tough, but compassionate. They are flexible in developing the processes and methods necessary to realize the vision. When others are down, leaders pick them up. When leaders are criticized, they listen. When they are praised, they give credit to their followers. They lead by example and have respect for others. They are fair and honest. Excellent leaders are also excellent communicators. They must be to reinforce their vision. They make people feel special when tough decisions are necessary, and they hurt when their people hurt. They always go the extra mile.

Success is an addiction, part of the DNA of leaders. If leadership was a sport, leaders would strive to outperform every competitor, even themselves. They live on the edge of risk and insist on negotiating life on their own terms. Anything less leaves them feeling unfulfilled.

Effective leaders know success comes from applying clear direction to real opportunities, not from fortuitous events. Fortuitous events do happen, but it's the ability to lead consistently that interests lightning rods. Systematic leadership encourages consistent results because, without it, leaders spend their time reacting to crises rather than leading success.

What makes a leader? Aside from the qualities already described, a leader is someone others are prepared to follow, even, as General Colin Powell puts it, if only out of curiosity. Whether leaders are born with the qualities to lead or leadership behavior is learned remains a long-standing debate. Neither position is completely true. Yes, you are born with a certain level of intelligence and personality to lead. What you do with it, though, is often a function of the environment in which you learn. We learn the social behavior that is necessary to gain leadership respect. We also learn the tools we need to manage effectively. The gray area is passion. Its existence depends upon your personality and your life experiences. Anxious personalities, for example, who measure everything by performance, may begin life with certain qualities to lead. If their formative years are unhappy or fraught with failure or a poor family environment, with no developmental encouragement, they may never have the confidence to display the passion to lead. Insecurity prevents their leading success. Conversely, leaders may develop a passion through positive formative years.

Two points are fundamental. First, successful leaders are passionate about their leadership. Second, even for leaders with passion, leadership development is a continuous learning process. Let's look at the traditional images of managers and leaders as outlined in Figure 2.1.

Many books have been written on leadership and managerial effectiveness. They tend to focus on the differences between leaders and managers. They stereotype leaders as creative people who think "outside the box" and do not manage detail well, and portray managers as less colorful people who must meet budgets and handle leaders. Such characterizations are myopic and misleading to the leaders of tomorrow because they do not address the growing need for successful leaders to be good managers — and vice versa. The information explosion, the impact of the Internet on business, and the increasing speed of change will force visionaries to be more directly involved with the daily implementation of their visions. Similarly, managers will be measured more and more by their ability to offer leadership ideas. Globalization and the empowerment of managers will force a closing of traditional gaps between leadership and managerial skills. Yes, there will always be people fulfilling only leadership or managerial functions. But as more traditionally managerial detail is handled by software, managers will be more frequently left to the task of leading human resources to grow sales and profit. They will develop vision as a demand of the new commercial era. Leaders, on the other hand, will not have the luxury of time to create a vision, obtain managerial buy-in, and wait for operations to catch up. They will want to drop directional change into a more receptive managerial group, which will be able to lead the rest of the organization to bring about better, faster, and more effective operational changes.

Contrasting Styles of Managers and Leaders

Traditional Manager	Leader
• controls business processes already in place	• encourages collective wisdom to develop improved business processes for the future
• uses managerial authority to force compliance with business rules	• encourages followers to share responsibility by offering team solutions
• a focused individual sufficiently bright and confident to make speedy decisions	• member of a team, shares power to deliberate the future direction of the business

Figure 2.1

Change will be institutionalized, and for a leader to be successful, he will have to encourage all his followers to be leaders too. There will be no time for division of leadership and managerial skills in the future. Consequently, *50 Steps to Business Success* crosses the traditional boundaries of leadership and management and, at times, interchanges the terminology. This will horrify traditional thinkers. But those who do not move in this direction will see their organizations decline as change comes at an even faster rate.

Let's explore.

BITE 1: DEVELOP A CLEAR VISION

A vision is your mental picture of future success. It's what you imagine your business to be in three, five, or ten years. What business do you see yourself in? What will your sales volume be? Products? Number of locations? Organization? Global integration? These questions figure prominently in the "mind's eye" of every business leader who struggles with the future. Your vision is heavily influenced by your values, ambitions, personality, and needs. A well-defined vision shows where your business is headed and defines your desires. It triggers a new direction for the organization and gives it meaning and purpose.

When it is properly articulated throughout an organization, a vision moves a business toward its actualization. A vision is the leader's definition of her own leadership. It's very personal, and it motivates the leader to project her passion and determination throughout the organization.

If vision is the end, then it is passion that drives leaders to develop goals, and then actions, to achieve that end. Visions come from open minds, not from those trapped inside old paradigms. They're built upon learning as much as upon the results the leader wants to see.

When a vision has been developed with the involvement of key members of an organization, it has a greater chance of becoming reality. It becomes a shared vision, and those responsible for its realization are more likely to adopt it. Since a vision always involves change, it will meet with organizational resistance if a leader does not share the process of developing it.

To lead your business without a vision is not leadership. At best, it encourages mediocrity. At worst, your business will fade away when competitors effectively implement their visions. And so, developing a clear vision is the first manageable bite if you are, or are about to become, a leader. Let's look at Hank Shepard's vision for his company, Atlantic Products Inc.

Atlantic Products Inc. is a public company that has manufactured paint for 31 years. Hank Shepard became president and chief executive officer of the $250 million company last year. The board of directors hired him to set a new direction for what had become a sleepy company that always made money, but wasn't growing in sales or market share.

Since he accepted the position, Hank had been building relationships internally to gain support for his leadership and knowledge about the company. His assistant gathered industry and competition data during the same period.

Atlantic operated from two locations on the eastern seaboard, retaining 780 employees. Sales occurred through direct selling, but had only increased an average of 6 percent per year during the last five years. The average increase for the industry was 12.6 percent for the same period. Hank took his four key executives off site for a weekend to study the industry, the company, and the future.

Hank wanted a clear picture of what the company should look like in five years. By Sunday afternoon the five executives had shook hands on the following components of a vision as outlined in Figure 3.1:

Atlantic Products
Components of a Vision

1.	A company with sales of $500 million.
2.	Industrial rather than household focus.
3.	An established and recognized brand.
4.	No-name branding to facilitate joint venture agreements.
5.	An elaborate network of distributors fanning the United States.
6.	Total employee headcount reduced to 600.

Figure 3.1

Hank had now developed a shared vision with his senior executives. It had become their vision — the first step to successful implementation. By doing so, he defined what his leadership would be about. Atlantic would shift its corporate culture from one of contentment with marginal growth to a dynamic, aggressive industrial paint supplier — a company reignited, one that would strive for growth and plant modernization.

Goals and action plans were then developed to move the company closer to that vision in each of the next five years.

BITE 2: KNOW YOUR LEADERSHIP STYLE

Leadership style is a leader's approach to people, events, and processes. It consists of his personal available assets to achieve his vision. Style is dependent upon the leader's motivation and personal make-up. Make-up can be influenced by a number of personal and environmental factors. Figure 4.1 depicts the major influences on our personal make-up, motivation, and leadership style.

We are driven by our motivation to accomplish objectives. The extent and complexity of those objectives manifest themselves from a cauldron of situations and the way our personality addresses those situations: with what level of maturity, at what acceptance of risk, and with what learning through education and experience.

There are numerous leadership styles, but most may be placed in the four major categories outlined on Figure 5.1. The effectiveness of any style is situational. Dictators, for example, perform well in military leadership roles, but lack the warmth to lead community volunteers. Benevolent dictators, too soft for military duty, lead business well when a firm hand and occasional smile motivate employee performance. Coaches are task-oriented, but tend to lead through growth and development of people. They seek to leave followers stronger than they found them. When difficult decisions are required, they become benevolent dictators until the mission is complete; then they return to coaching. When operations are exceptional, they become missionaries, giving more care to followers. Missionaries are usually not successful in business over the long term because their focus is often limited to humanitarian goals. It is only a matter of time before change forces a tough new direction, the discipline of a stray employee, or the ability to use the word no. In such difficult situations, they do not lead well. Those who follow missionaries do so out of faith rather than out of recognition of authority or vision.

Leaders may be motivated by profit, sales growth, or employee morale. Those who measure everything by profit may be dictators who demand profit or death. Those focusing on revenue growth are often motivators who continuously coach employees to new heights. Leaders concerned only with morale will often tend to be oversupportive to achieve happiness. Regardless of style, a leader's motivational techniques are always influenced by his experiences — some controllable, others not.

Controllable experiences include leadership techniques, business knowledge, and human and financial resources. Each becomes an asset for success. Uncontrollable experiences are unplanned crises such as key decision-maker resignations, competitor product advantages, and acts of God. Leaders must face customers, bankers, suppliers, employees, and shareholders with all of their personal experiences, whether controlled or not.

While many factors influence success, personal make-up is often the least understood. Leaders may have the best education, yet lack courage to lead. Others with 20 years of leadership experience have egos that prevent them from learning new techniques. Moods affect our ability to lead as well. When we react poorly to others, we lead poorly. When our spirits are high, leadership skills are usually at their peak.

Knowing your style is more important than your style itself. Awareness of personal strengths and weaknesses are prerequisites to understanding your limitations to lead a business. If you fail to understand yourself, it's unlikely you will successfully lead others. Determine the style that is likely to be most effective for the business. If it's your style, you are the optimum. If it is not, then you need to find the skills required to make the management team successful.

The DNA of Leadership Style

Figure 4.1

Major Leadership Styles

Style	Characteristics	Effective Application
Dictator	• gives orders • no emotion given to or tolerated from employees • one-way communication • little concern for people • motivates by command	• military • emergency business action • natural disasters
Benevolent Dictator	• directive • does not push employees to extreme • listens to feedback, but only from those he or she grants privilege • some concern for people • motivates by cause	• labor-intensive mass business • emergency measures • government
Coach	• encourages full participation • sets vision for management to build • mentors • rewards • substantial concern for people growth • motivates by vision and support	• building business growth • community affairs • charities
Missionary	• concern only for people • no direction • provides comfort • motivates by care	• humanitarian organizations • government policy • religion

Figure 5.1

Know when to compensate for yourself through other people. Manage your personal make-up well and you'll tend to lead well. Gerry Leftson of Leftson Industries Ltd. highlights the bite.

Gerry manages the family's small foundry, which produces several hundred tons of steel products a year and employs 250 people. He graduated third in his business class, demonstrating a firm grasp of management and analytical techniques.

During the first five years of Gerry's leadership, sales grew slowly. Consistent growth was easy to manage, and manage Gerry did, playing a significant role in virtually all daily planning, marketing, and purchasing for the company. Then, in year seven, the pace increased. A Leftson competitor holding 18 percent market share fell into financial difficulty and filed for bankruptcy protection.

When Leftson successfully landed the competitor's market share, Gerry's plant capacity was stretched. Space was at a premium, forcing production rescheduling to cope with escalating demand. Virtually overnight, Leftson was transformed from a small business into a medium-sized one. As a result, the company became much more difficult to manage.

By year eight, Gerry fell victim to stress. Worrying about his business most of the time, he suffered from sleepless nights and enjoyed life much less — even though his leadership effectively sustained Leftson's growth. Seeing a major change in her husband, Gerry's wife urged him to seek advice from his father's business partner, Hector Goddard. Hector's observations were simple.

Gerry's business is small by steel industry standards. But though it had grown in both size and complexity, he still managed it as a small business, insisting on planning daily operations, meeting key customers, and negotiating raw material purchases. It was simply too much. Hector's advice was to hire a plant manager and a salesperson.

Gerry didn't understand his personal make-up or style until it almost cost him his health. His benevolent dictator style and everyday involvement worked well when business was simple, but not when it reached a certain level of complexity. During rapid growth, his style was not workable.

Gerry was lucky. Not everyone is fortunate enough to have a Hector Goddard to open his eyes. Many burn out first and lose their businesses as a result. Hector helped Gerry examine his leadership style and make adjustments to avoid burnout.

While Gerry's story illustrates the problems with micromanaging, Alfie Saunders's demonstrates the possible effects of dictatorship.

Alfie's Repairs consisted of eight automobile repair centers generating $6.8 million in sales with 52 employees. Each repair center was managed by its most senior mechanic, who reported directly to Alfie. At the beginning of each planning year, Alfie distributed sales and profit expectations to each location manager. Managers were expected to accept Alfie's targets at face value. He lost his temper if anyone challenged his goals. One year, frustrated because he hadn't met profit plans, Alfie was determined to achieve success — or heads would roll!

Quarterly management meetings were held to review financial results. Those failing to meet the targets earned Alfie's ridicule in front of the others. By the third quarter, each manager had endured enough abuse. Following the meeting, one by one, each manager turned in the keys to his location and resigned. Alfie now had no one to open stores the next day!

Alfie Saunders is one of many leaders who believe business goals are achieved by force. Bewildered when everyone quit, he did not understand the impact of his leadership style. Rather than ask managers to contribute to the planning process by preparing store budgets, he dictated acceptance of his own plan. His poor people skills deprived him of people to lead.

Given the importance of knowing your leadership style, one more case study is in order.

William Kraftstar owns and manages Kraftstar Homes. A manufacturer of cottage homes, Kraftstar employs 73 people to sell $13 million of precut log homes each year. Most of the 73 staff members have been employed by Kraftstar since its inception, 14 years ago.

Each morning, William walks through the plant, talking and joking with his employees. Godfather to 28 of their children, William believes employees are extensions of his own family.

Every employee is on a profit-sharing program. Everyone is encouraged to offer productivity improvement suggestions. When productivity and profit targets are exceeded, even the newest employee receives an extra monthly paycheck.

Monthly meetings set the number of cottage packages to be delivered from production the following month. Setting ever higher productivity goals becomes a game and a challenge for the production team. In almost every meeting, targets adopted are tougher than William believes possible. But his employees enjoy setting challenging goals — and exceeding them. Full employee participation encourages higher productivity and greater financial rewards for everyone at Kraftstar Homes.

William is a coach. Unlike Alfie, he encourages employee participation in both management and profit sharing. Teamwork generates unusual levels of loyalty, productivity, and profit — certainly greater than Alfie Saunders experienced.

The leaders of Leftson Industries, Alfie's Repairs, and Kraftstar Homes demonstrate significant differences in leadership style, with equally varying results. If you fail to understand your style, it will be impossible to foresee your effect on people and the business — and thus impossible to lead effectively.

BITE 3: KNOW YOUR RISK TOLERANCE

Risk is a tantalizing lover. On one hand, you negotiate every decision to minimize it; on the other hand, you're seduced by its temptation for greater gain. It's what you measure before you begin a business, and agonize over before every decision thereafter. It is one of the most potent ingredients in your personal make-up cauldron.

Risk tolerance is very personal, as individual as personality itself. What matters is how you reconcile the risk you are prepared to accept with the actual risk required to achieve goals. It means truly understanding your tolerance threshold, then adjusting goal aggressiveness to match. Sound simple? It's not. Few people ever achieve *risk peace of mind*. Yet every soul who leads a business strives to find that perfect balance.

Risk acceptance is affected very much by the people you lead. If employees are well trained and perform with excellence, leadership is more comfortable. You have more confidence to accept risk. If your followers are weak, your energies will be depleted just ensuring they meet expectations. You'll have little energy left to manage new risk. The stronger the team contribution, the greater a leader's tolerance for risk. The case of Laura Harding and Luxury Homes Ltd. illustrates this point.

When they graduated from university, Laura and two friends started an interior design firm. At the time, there were no designers for the expensive housing market in the city, so sales increased at a faster rate than expected. With Laura's penchant for business detail and finance, Margot's for creativity, and Ann's for sales and marketing, the three formed a strong team. When they considered additional outlets, Laura studied the demographics, cost of premises, and break-even volume. Natural team dynamics led Ann to project sales volume, while Margot examined suitable design products.

When it came time to open the south-end store, management dynamics changed. Margot strenuously argued against opening, fearing sales would not support a store. Ann insisted that more than sufficient potential volume existed for a profitable outlet. Laura found herself in the position of referee. She had data to support the decision and a proven blueprint from previous successes. Why not just go ahead?

The three were deadlocked. Then, Laura had an idea. The three spent a day in the south end: they lunched at a local café and drove through neighborhoods looking at age, style, and size of homes, street by street. At the end of the day, they weren't sure the number of wealthy, aging homes would sustain profitable business volumes. Surprised at their own uncertainty, they postponed the final decision one week. When the week ended, they all said no to the opening.

What happened here? Margot stepped away from her normal creative role and into sales and marketing when she couldn't accept the level of risk associated with the new store. To her, risk was not in balance. When her level of risk tolerance was rejected by the other two, she rebelled, forcing a new risk balance for the team and perhaps avoiding a major financial disaster in the process. Laura and Ann were persuaded away from a risky opportunity and toward preventing a loss.

The pursuit of opportunity versus the prevention of loss is the fulcrum of risk tolerance! It is a matter of balance. Wholesale opportunity pursuit indicates high tolerance of risk. Total focus on loss prevention indicates low tolerance. Everything is a matter of degree.

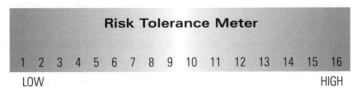

Figure 6.1

The risk tolerance meter in Figure 6.1 demonstrates degrees of risk acceptance. Leaders scoring 1 are completely risk averse. Found mostly in government positions or business maintenance roles, these people have trouble deciding on lunch. At the other extreme, leaders scoring 16 will play at the $1,000 blackjack table with their retirement funds. Most leaders are somewhere between 7 and 10 on the scale — prepared to take calculated risks at certain levels. In the Luxury Homes example, Ann demonstrated the highest tolerance, probably at level 8 or 9. Margot would be the lowest at 4 or 5, and Laura would be somewhere in between. Team risk balance benefited the business. The strengths and weaknesses of each individual balanced the others. Enough risk tolerance exists for growth, but not reckless growth. If Margot was the only leader, Luxury Homes may not have opened its first store. Ann's overanxious risk tolerance may have eventually gotten the company into difficulty.

Leadership changes when team risk tolerance alters. Declines result in shifts toward more conservative decisions; increases lead to more aggressive strategies. Total loss prevention tolerance, between 1 and 5, often brings about stagnation. These businesses do not fulfill their potential. Leaders with risk scores higher than 10 are many times more likely to lose because they gamble. A couple of examples will illustrate both ends of the scale. First, let's look at Aquabar Inc. and its conservative principal John Lavender.

John started commercial welding in 1967 with $50,000 capital, a $100,000 loan from his brother, and a bank line of credit for a similar amount. Four entrepreneurs earned a living during the first five years. Sales grew from zero at the start to $837,000 in year five, when John hired more welders to meet growth demands. He managed three locations and consistently banked $53,000 each year. He was a long way from his childhood days of poverty in Poland, and better off than any of his friends from the old country.

Business continued to flourish through the years. He avoided expansion beyond the original three outlets, choosing instead to apply cash flow to retire corporate debts ahead of schedule. He thought there was little point taking more risk, remembering the effects of the Depression and World War II on his father's business.

In his 28th year of business, he decided to sell the operation so he and his wife could travel. Now their daughters were attending university. A friend urged him to hire a business adviser to appraise the value of his enterprise to establish a selling price. Much to his horror, it was valued at $500,000, only half the value he had projected!

By maintaining a small, conservative business, he had limited future profits, thereby reducing the value of the company to potential purchasers. Now, at age 56, he had little working time left to save for retirement. For 28 years, his pride had prevented him from seeing the weakness in his strategy. Doomed to additional years of hard work to fund retirement, John was forced to let go of his dream of leisure and travel. It was too late.

John lacked the luxury of the management team enjoyed by Laura. Without a partner to act as a sanity check, he lacked risk tolerance balance and his business failed to meet his own expectations — a leader's worst nightmare. As is always the case with poorly managed risk, the penalty is anxiety.

Other leaders can be too aggressive, and their pain is acute when excessive risk leads to a financial crisis. Buildcorp Construction makes the point:

Buildcorp successfully constructed four- and six-unit apartment buildings for various investor groups. During its 15-year history, investors never caused cash flow problems with late progress payments. The company always experienced a relatively smooth cycle from contract signing to completion. After several years of profit, Buildcorp decided it could make greater profits building a proposed 20-story office complex next to city hall. The project was large enough to generate the profit of three apartment buildings. There is no difference between building an office building and an apartment building, the company's leaders thought. Construction is construction, right?

Wrong! Buildcorp had no experience with large subcontractors and their tendency to add scheduling problems. A building foundation normally requiring a week to form, pour, and set managed to separate before completion. This meant extra wages not originally budgeted in the fixed price contract. Cost overruns drew additional funds from an already stretched bank line of credit. The company's financial house all but fell when the project owner delayed a progress payment by 30 days. The company was saved only by a last-minute financial arrangement with its banker.

Buildcorp, motivated by greed, didn't bother to anticipate the particularities of high-rise construction. Risk levels were beyond balance for the company. Shareholder equity, accumulated during 15 successful years, was eliminated and company survival threatened — all due to just one contract.

Buildcorp leadership fell into John Lavender's trap. Neither had support networks to balance risk assessments. Both suffered from leadership loneliness — one of the greatest threats to entrepreneurial success.

BITE 4: CHOOSE A SOUL MATE

One of the most effective ways to balance your own risk tolerance comes through consulting with an independent sounding board — a soul mate. A soul mate provides a sanity check, offering reflection before major decisions are taken. A lonely decision-maker travels many rationalization paths and often becomes so confused in the process that he's capable of convincing himself of just about anything. Without a soul mate as a sounding board, such a leader is also often consumed by fear.

Evidence of the value of soul mates is plentiful in the business world.

Had Gerry Leftson not had his father's partner as his soul mate, he could very well have ended up dead from overwork. Laura Harding and her partners in Luxury Homes Ltd. acted as soul mates for each other, and together they prevented a potentially serious business error. John Lavender managed Aquabar Inc. without a soul mate and he paid a dear price. The advantage is clear. Leaders with soul mates have a safety valve built into their decision-making processes. Although it doesn't guarantee success, consultation at least forces them to pause and consider every aspect of the risk. It is a logic check with someone who doesn't carry the emotional baggage of the decision. Soul mates are often able to provide objective risk assessments when leaders are flummoxed.

It's true that there are successful people who do not consult, though our increasingly complex business world places them clearly in the minority. They are, as John Lavender discovered, lonely. Some are proud, and view consulting as a weakness. Successful people, though, realize that it is the failure to consult that is the weakness. Others see consultation as too time-consuming. These leaders are the most difficult to convert because they can't seem to see the link between sober second opinions and bottom lines. Decisions per second is their primary measurement, so they see time spent on second opinions as impeding their productivity. As we've seen, the reverse is often true.

A compatible soul mate will possess characteristics special to you. Knowledge and experience are givens. Successful soul mate candidates will also have a level of risk tolerance that is complementary to yours — but not too complementary. You shouldn't match government bond investors with penny stock adventurers. Mutual respect is always a prerequisite. Those who are too conservative, though, should be exposed to more liberal mates to encourage more balanced decision making.

On the other hand, if you assess your nature as slightly left of a river-boat gambler, a more conservative adviser will help keep you in a harness. You're trying to balance your risk tolerance, not reinforce it. Soul mates should average your risk tolerance up or down, whichever is necessary to balance your aggressiveness in goal pursuit. Nothing more, nothing less. They cannot, and should not, make decisions for you. Remember, you are a leader seeking risk balance, not refuge. Refuge is abdication of your role as leader. And that's not leadership.

You will instinctively recognize the person most suitable to be your soul mate. Finding them is another matter. Look around you; select the most successful people, those with skills you admire. If they possess a risk tolerance to balance yours, they're soul mate candidates. If you have no obvious candidates, you must continue to sift through personal contacts, and meet new ones, until you identify the most appropriate person.

Identification of a soul mate does not guarantee their willingness to assume the role. Personality match and comfort come into play. There is a certain time commitment. Sufficient trust for an open discussion on any matter is the true test. Considerable trial and error may be necessary. But don't despair. You must choose wisely, not quickly. Lunar Holidays Inc. provides an excellent example of what can happen on the search.

Julie Francis operates a travel agency in a city of eight million people. Blessed with six commercial accounts, Julie manages Lunar Holidays Inc. at a high profit level compared to her competition in the City Center Shopping Complex. Julie has always been frightened of managing the business alone, especially during difficult air rate negotiations and frequent bouts of tight cash flow.

She read a brochure recently offering management tips for small owner-managed businesses. As she scanned the document, her eye caught a recommendation for corporate soul mates as a sounding board for management ideas and decisions. The idea was appealing.

She discussed the concept of soul mates with her husband who worked for an air cargo company. He suggested his own boss for the role and, when Julie agreed, invited him and his wife to dinner. During the evening Julie seized an opportunity to discuss the possibility of a soul mate role with him, but felt uneasy with the discussion.

He appeared too aggressive for her, encouraging multiple agency locations around the city. Julie was uncomfortable with the risk, especially considering the current excess industry capacity. She believed a number of agencies would close as airlines downsized further. She truly couldn't reconcile her risk tolerance with his.

She discussed it with Jurg Heller, a friend in an airline business center. Jurg listened carefully to Julie's assessment of her husband's boss. They talked for hours about Julie's desire to grow the agency. As time passed, it became obvious Julie had found her corporate soul mate in the last person she expected — a friend. Although Jurg was not as experienced in business as her husband's superior, he possessed the appropriate risk tolerance and temperament to help her reach decisions comfortably.

The next day she approached Jurg to be her soul mate. Much to her surprise, he declined, saying he didn't want the responsibility for her business future. Julie was totally demoralized and turned to her husband for consultation.

They talked extensively about her business. Julie's inability to find a soul mate actually brought her closer to her husband. His encouragement strengthened her self-confidence and decision-making ability. In the final analysis, Julie's husband became her business soul mate.

Julie's scenario teaches us to take time to find and build a soul mate relationship. Next to a lifelong personal relationship, it's the most important one you'll ever have. It is only a coincidence that Julie's lifelong partner also became her business soul mate.

Leadership without a soul mate is lonely, and loneliness is often likened to a fear of darkness. When alone, your decision-making abilities may become paralyzed as you revisit the same rationalizations again and again. Paralysis becomes anxiety. Anxiety becomes panic. And panic translates into one of two results: leaders either pounce on quick solutions or opt for the status quo. Most often, neither choice achieves the optimum result. At worst, they fail. At best, they stagnate. Other leaders aren't paralyzed by fear but by pride. They choose to remain in the darkness because they aren't prepared to accept help from a potential soul mate. While not as acute as panic, pride can create some dreadful results of its own. Guido's Pizza makes the point.

Guido owned and managed 18 take-out pizza stores with sales of $1.6 million, and with total net income in excess of $430,000 per year, he was satisfied with the financial performance of the business.

Cousin Hugo also owned and managed a similar company of 14 stores. His total net income exceeded $563,000, in excess of $130,000 more than Guido — with fewer stores.

Hugo constantly pursued Guido to discuss common business matters and believed that comparing notes would strengthen both businesses. Guido didn't feel he needed help from his cousin, even though Hugo earned more and did not compete in the same area. Seeking advice from his younger cousin was unthinkable. Being the older businessman, Guido thought, he must be stronger.

At a family get-together, Hugo suggested they combine buying power to purchase pizza ingredients at lower prices. By reducing the average cost per pizza in both companies, they would each prosper. Hugo also whispered his intention to reduce quantity of toppings by 5 percent and increase prices of larger pizzas by a similar amount — further increasing gross margins.

Guido rejected the advice, continuing his historical purchasing, recipe, and pricing strategies. When financial results were tallied the next year, Guido's net income declined to $398,000 while Hugo's increased to $610,000 — with four fewer stores!

Guido's stubborn resistance to a soul mate cost him an opportunity for profit improvement. His profit declined while Hugo's increased. Pride denied him a sanity check for a more cost-effective operation. Lost profits, in excess of $212,000, was the price.

Earl Dawson offers us a final case study on soul mates:

Earl Dawson, owner and manager of Earl's Taxi, operated a fleet of 148 cars, 75 owned personally. All remaining 73 cars were leased directly by their drivers, who paid variable stand fees based on the number of calls. Current revenues approximated $110 per week per driver.

Over seven years, stand expenses had increased and exceeded the $110 charged to the drivers. Earl's accountant advised him to increase fees to $150 per week.

Earl was worried that his accountant's advice would result in drivers refusing to work, and discussed the matter with Art Risling, a fellow member of a local investment club and small businessman. Art probed for details about his operations and discovered expenses had increased 20 percent during the past three years, while the number of fares per driver per day declined — leaving him with $110 per week per driver. What Earl thought was rising costs was, in fact, a driver productivity problem. Customer pickup delays were causing volume declines, and hence no increase in variable revenue, even though meter rates had increased.

Earl investigated driver shift habits and learned that a number of his employees met for coffee throughout the day. Coffee time meant lost fares and lower volume for Earl.

Art suggested two approaches to the problem. Charge the $40 cost increase only and risk losing drivers, or charge $40 and apply it to an incentive pool, from which refunds of $20 would be given to those who increased their number of fares by 30 percent. Option one forces everyone to pay for inefficiency while option two creates an incentive to improve fare volume. If accomplished, volume increases would increase both stand fees and income for productive drivers, while penalizing those who failed to improve. Earl believed option two would encourage the desired behavior. Within eight months, stand fees rose to $155.

By assuming the role of soul mate, Art Risling led Earl to a better conclusion. On his own, Earl had concluded inflation was his only problem. With Art, he discovered that, in fact, stand revenue didn't keep pace because of low productivity. Soul mate involvement also led to the choice of a reward system over penalties.

BITE 5: BREAK MAJOR OBJECTIVES INTO SMALLER GOALS

Planning goals is intimidating because pressure to succeed frightens people. No one likes to fail. But sometimes failure doesn't come from an inability to do the work to reach a goal. Rather, it comes from setting unrealistic goals in the first place.

Not surprisingly, in the world of business, goal magnitude is a frequent cause of failure. For example, planning to increase production 25 percent in one quarter is too ambitious. Similarly, improving gross product margin by 52 percent in one year may be impossible. Here, goal failure occurs at the moment the goal is set, not when actions are implemented to reach it.

The 25 percent production increase is an objective, not a goal. It is a longer-term aim that must be broken into smaller, more manageable goals in order to be approached with any kind of confidence. Continuing the example, it may be possible to increase production by 3 percent during the first quarter if certain production line procedures are improved, and perhaps a further 6 percent in quarter two if additional productivity training is available to production people. The purchase of modern machinery in the third quarter may increase production by an additional 10 percent and revised production scheduling in quarter four may yield further gains of 6 percent. By year end, production will have increased by 25 percent through the achievement of four separate goals. Converting a 25-percent production increase objective into four goals over a slightly longer period creates a concentrated focus that yields results.

Smaller, more specific, goals lend themselves to specific actions. Larger, less-defined, objectives make specific action difficult, as the lack of focus leads to decision paralysis. So, why do certain leaders prefer general objectives rather than specific goals? Human nature.

Specific goals provide leaders, and others, with trails to measure performance. The more general the objective, the easier it is to claim success when it has not been achieved. Confusing? Not really. Leaders with a number of smaller goals laying out a trail to success are exposed to accountability everywhere along the trail. Unaccomplished goals attract attention and leadership follow-up. Large, general objectives, on the other hand, leave room for creative excuses when the desired outcome is not achieved. In the end, leaders with more focused goals generally enjoy greater success. Let's look to Pot Kiln Ltd. for our case study on point.

Pot Kiln Ltd. was incorporated in 1983 by three women whose children had grown up and left home. Lisa Moll, Beth Shale, and Irma Cummings each wanted to put their pottery-making skills to a test and use their newfound freedom to become entrepreneurs. Lisa is the financial manager, Beth creates new designs, and Irma is responsible for production. Each year they prepare a business plan, which becomes Lisa's agenda for monthly informal management meetings.

Sales were $600,000 in 1987, generating income of $17,000 for each shareholder. Lisa and Irma were satisfied with this income level because their husbands enjoyed high-income professions. Beth was unhappy. Her husband had died two years earlier, leaving her with only a small life insurance settlement.

During the 1988 business planning meeting, Beth argued for an increase in targeted sales revenue of $300,000 to a revenue goal of $900,000 — a 50-percent increase. This would allow her to double her income from the company. Although doubtful it could be achieved, Lisa and Irma agreed to Beth's goal.

Throughout 1988, each shareholder sold aggressively, encouraging additional pottery sales through price reductions with volume thresholds. Volume increases did occur, but they knew even before year-end accounting was complete that they hadn't achieved the $900,000 sales goal.

Financial statements revealed an increase from $600,000 to $750,000, but volume discounts decreased gross margins by 7 percent. Net income available for each shareholder amounted to $19,000, far from Beth's personal objective to double her income.

Was Pot Kiln Ltd. a success or failure? After all, sales did increase by 25 percent and shareholders' income climbed by almost 12 percent. Admirable progress, unless your goal is to double your income from $17,000 to $34,000. Then, it seems like a failure. It wasn't enough to have a company objective to increase sales by 50 percent. The magnitude of Beth's personal objective demanded a detailed trail of smaller company goals to be developed and implemented. Working harder at traditional sales plans failed to produce the desired results. Let's look at what they did in 1989.

During 1989 planning, they met with their accountant to determine how to improve performance. Reviewing 1988 performance, he suggested replacing their one major revenue objective with 12 less ambitious monthly goals as outlined in Figure 7.1.

For each goal, specific action plans were devised and responsibilities assigned to each shareholder. Much to their delight, sales increased to $825,000, all at normal gross margins. Even though the $900,000 sales target had not been met, above-average sales growth had been sustained without giving away margins. Shareholder incomes grew from $19,000 to $27,000 that year.

Pot Kiln's 1989 objectives were broken into a series of smaller ones, providing a trail for each shareholder to follow. A new goal each month encouraged a more methodical approach to reaching the overall sales objectives. Achieving each monthly goal brings the shareholders another step closer to realizing their overall objective.

Pot Kiln
Monthly Goals to Increase 1989 Sales by 50 Percent

Month	Goal
1	Set monthly sales targets by salesperson.
2	Hire a key account salesperson.
3	Identify 20 potential new sales accounts and assign responsibility.
4	Re-engineer advertising and marketing program.
5	Hire a second key account salesperson.
6	Review and reassign territory and account responsibility.
7	Examine fall sales plans.
8–12	Hold monthly progress meetings.

Figure 7.1

Echomart Inc. provides another excellent example of this bite.

Echomart Inc., a chain of convenience stores, is owned by William Denning. Bill opened his first corner store in 1972 followed by a second in 1974. The two stores grew successfully, earning Bill three prestigious retail sales awards.

When his five sons each reached their late teens, they demonstrated an interest in the business. It became Bill's dream to have each son operate a store of his own. But the timing had to be right. At the insistence of his business adviser, Bill trained his sons in the two existing operations and worked to pass on basic skills for managing both inventory and cash.

By the time the first son reached age 20, he had a total of six years of service helping his father and was ready to manage a store on his own. Bill used the equity in the two original stores to finance a third, reducing the burden of start-up. The oldest boy is now managing his own store. Bill achieved his expansion goal while at the same time carefully managing his business risk. He repeated the process with each boy thereafter.

Bill expanded operations without harming the sales volumes of existing stores — and provided a future for his five sons. Opening each new store is a separate goal. Training each son to manage over time, not overnight, is a separate action to achieve that goal. The financial success of each new store is always intact before the next is opened. The time line for completion was 10 years. How many businessmen are patient enough to wait 10 years to complete a goal? Bill was, and it paid off.

Top Sound Music Stores provides a third case for this bite.

Jim Sloan, president of Top Sound Music Stores, owned and managed five music stores selling instruments, compact discs, cassettes, and sheet music. Annual sales of $1.9 million were segregated by line of business and by store.

Jim's examination of segmented financial statements showed the company losing money on instrument sales in every location. On the advice of soul mate and chief financial adviser Garth Weymouth, Jim decided to discontinue selling musical instruments.

With a goal to phase out instrument sales, Jim had to be careful not to upset customers and staff. Change had to be managed well to minimize losses. Garth persuaded him to list key steps for the phase-out and which people, if any, would be hurt by each step. When Jim analyzed the goal, he found five smaller goals, as outlined in Figure 8.1. Following his detailed plan, the shift in focus was implemented smoothly.

Top Sound Music Stores
Instrument Phase-out Plan

1.	Negotiate the sale of instrument business with one of three major competitors.
2.	Meet with manufacturers of instruments to ensure consent to transfer manufacturer agreements.
3.	Gradually reduce inventory of each instrument to one to five units.
4.	Draft a letter to all customers announcing the sale of instrument lines to the competitor.
5.	Ensure open internal communication among employees.

Figure 8.1

LSM Auto Sales Ltd. is our final case.

> Bob Smithers was president and chief executive officer of LSM Auto
> Sales Ltd., operating eight locations in two cities. Specializing in late
> model pre-owned automobiles, Bob built the company to sales of
> $28 million. His vision included expanding the number of locations
> to 12 and sales to $45 million.
>
> During strategy meetings to plan expansion, Bob's soul mate Frank
> Carson insisted the goal was too general. Many action plans would
> have to be achieved to lay a trail of sales growth to reach the target
> of $45 million. Frank argued that sales staff wouldn't relate well to
> such visionary goals and would require practical day-to-day tasks. Vice
> president Bill Waverly agreed. In his experience, salespeople performed
> better when given short-term, specific goals. A salesperson's quest for
> achievement really happens daily with each sale.
>
> Both men's arguments persuaded Bob to refine his objective.
> Remaining strategy meetings were spent agreeing to a number of actions
> required to achieve the overall goal as outlined in Figure 9.1.
>
> Bob was surprised when the actions required to grow to $45 million
> in sales numbered more than nine. The steps included a very detailed,
> well-programmed media campaign to increase LSM name recognition,
> incentive programs to push each salesperson to surpass the threshold
> of 30 car sales per month, and careful site selection for each new loca-
> tion. When the meetings were complete, Bob was encouraged by the
> trail of events to success.

The puzzle depicting the foundations of success is reflected in Figure
10.1. Soul mates help bring objectivity to leadership style. They help
balance both our tolerance for risk and our personal make-up. They
provide a valuable second opinion during goal setting and decision
making, and help to minimize that feeling of fear and loneliness that creeps
over us all during the challenges of leadership.

LSM Auto Sales
Expansion Plan

	Goal	Responsibility	Due Date
1.	Approve, design, and implement a $465,000 media campaign to develop name recognition.	Bob Smithers	March 31
2.	Increase salesperson's commissions by 1 percent for those who sell more than 30 cars per month.	Bill Waverly	April 2
3.	Identify 9th viable location for a store.	Bob Smithers	April 23
4.	Hire new store manager.	Art Black	June 13
5.	View store opening promotion campaign.	Julie Smithers	June 15
6.	Implement mailings to neighborhood homes.	Sally Penchant	June 21
7.	Launch bonus trade-in plan.	Herman Sky	July 5
8.	Negotiate preferred exchange program with five new car dealers.	Bob Smithers	July 19
9.	Search for most appropriate 10th location.	Bob Smithers	October 16

Figure 9.1

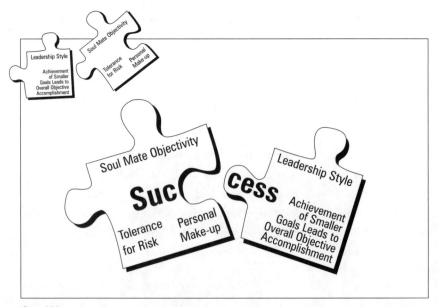

Figure 10.1

Leadership Triage

The Concise Oxford Dictionary defines the word *triage* as the assignment of degrees of urgency when deciding the order of treatment of wounded. Although its common usage is medical, the term can also usefully describe the business planning process that successful companies use to identify matters for urgent management attention.

Through a triage process, leaders are able to determine management priorities, reconfirm corporate missions, and set measurable and attainable goals. With this knowledge, they can set specific action plans, which become the vehicle for goal achievement through the assignment of responsibilities and dates for completion.

When action plans are accomplished, a company is able to move on to new priorities during the next year's triage. Unsuccessful action plans receive remedial attention. Over the life of a company, the sum of its business plan accomplishments reflects its success in achieving its corporate mission.

Figure 11.2 depicts the circular flow of the planning process both through the organization and through time. It resembles a subway system that transports commitments, goals, and actions through the company. It is the mechanism by which all leadership direction is communicated to every level of the organization, and the way the performance of those levels is compared with the expectations of leadership. Communication is two-way, going from employee to leader and vice versa. Performance and action plans move upward. Expectations and performance evaluations move downward. Both are interdependent, and should be modified frequently to achieve congruity through the planning process. A leader's expectations are based upon the corporate mission statement, the competitive environment, and the capabilities of the organization. To achieve optimum performance, these expectations should push the organization hard. Performance and action plans reflect the organization's capabilities. Leadership expectations need to be in line with the organization's commitment to performance in order to achieve congruency. Leadership and the organization play different roles in reaching congruence. Leadership challenges the organization to higher performance, and the organization tempers leadership expectations to realistic levels.

Fundamentals of Annual Triage

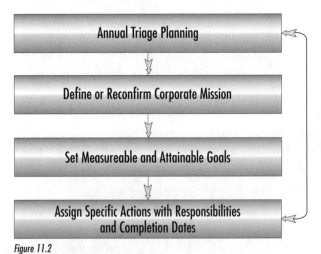

Annual Triage Planning

Define or Reconfirm Corporate Mission

Set Measureable and Attainable Goals

Assign Specific Actions with Responsibilities and Completion Dates

Figure 11.2

BITE 6: CONDUCT AN ANNUAL PLANNING PROCESS

Business plans must be an annual affair. Without them, leaders have no objective mechanism to identify goals and action plans for implementation. Without a plan, success will come only by chance, and failure is a matter of time.

Planning is used in every type of business and industry, whether service or manufacturing, and regardless of size. If we look at a business as a ship, triage is like an automatic ballast system, keeping things running smoothly on the journey. Triage identifies matters to be addressed, marshals goal achievement, and exposes poor performance for rehabilitation.

Achievement of ballast is not possible without first identifying your company's strengths and weaknesses. Historical and projected data should be carefully reviewed. Interviews are conducted with key decision-makers to ensure accurate information is gathered and properly understood. A preliminary plan containing preliminary goals for discussion is prepared as a communication medium and used as a working document.

But before examining planning in detail, it's important to acknowledge a point or two. Business planning is certainly not a new tool. Its theory has existed for several decades, although practical implementation has trailed. Finding leaders who disagree with the merits of business planning is difficult. Finding those who fail to employ it properly is surprisingly easy. There remains a constituency of leaders who support the theory but not the practice. They may fear either the cost of the process or lack the patience and discipline to implement it. In either case, an improperly implemented planning process encourages failure — a far greater cost!

Plan focus depends substantially upon the maturity of the business. Plans for start-up operations are quite different from those of mature companies. Newborns struggle for survival: every management activity is focused on product development and cash flow. Established companies are more concerned with growing market share and expansion.

The time line in Figure 12.2 depicts phases of business evolution. Determining the stage of a particular business is not as simple as one might think. Overconfident leaders whose new businesses are still in survival stage often act as if they are in the growth phase. This can lead to overly aggressive plans that unnecessarily risk a company's viability. At the other extreme, profits stagnate in mature companies when leaders are too timid. Risk tolerance and personal make-up make the difference. Soul mates must be consulted for objectivity.

Once the phase of business maturity has been accurately determined, the planning process can begin.

Phases of Business Life

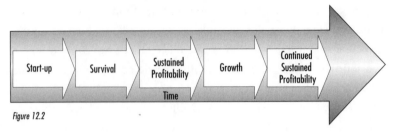

Figure 12.2

Ludwig Inc. is our case study as we understand the process of systematically building an annual business plan.

> Ludwig Inc. employs 626 people to manufacture and sell $964 million in computer equipment worldwide. Each year its leadership team conducts a formal planning process to identify strengths and weaknesses in each functional area, confirm the corporate mission, and identify specific goals and action plans for the upcoming year.
>
> Leaders of each of five functional areas assess their priorities in comparison with those of the company. Leaders in the areas of general management, finance, marketing and sales, production, and human resources then meet to ensure their goals are compatible. When all are in agreement with the specific plan, it is committed in writing and guides each day's activity for the upcoming year.

BITE 7: DEFINE YOUR CORPORATE MISSION

Business plans are composed of three pillars: mission statements, specific functional goals, and detailed action plans to achieve those goals.

Corporate mission statements depict a company's *raison d'être*, its reason for being in business. Typically a four- or five-line general statement of corporate values or direction, it becomes the corporate constitution. Some leaders have little use for the statement, considering it too general to have meaning. Employees frequently don't understand it, and customers may not relate to it. They all fail to appreciate the value of a mission statement and its potential contribution to corporate success.

The mission statement sets the tone for goal development and specific action plans by encouraging a cascading effect to planning — from the very general mission statement to very specific action steps, or manageable bites!

Mission statements are found in companies of any size, industry, or profession. The complexity of a mission statement does not necessarily vary from corner store to multinational corporation, although, of course, they're likely to be more complex for the latter. Let's turn to Ludwig's mission statement for an example.

> Ludwig Inc. is the leading most profitable manufacturer of computer equipment, with worldwide distribution, providing exceptional customer service and challenging careers for our employees.

What can we learn about the company by examining its mission statement? For starters, the word "leading" implies that the company develops products, lines, or markets ahead of its competition. By this, we can be pretty sure that the company puts research and development efforts high on its list of priorities in order to stay ahead of everyone else in the industry.

The phrase "most profitable" suggests that any development plans are carefully weighed against profit expectations, both short- and long-term. To be "leading" and "most profitable" at the same time, all the time, is a formidable leadership balancing act indeed. It requires split-second timing for product development to reach market readiness when the market is ready. Probability of success is not on Ludwig's side here.

We also have to look at Ludwig's product line. Computer equipment is manufactured by a number of worldwide companies. Substantial competition creates a greater need for precision management planning, not to mention effective "worldwide distribution."

"Exceptional customer service" is expensive and difficult to manage consistently worldwide.

"Challenging careers for our employees" suggests fair measurement policies are applied regardless of country and culture.

So much for those who believe mission statements are worthless. We've taken an unknown company, broken its mission statement into manageable bites, and were able to develop realistic expectations of what the organization might be about. That doesn't mean we are accurate, but if we walked into Ludwig's head office we would be armed with a respectable list of questions — more so than if we hadn't seen the mission statement.

The same approach applies to 5-, 10- or 50-employee businesses. The company in question doesn't have to be "worldwide" to have a mission. It may be the "most profitable manufacturer" while providing "exceptional customer service and challenging careers for our employees" even if it is small and owner-managed.

It's fun to dissect a company through its mission statement, but what does the statement do for Ludwig's management? How does it help continuous leadership triage, the company's ballast mechanism?

Well, when it is dissected into smaller, manageable bites and analyzed, the mission statement spells out the keys to Ludwig's success. It is the wellspring, if you like, from which all company direction cascades. Each phrase represents a functional area to be addressed by specific goals and objectives. If specific goals could not be gleaned from a company's mission statement, it would serve little purpose to the company, and critics of mission statements would have a point. Setting goals for each functional area of a business also sets up a system of accountability. If managers accept responsibility for goal achievement, they may be held accountable for success or failure. Without accountability, how could a company profess to provide "challenging careers for our employees"? More important, how would it know when it had achieved anything? It wouldn't.

Mission statements, as corporate constitutions, have longer shelf lives than goals. Goals are short-term desires, the breadcrumbs on the trail to mission achievement. Annual revision of goals can prevent a company from straying too far from its intentions as expressed in its mission. Changes in risk assessments and industry and economic environments influence the nature of each year's goals, but they are always prepared with the mission in mind.

Although financial information is an essential ingredient in the triage process, it alone does not ensure success. Other key ingredients include assessments of markets, competition, product or service acceptability, pricing, costs of production, productivity, customer service, new product development, overhead expenditure levels, and, of course, people.

Each year, triage information is presented internally to all senior management by those responsible for each functional area. Leaders interview managers seeking a clear understanding of the information so they can form accurate opinions of performance.

Ludwig's planning process, illustrated in Figure 13.2, provides an excellent checklist for businesses of all size to ensure important considerations are not overlooked.

Ludwig, as we suspected, prepares its annual goals by major mission statement category. Each year, managers from all locations submit goals to key decision-makers. The company then updates planning forms to ensure management works with the most current business data — the first assurance the ballast is in check. One department may provide functions for others; interviewing each manager ensures that the goals of users match those of suppliers. Incongruities are negotiated before proceeding further.

Ludwig managers then list the strengths and weaknesses of each supplier department in the company. When lists are combined in a written business plan, strengths and weaknesses are cross-referenced to see where the company needs to set corrective goals to improve the function of one or more internal supplier.

The company chairman evaluates senior management performance and identifies mediocrity for corrective action. Mediocre performance means the company will not achieve full potential. Mediocre management prepares mediocre plans. Lost profit is the outcome. Cross-referencing strengths and weaknesses helps Ludwig reveal any traces of mediocrity. The chairman and board of directors ensure everyone takes ownership of the planning process. This provides a second ballast for the senior leadership triage team.

In turn, senior leaders ensure operating managers accept responsibility for the plan, so similar ballast occurs at this level. Cascading responsibilities from senior to junior management levels reflect the downward flow of the manageable bites business plan. Operating managers identify goals for day-to-day operations that are in line with the corporate mission.

Cascading responsibility for the business plan ensures all hands on deck sail together. Planning and implementation roles are shared.

Ludwig Inc.
Planning Process

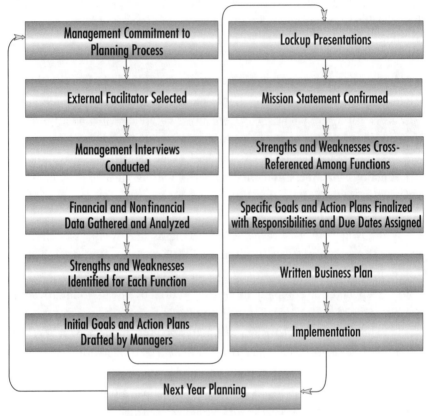

Figure 13.2

Everyone in the company must be in harmony for maximum goal potential and effective implementation. If Ludwig leadership does not truly believe harmony has been achieved, they have failed to accomplish maximum potential, failed to achieve its mission statement. Harmony of implementation is not only key; it is as essential as the business plan itself.

BITE 8: COMMIT ONLY TO ATTAINABLE AND MEASURABLE GOALS

In any successful business plan, goals must be both attainable and measurable. The statement "we will maximize profit," for example, is often thought to be a goal. It's not. When does anyone ever maximize profit? It's an infinite statement without a finish line. It can't be attained without a definite financial target. There's no way to measure it if no completion date is specified.

For goals to be attained, they must be considered realistic by the workers who will strive to reach them. Managers will avoid taking ownership of goals if they do not believe they are achievable. Ludwig, for example, has increased profits annually by an average of 6 percent. It would be unrealistic to set 15 percent growth as a goal for next year. It is unlikely to be attainable, and forcing its acceptance would create mistrust, especially if employee bonuses are tied to the profit performance exceeding the goals. Ludwig would be setting goals beyond management's reach, preventing these workers from maximizing their income.

If, instead, Ludwig says, "We will increase corporate profit by 7 percent during the next 12 months," then the company knows the goal is attained if net income is 7 percent higher than the previous year at the expiration of the 12-month period. It is measurable and it is likely to be perceived as attainable as well, since the 7 percent goal is in line with the company's historic performance. This type of plan encourages management to reach just a little higher for success.

Once triage identifies industry and economic environment data, strengths and weaknesses of management, and areas for improvement, Ludwig schedules a three-day "lockup" planning session for senior managers. A lockup is just that. Senior people lock themselves in a hotel meeting room to pour over data and contemplate company goals and action plans. No one leaves until the corporate mission is reaffirmed and agreement is reached on specific areas for improvement, with corresponding goals and action plans set to achieve the desired improvement.

The lockup serves three major purposes. It ensures a degree of quality control. With all managers present, room dynamics prevent one management group from setting goals that negatively impact another. An example would be the marketing group planning to spend $300,000 to promote a lagging product that research and development is convinced is obsolete. Lockups reveal such dysfunctional goal setting.

The second purpose is completion of the actual plan itself. Completing comprehensive business plans without managers coming face to face doesn't work — or at least not very well. Lockups foster room dynamics and group creativity. They are incubators for group thought processes that consider the well-being of the company as a whole. Shareholders expect leaders to pull together as a team. If leaders don't physically come together, it is difficult for them to do so. They tend not to develop that commonality of thought so often characteristic of a successful well-oiled team.

Continuous Leadership Triage: Your Business Ballast Process

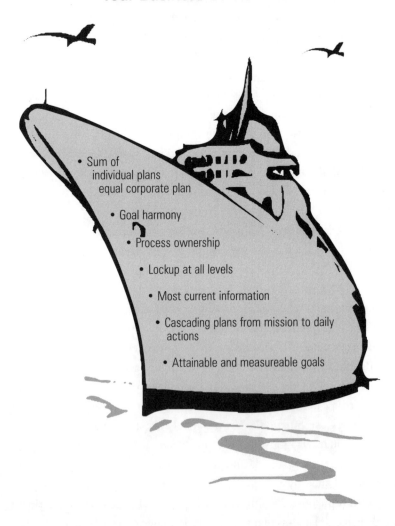

- Sum of individual plans equal corporate plan

- Goal harmony

- Process ownership

- Lockup at all levels

- Most current information

- Cascading plans from mission to daily actions

- Attainable and measureable goals

Figure 14.2

The third purpose is goal acceptance. Managers who participate in the creation of goals are more likely to assume responsibility for their achievements. If the plan has a manager's stamp, she is more likely to take its success personally.

Managers often come away from lockups with a greater feeling of self-worth — proportional, of course, to their level of participation. If properly detailed triage and planning take place beforehand, a well-prepared lockup agenda encourages wide participation, which, in turn, enriches the meeting for everyone.

Lockup goals require champions — those who assume responsibility for goal achievement. When prospects for career enhancement are bonded with goals, there are incentives and rewards to performance. No bonding usually means no goal ownership, and no ownership means no progress.

Let's look at the issues arising from Ludwig's lockup.

On the first day of Ludwig's lockup, the vice president of marketing begins the presentation, following opening remarks from the chairman. He teases the room of managers with such questions as:

▲ How aggressive is our competition? What products do they have on the drawing board? Do these products match customer expectations with respect to purpose, use, and availability?
▲ At what price can their new product be sold and still generate a profit? Is that greater than our estimate of their cost to produce?
▲ How reliable is our industrial intelligence of the competition?

The questions continue, each followed by extensive discussions until consensus is reached. Starting with the background of competitors, the group works methodically toward details of market positioning for each product.

It is imperative to know how the company's marketing approach measures against that of its competition. There is no point talking about production and distribution if the marketing and sales departments cannot lay down a winning formula to sell the product. If you can't sell it at a profit, you don't make it.

Once details of marketing and sales environments are agreed upon, foundations for goals begin to form. Differences between company and competitor marketing are among the first observations to bear fruit for current year goals. Everything is related back to the company's mission statement. What is necessary to become the "leading" manufacturer of computer equipment? Care is taken to ensure goal compatibility, so "leading" will not be accomplished at the expense of "profitable."

Presentations from vice presidents of distribution, production, quality control, research and development, finance, and human resources follow one by one. Each VP carefully tailors goals to fit the marketing and sales decisions already taken. All goals emanate from market demand.

For example, the new Ludwig laptop computer model is expected to gain 3 percent of its target market share. By company estimations, that will yield $50–60 million of additional sales — at a net contribution margin of 12 percent, after all direct marginal expenses, for approximately $6–7 million of additional profit. The vice president of production advised the group that approximately 30 percent of raw materials required to construct the units are currently on hand, having been purchased for similar products last year. Other components may be altered to accommodate certain functional advancements in the new model.

People requirements to match the plan are handled in the same manner as other resources. Skills not available in-house are acquired or existing people are trained. Skill and employee competence levels are an integral part of any corporate planning process.

Management is committed to March 31 for market introduction of the computer. To accomplish that goal, laptop production must begin by January 18. Even then, units will not be available in certain parts of the world until July. Quality control tests for durability of units must be finalized by February 1. Financing has to be in place before demands are felt on the company lines of credit. This pressure will be felt shortly after production for the new model commences. Certain training programs must also be planned to prepare production floor assembly staff and salespeople.

The drive for successful marketing and sales touches virtually every management function in the company. Ludwig truly believes customer satisfaction is the most important focus.

Ludwig's actual list of goals is quite long and too difficult to reproduce as an example here. It is important, though, to review a summary of goals to appreciate the principles discussed. Although goals listed for worldwide distribution, customer service, and challenging careers have not been discussed, they are included in Figure 15.2 to complete our example of goals for the whole mission statement.

Ludwig Inc.
Schedule of Corporate Goals

Mission Functional Area	Corresponding Goal
1. Leading computer manufacturer	• To increase Company's share of laptop computer market by 3 percent, introducing the new model by March 31.
2. Most profitable manufacturer	• To increase corporate profit by 7 percent within 12 months.
3. Worldwide distribution	• To maintain one month's sales in inventory in each warehouse location throughout the world.
4. Customer service	• To respond to customer service calls within two hours of contact.
5. Challenging careers	• To review the performance of each employee, by major category, by July 30, to determine career advancements.

Figure 15.2

A sample of Ludwig's goals are matched with a manageable bites version of the mission statement to reveal what must be achieved within specified time periods. Where specific dates have not been applied, respect is given to the nature of the goal. For example, a 7 percent increase in profit may be determined only on the expiration of the entire year planned. Similarly, inventory maintenance around the world is an ongoing process. At any given time, goal achievement or failure is determined by the quantities of product available to be consumed. As well, the speed of customer service can be referenced only to the customer call itself. Goal success is linked to response time, not real time.

Although Ludwig now has defined business goals, a road map for achievement does not yet exist. Goals must be reduced to smaller, more manageable bites that can be more easily translated into daily management activity.

BITE 9: COMMIT ONLY TO SPECIFIC ACTIONS WITH RESPONSIBILITIES AND COMPLETION DATES ASSIGNED

Morsels of success are accomplished with action plans — individual milestones to be achieved if goals are to be achieved. Although each goal must have at least one action plan assigned to it, most have more than one. Without actions, a goal is nothing more than a wish with nothing to propel it. Action plans are always the means, goals the end.

Action plans have to be specific to pass the measurement test. An example is required.

To acquire 10 new customers during the month of June, it's not sufficient to "call 20 contacts by May 31." That's a goal, not an action plan. A better example would be: "John Smith of the sales department will call upon Mr. H. Lawson of Company A on March 15, Mr. D. Sloan of Company B on March 21, Mr. L. Barry of Company C on May 28, etc., to ask each for a sales order." The difference between the two is the latter permits the measurement of John's progress toward his goal. It is detailed enough to monitor as time passes and avoids waiting until May 31 to determine success or failure.

Ludwig believes goals will not be achieved unless specific action plans are assigned to key decision-makers during lockup. An integral part of goal ownership takes place when managers are identified as champions. When managers accept responsibility, peer pressure brings embarrassment to those who do not perform their actions. Pressure is compounded when specific completion dates are assigned to each action.

Completion dates establish milestones, deadlines for each action to be accomplished. In our example, John Smith has been assigned responsibility to make 20 contact calls, each by a specified date. John must initiate those calls by each date; he knows the whole company is watching. Failure to do so affects John personally, and it is published each time the plan is reviewed. He will be called on to explain his lack of success at the next progress meeting and, thanks to peer pressure, will likely be more motivated to perform.

Assigning personal responsibility for success or failure encourages everyone to adopt the business as their own. When their future is at stake, more adrenaline drives leaders to succeed at their plans.

The larger the organization, the more critical action ownership becomes, simply because a high volume of actions is difficult to manage. Ownership flushes out those who hide from accountability. Those who avoid accountability have limited career options. No leader grants more responsibility to those who spend their careers avoiding it. It's not fair to those who earn their growth honestly and it's not fair to a company trying to avoid mediocrity.

Let's see what action plans Ludwig prepared to achieve its goals.

When the company addressed its mission to be the leading manufacturer of computer equipment, the goal discussed was, "To increase Company's share of laptop computer market by 3 percent, introducing the new model by March 31." To accomplish this goal, those who take ownership begin with the March 31 deadline and work backward to determine what must be completed by whom and when in order for the product to be ready by that date.

Timelines may be forced by the nature of the industry or by the company itself. For example, Ludwig's prototype computer model must be designed nine months before market introduction to permit time for testing and design changes. Further testing of final designs is necessary before instruction booklets are printed. These demand a lead time of two months for outside printers. These time lines are industry normal, while the deadline of March 31 is set by Ludwig's desire to be first to market.

Sales training manuals are designed and tested for effectiveness with a sample group of sales people. Production scheduling for the actual building of the computers must commence at least two months before the introduction date — in this case it's a January 18 production launch for the March 31 introduction. Finally, the market introduction strategy must be determined along with distribution timing worldwide, also two months before the launch. A number of activities are now happening concurrently to accommodate a launch date specified by the goal.

Senior executives asked Harry Taylor, of the new product group, to head up the introduction of the new laptop. Harry, seeing the request as a vote of confidence from the board, accepted the challenge, personalizing the goal as "Harry Taylor's." This satisfied a critical success factor for goal success.

He established his new product launch team with little difficulty because those asked saw the project as a career enhancer. Harry appointed champions and scheduled actions, creating plans for each functional area.

Ludwig Inc.
Functional Planning

QUALITY CONTROL ACTION PLAN:

"Leonard Zolisky will test the model five times for quality, during five consecutive weeks, commencing May 1 of the year prior to market introduction, reporting quality satisfaction levels together with any recommended design changes and follow-up testing dates to the launch team, no later than June 15."

PRODUCTION ACTION PLAN:

"Arthur Kellarman will implement final design changes to the production line by December 15, complete testing by December 31 and training of assemblers by January 15 for production readiness on January 18; status reports due to the committee the day following each milestone date."

MARKETING AND SALES ACTION PLAN:

"John Lexon will write the introduction marketing plan by December 1, for amendment and approval by the committee on December 15, facilitate marketing and sales training courses worldwide by January 15, with finalized instruction updates to all staff by February 15."

PERSONNEL ACTION PLAN:

"Alanna Belcher will write the training course with John Lexon by December 19, provide a final production shift list of names to Arthur Kellarman by January 4, and assist with training courses through to January 31."

Figure 16.2

Each action is very detailed and complements the activities of other launch team members working toward specific completion dates. Each department head assumes ownership of a functional piece to the goal puzzle. Any breakdown during implementation can now be traced to an individual's activity. The breakdown can then be addressed and repaired. Those who successfully complete actions on time are recognized and rewarded, and those who don't are embarrassed.

Before a business plan is finalized, action plans are compared with the desired results from all goals — a sanity check to make sure that plans are reasonable and resources are available to match the effort demanded by the goal. Expectation adjustments are usually required when resources are not sufficient to ensure success.

When agreement for goals and action plans is reached among senior managers, Ludwig prepares its final written plan. Figure 16.2 represents the functional planning schematic used by Ludwig leaders.

The business plan is available to all participants and becomes the guide for next year's activity. To be effective, a copy of the plan must be kept on the desk of every leader as a constant reference. Storing them in drawers increases the probability of failure. Plans far from sight are far from accomplishment. The document must be a working one — another reason why detail, individual ownership, and completion dates are critical for successful implementation.

Haggerty Construction offers a second case example for business triage planning.

Jim Haggerty incorporated Haggerty Construction in 1955 and has grown sales to $350 million and employees to 625. With the mission to become the city's preeminent contractor for industrial and commercial properties, Jim estimates his market share stands at 32 percent. During the first 20 years of corporate life, sales growth was slow but steady, followed by a more robust rate of growth for the next 11 years. A return to slower growth rates during the past 5 years frustrated Jim, and growth became his priority-planning goal once again.

Vice president Bruce Sinder argued the slow sales growth resulted from a lack of human resources. In rapid growth years, Haggerty employed strong estimators and purchasing agents skilled in sourcing favorable material prices. Foremen were more experienced, completing construction contracts under time and manpower budgets. Bruce observed that average foreman experience had declined from 15 years to 7.

Marketing manager Clarence Drew agreed with Bruce but felt that marketing, personal relationships with customers, and promotional material would help them to gain market share. Vice president of finance Lewis Spalding, on the other hand, believed more purchase discounts would permit more competitive bids. He felt better financial controls would help produce stronger net profit growth. Purchasing agent Sally Majors agreed with Lewis.

Each Haggerty leader identified strengths and weaknesses in his or her area and developed goals and action plans for profitable growth. Lockup meetings lasted one and a half days as each of the seven leaders presented findings and lobbied for company acceptance of personal goals and action plans. When the meetings ended, the company had agreed upon a list of goals and actions for each department. These were recorded for company use as shown in Figure 17.2.

Jim Haggerty articulated a vision for the company to senior leadership. He expected sales growth to continue at higher rates. Each leader was asked to support this overall corporate mission. Goals and action plans were developed by each leader while lockup meetings served to ensure their support and goal compatibility.

Not all is satisfactory with the Haggerty example, though. Notice the general statements used for goals and action plans. Estimating goal 2, for example, states, "Where necessary, bid closer to cost to eliminate competition." The action plan states, "Log estimating time required to handle jobs less than $100,000; compare to expected profit." Such examples lack the specificity seen in those presented by Ludwig.

How do we know when bidding closer to cost eliminates competition? It cannot be measured or proven attainable. Even more puzzling is how an action plan to log estimating time for jobs under certain thresholds could eliminate competition. With such lack of specificity, it's not surprising Jim Haggerty was disappointed when he analyzed goal achievement the following year. Although progress was made, he couldn't point to

Haggerty Construction
Management Goals and Action Plans 1992

Department	Goals	Action Plans	Completion Dates	Responsibility
Estimating	1. Keep competition weak through selective high volume bidding.	1. Analyze profitability of jobs less than $100,000 compared to long-term profitability goals.	October 31	Bill Sloan
	2. Where necessary, bid closer to cost to eliminate competition.	2. Log estimating time required to handle jobs less than $100,000; compare to expected profit.	October 31	Bill Sloan
Human Resources	1. Review all support staff for continuity and strength in the event of turnover and retirement.	1. Key personnel to select 10 support persons for training, development.	October 31	Bruce Sinder
	2. Review foremen bonus plan to provide incentive to use worker hours efficiently.	2. Develop and implement guidelines for foremen bonus scheme tied to 10 percent efficiency improvement.	October 31	Bruce Sinder
	3. Plan work to avoid labor layoffs.	3. Initiate quarterly staff level meetings to schedule and set actions to encourage work for slow periods.	October 31	Bruce Sinder

Figure 17.2

Haggerty Construction
Management Goals and Action Plans 1992

Department	Goals	Action Plans	Completion Dates	Responsibility
Marketing	1. Develop a company brochure outlining past projects, product lines, etc.	1. Distribute brochure to existing customers, contacts, and potential customers.	October 31	Clarence Drew
	2. Increase personal contacts • by 20 for industrial • by 35 for commercial • and by 10 for other.	2. Coordinate a marketing program, assigning specific responsibilities to employees: • listing potential markets • specifically assigning industrial and commercial contacts • following up developments at management meetings monthly.	October 31	Clarence Drew
	3. Establish a follow-up program for customer contacts.	3. Consider distributing to customers/contacts any relevant government research material.	October 31	Jim Barnaby
	4. Establish a follow-up program for tenders submitted.	4. Analyze successful bids • reasons for success or failure.	October 31	Jim Barnaby

Figure 17.2 (cont.)

Haggerty Construction
Management Goals and Action Plans 1992

Department	Goals	Action Plans	Completion Dates	Responsibility
Marketing (cont.)	5. Review effectiveness of implementing customer/contact give-aways (tickets, bottles, golf tournament) as a promotional tool.	5. Analyze source of repeat business.	November 30	Jim Barnaby
	6. Consider promotional mailings.	6. Review analysis of sources of business.	December 15	Jim Barnaby
Finance	1. Prepare overhead budgets.	1. Investigate overhead accounts for potential savings.	September 30	Lewis Spalding
	2. Identify, on a timely basis, those jobs losing money and identify reasons: • slow collection of accounts receivable • labor inefficiencies • material costs.	2. Investigate all losing jobs on a weekly basis, setting corrective actions to prevent further losses.	September 30	Lewis Spalding
	3. Take advantage of discounts where possible.	3. Analyze and compare cost of money vs. benefit of discounts.	September 30	Lewis Spalding

Figure 17.2 (cont.)

Haggerty Construction
Management Goals and Action Plans 1992

Department	Goals	Action Plans	Completion Dates	Responsibility
Finance (cont.)	4. Management review of monthly balance sheet (not just divisional income statements).	4. Analyze and question monthly expenses on an actual vs. budget basis.	September 30	Lewis Spalding
	5. Initiate preauthorizing certain expenses (part of budgetary process).	5. Prepare cost-benefit and break-even analysis of new products.	December 31	Lewis Spalding
	6. Analyze all job costs each month.	6. Prepare analysis as part of month-end reports.	September 30	Lewis Spalding
	7. Review development and profitability of complementary product lines.	7. Contract profitability analysis prepared.	December 31	Lewis Spalding
Purchasing	1. Review purchasing arrangements to ensure best prices are achieved based on expected usage (concentrate on major suppliers).	1. Review purchasing arrangements for volume discounts, rebates.	September 30	Sally Majors

Figure 17.2 (cont.)

Haggerty Construction
Management Goals and Action Plans 1992

Department	Goals	Action Plans	Completion Dates	Responsibility
Purchasing (cont.)	2. Review purchasing terms with major suppliers to achieve more cash discounts, rebates.	2. Review existing terms to take advantage of potential discounts. Consider negotiating new ones.	September 30	Sally Majors
General Management	1. Ensure key management is provided with timely information to permit immediate follow-up.	1. Information must include at least: • complete monthly financial statements • overhead actual vs. budget analysis • feedback concerning employee morale • contract profitability analysis • a report on foremen efficiency bonus plan.	October 31	Jim Haggerty
		2. Monthly management meetings agenda distributed to allow participants lead time to prepare for meetings.	October 31	Jim Haggerty

Figure 17.2 (cont.)

individual goal success. Determined to lead a more successful plan, he insisted each manager produce just one very specific goal for the following year. When plans were written and lockup meetings completed for the following year, goals were much clearer, as outlined in Figure 18.2.

Goals and actions are few, but those that are there are much more focused. Now Jim can determine what actions are necessary for goal achievement. Managers are unable to hide behind general statements when definitive actions are assigned responsibilities and completion dates. Although responsibilities and completion dates existed for previous plans, the generality of goals and actions left room to argue whether success was the outcome — an unacceptable situation for ensuring leadership accountability.

Little has been said of soul mates throughout this process. Chairs, senior executives, and middle and lower managers alike consult soul mates frequently for opinions on procedure, timing, and communication matters. For some, mates offer insight into weaknesses identified during triage. Others receive advice about lockup presentations — the mate acting as mock audience, critiquing style and delivery. Practicality of goals and action plans is a favorite topic when soul mates review plans. No matter what the soul mate's role, his or her opinion should help strengthen or alter your resolve.

Business planning, then, with all its components, is leadership triage in an orderly fashion. Weaknesses are identified, goals set, and actions agreed to — both by individual leaders and together as a team. Management teams monitor individual success and individuals monitor team success — all in manageable bites.

Haggerty Construction
Management Goals and Action Plans 1993

Department	Goals	Action Plans	Completion Dates	Responsibility
Estimating	To increase the number of successful tenders by 5 percent	Negotiate a 2 percent reduction of costs of all supplier materials by January 15 and pass resulting savings on to clients through new tenders.	January 15	Bill Sloan
Human Resources	To offer a three-day training course for foremen to gain additional experience in project management.	Analyze each contract completed during the past 12 months to identify areas of labor waste to discuss at training meetings to be held by July 31.	July 31	Bruce Sinder
Marketing	To solicit customer views of Haggerty's quality, service, and completion satisfaction from past customers.	Design a customer questionnaire by February 2 to be distributed to all customers served during the past three years.	March 31	Clarence Drew
Finance	To simplify job costing and produce project accounting updates by Friday noon of each week.	Consolidate project costing on a one-page summary showing deviations for labor and materials consumed and highlighting cost and scheduling items to be reviewed.	March 12	Lewis Spalding

Figure 18.2

III
Leading Core Competence

"The problem with building a relationship
is that too many people use a hammer."
— *ANONYMOUS*

Your success in business is dependent upon the competence of your people. The relationship is clear: lack of competence will result in lack of success. But identifying the skills necessary for success, though important, is just a small part of core competence leadership. Determining what employees do or do not do well consumes the most leadership time. This is a fluid matter that demands continuous attention. It takes time, energy, and patience to establish a fair and equitable process for consistently making quality decisions regarding new hires, promotions, dehires, and retirements. Essentially, leaders need a mechanism to track performance and encourage employee growth. This mechanism should identify and reward high achievers while ensuring poor performers receive an opportunity to improve through rehabilitation plans. It should encourage all employees to personally adopt leadership's vision, culture, goals, and action plans. Those who can't will move on. Rewarding those who do reinforces positive behavior. Whatever form reinforcement takes, it should solidify employee commitment to the corporate vision.

Businesses are never static and often undergo significant change. Major customers are gained or lost. Divisions are acquired or divested. Each activity has its own competence demands. Increasing world competitiveness will force more, rather than less, business change at more rapid rates in the future. To be competitive, leaders will demand more rapid changes in core competence to meet those challenges.

BITE 10: IDENTIFY COMPETENCE FOR GOAL ACHIEVEMENT

Leadership triage provides insight into available and required employee skills. Employee strengths and weaknesses, both as individuals and as a team, become your inventory of core competence. To be truly informative, triage needs to involve a process of analyzing employee performance, as illustrated in Figure 19.3, in different situations.

Leading Core Competence

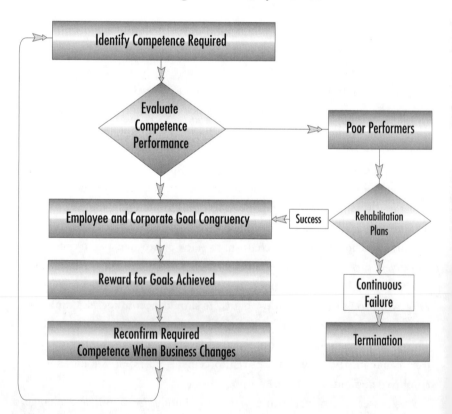

Figure 19.3

Successful companies assess competence as annual goals are finalized. When goal development and performance reviews are fresh in the minds of managers, they are best able to update competence data. Ludwig Inc. lists available and required skills when it compares strengths and weaknesses of employees with the goals to be achieved. Levels of competence become clearer when planning turns to implementation. Attention shifts from goal creation to action completion, forcing management to match skills with proposed tasks. First, competent employees are assigned to each action plan, then missing skills are identified so training can begin. Igloo Ice Cream offers an excellent illustration of the process.

Igloo Ice Cream is a small chain of retail ice cream stores with sales of $4 million and 30 employees. Art Thatcher, the president, leads the annual management triage process with only four managers. He drafts a plan, then holds a one-day lockup at his farm with his four managers to reshape the draft.

For the current year, one goal is to open two additional ice cream outlets by July 31. Management believes the expansion requires an additional manager be hired or developed. Art prefers to promote from within his organization rather than incur the expense and risk of an outside search. Art asked one of his managers, Bill Moody, to assess Igloo's core competence below the management level. Bill accepted responsibility for the action, producing the assessment in Figure 20.3 for Art a week later.

Bill selected employees with two or more years' service. Dependability ratings range from 1 to 5, five being the most dependable, one the least. He used the same scale to rate their ability to manage people.

Employees with the longest service were not necessarily the most dependable, and the most dependable were not necessarily the best people-managers. Bill recommended that Louise York be trained as the fifth manager in Igloo Ice Cream and that Sid Cameron be replaced for poor performance.

Igloo Ice Cream
Assessment of Core Competence

Employee	Years of Service	Dependability Rating	Ability to Manage People
Susan Blake	6	3	2
Louise York	5	4	5
John Zenner	2	5	3
Sid Cameron	4	2	2

Figure 20.3

Bill's system of analysis permits managers to employ as many columns of characteristics as necessary to rate competence. His analysis compares employee strengths and weaknesses with criteria most important to management. Tools like Bill's analysis increase the likelihood of successfully matching skills with tasks to be completed. Simzer Chemical provides a great example of matching superior performers with difficult projects.

Simzer Chemical, a $60 million producer of chemical agents for food and beverages, operates four manufacturing plants. Managers are responsible for evaluating and ranking performance of key employees in each of the company's eight divisions.

Evaluations are prepared based on such factors as desire to advance, skill improvement, adoption of corporate goals, hours of overtime, and creativity. Weights are assigned to each category to form an overall composite evaluation for each employee as outlined in Figure 21.3. Employees, ranked in descending order of composite evaluation, are matched with goals developed during annual triage. More complex goals are assigned to high performers, while simpler responsibilities go to those with lesser ratings. Engineering determined the cleaning process to be the most complex, involving many suppliers and multiple sections of the production floor. Responsibility is allocated to the highest performer, Bradshaw. Remaining projects are ranked by complexity and matched with comparable competence as evaluated by the manager of engineering.

Simzer Chemical
Core Competence Allocation, Engineering Department

Engineers by Evaluation	Composite Evaluations	Future Projects by Complexity
1. Bradshaw	5	• Cleaning process
2. White	4	• Line redesign
3. Gladstone	4	• Bottling efficiency
4. Laurence	3	• Ventilation
5. Lance	3	• Maintenance

Figure 21.3

Simzer's method of matching competence to the complexity of the task to be performed works for two reasons. More difficult tasks are assigned to more capable people, improving the potential for goal success. And allocation of projects is a public expression of confidence in each employee. It's part of the reward system. Peer pressure encourages growth in lesser performers who desire more complex tasks the following year. A competitive atmosphere demands constant improvement, ensuring Simzer's system not only allocates actions by performance, but also enriches core competence over time.

Training is another essential tool for enriching core competence. African Trading Inc. makes the point well.

African Trading Inc. is a worldwide import/export business of African-made goods. President Leo Barley incorporated it in 1956, when he and five buddies began importing African products. Aggressive annual business plans grew the company to 450 employees and average annual sales of $98 million.

The majority of worldwide employees were salespeople, accounting for 383 of the 450 total. North America contributes both the greatest sales volume and greatest number of people. Europe was the most profitable region, selling $28 million through 78 salespeople. Japan and a number of smaller countries had poor results.

Leo's sales goal was to achieve $300,000 per salesperson worldwide. Peter Henzel, vice president of finance, prepared a sales competence analysis to determine current sales per person as outlined in Figure 22.3.

Peter's analysis laid out Leo's challenge. Only Europe and the Middle East meet the $300,000 criteria. North America's $34 million averages only $272,000 — with Southeast Asia, Japan, and other smaller countries falling substantially behind. Only 108 salespeople, or 29 percent of the sales force, currently achieves the $300,000 goal. Leo realized sales competence issues had to be addressed and asked the vice president of human resources, Avrum Wentzell, to study the matter.

African Trading
Sales Competence Analysis

Area	Number of Salespeople	Total Sales ($ millions)	Average Sales per Salesperson ($000s)
North America	125	$34	$272
Southeast Asia	60	12	200
Europe	78	28	359
Middle East	30	9	300
Japan	63	11	175
Other	27	4	148
Company Total	383	$98	$256

Figure 22.3

Two weeks later, Avrum returned, having interviewed both the most and the least successful salespeople. The findings he presented to Leo suggested a number of inconsistencies in sales training around the world. European and Middle East salespeople spent an average of 10 days in sales training annually, addressing, among other topics, key accounts management, customer satisfaction, interview techniques, and deal closings. Training elsewhere in the world was more sporadic, occurring only when time permitted. Salespeople in Europe and the Middle East viewed training as necessary while others felt it interfered with productive selling time.

Leo had two challenges. He had to foster a healthy attitude toward training everywhere in the company. Then, he needed to administer training at European and Middle East quality standards to all salespeople throughout the year. Avrum Wentzell accepted these challenges as personal goals.

African Trading Inc. set its goal for average sales per salesperson first, then evaluated competence to determine what was required to achieve that goal. The evaluation indicated the company already had a sufficient number of salespeople to meet the goal, but concluded they were ill-trained. Triage led to the adoption of specific training goals and responsibility for achievement was assigned to Avrum Wentzell.

BITE 11: COMPLETE ANNUAL PERFORMANCE EVALUATIONS

Identifying the competence necessary to achieve a corporate mission is one thing. Maintaining it is quite another. Competence levels are in perpetual turmoil. As personnel are promoted, leave the company, and simply go through periods of high or low motivation, there is rarely a moment when some competence issue doesn't require attention. Think of core competence as a battery. If left without recharging, it loses strength and fails to perform at peak efficiency. Recharging begins with triage when needs are analyzed. It's completed when action plans are fulfilled. Then the process begins again.

Continuous triage assesses the quality of your competence inventory — checking the life of the battery. You may have engineering skills, for example, but how competent are they? Remember Igloo Ice Cream. Those with similar skills do not necessarily have them in equal portions. All production managers, for example, are not excellent schedulers, shift planners, or line motivators. Each is blessed with different levels of skill quality — levels that can be determined from objective performance evaluation only.

Without performance evaluation, decisions for promotions or terminations are just emotional reactions between manager and subordinate. No opportunity exists to formally encourage improved performance or link corporate goals to employee goals. Without evaluation, even determining the causes of poor performance becomes a random act rather than an integral part of a larger process. In the example of a service department that receives numerous customer complaints, performance evaluations would be needed to determine whether the complaints arise from too few service people or the incompetence of existing ones. Each conclusion requires different corrective action. If the evaluation shows a lack of human resources, more people can be hired. If current employees are performing poorly, training can be implemented or staff changes made. Only systematic performance documentation will determine the difference. In either case, strong performers are identified for reward and poor performers for rehabilitation.

Annual performance evaluations also help ensure that leaders think carefully about each employee. Through the process, leaders are able to maintain up-to-date human resource files and provide career guidance where necessary. Knowing employee strengths and weaknesses also enables supervisors to compare existing competence with that required for goal achievement. Annual employee interviews assess each individual's contribution to core competence and objectively evaluate technical excellence, team participation, attitude, ability to train and be trained, and flexibility for special tasks.

Performance criteria that require improvement may be addressed with training and rehabilitation, while performance areas that exceed expectations receive praise and encouragement.

An employee's activities outside the workplace are not necessarily critical to performance evaluation, but they are important to personal growth and development and they do have relevance to job performance and potential. Community leadership, for example, often signals skills suitable for higher positions and indicates balance in employee lives, contributing to happier, more productive work habits.

Stellar Communications Inc. provides an excellent example of performance evaluation.

Stellar Communications Inc. is a public-relations company with 43 employees. Each year, during planning, Frank Stellar conducts a formal performance interview and evaluation of the 10 most senior people. These 10, who report directly to Frank, are responsible for conducting the same performance evaluation for remaining employees.

Performance evaluations at Stellar have evolved over the years, as Frank amends the process regularly. Stellar's performance review form, illustrated in Figure 23.3, is adaptable to any job in any company.

Stellar Communications
Employee Performance Review

Name _____ Position _____

Responsibilities _____ Previous Positions _____

_____

_____

_____

Years of Service _____

REQUIREMENT

A review must be completed annually. It is the obligation of the person being reviewed as well as the reviewer to ensure the review takes place.

HOW TO USE THIS FORM

The primary purpose of the review is to provide immediate feedback on selected performance areas to employees upon completion of a year of service. The secondary purpose is to document the performance assessment and feedback, and to place this review form in the employee's personnel file for reference at the next annual review. The area or areas to be covered in the review should be based on the categories below and jointly selected by the reviewer and reviewee with reference to improvement targets established in the last annual review.

SUMMARY ASSESSMENT
Degree of difficulty of position being assessed:

Below ☐   **Average** ☐   **Above Average** ☐

Indicate your assessment of performance according to the following code:

AA = Above average; SP = Satisfactory performance; NI = Needs improvement

Add comments below.

Figure 23.3

Stellar Communications
Employee Performance Review

1. Relationship Management ☐

Employee and Management Relations ☐

Technical and Problem-solving Ability ☐

General Business Knowledge ☐

2. Individual and Team Excellence ☐

Team Involvement and Leadership ☐

Development and On-the-job Training of Assistants ☐

Continuing Training Activities ☐

Personal Development ☐

3. Growth ☐

Marketing and Selling (if applicable) ☐

Personal Business Development Program ☐

Business Positioning in Community ☐

Portfolio of Business Capabilities ☐

4. Productivity ☐

Quality and Service Improvement ☐

Effective Management of Resources ☐

Effective Task/Assignment Management ☐

5. Reviewer's Opinion ☐

Communication ☐

Energy and Enthusiasm ☐

Consistency of Performance ☐

Ability to Achieve Improvement Targets ☐

Commitment ☐

OUTSIDE ACTIVITIES

Figure 23.3 (cont.)

Stellar Communications
Employee Performance Review

COMMENTS ON ASSESSMENT

_____

_____

_____

REHABILITATION PLANS (IF REQUIRED)

_____

_____

GENERAL COMMENTS ON REVIEWEE'S
PERFORMANCE AND DEVELOPMENT

Where possible, state whether the reviewee's performance has improved.

_____

_____

_____

_____

CAREER GOALS

_____

_____

_____

REVIEWEE'S COMMENTS

_____

_____

_____

SIGNATURES

Reviewer _____ Date _____

Reviewee _____ Date _____

Figure 23.3 (cont.)

> Once Stellar managers complete written assessments, an employee interview takes place. The interview allows the manager to provide performance feedback, offer praise and reward or rehabilitative actions, and give career development suggestions.

Feedback encourages improved performance by reconciling employee and manager perceptions of performance. There is always a difference in the perceptions, and it's healthy for the relationship for this difference to be identified. Interaction throughout the year fosters perception differences. For example, a manager may follow implementation of a sales plan closely to ensure important activity is not overlooked. Salespeople interpret this as stifling micromanagement. Where performance perceptions do not match, interviews provide a forum for voicing opinions and coming to some mutual understanding.

Frank Stellar also believed he, himself, was not above a leadership review. To lead, he felt he had to know what his senior people thought of his performance as leader — what they felt were his strengths and weaknesses. The first year he asked them to perform this role, they were timid and somewhat afraid to speak their mind. But Frank's lighthearted approach to his own weaknesses eventually won their confidence to participate honestly. Over a couple of years he perfected his own version of the 360° review, shown in Figure 24.3.

BITE 12: ENSURE CORPORATE AND EMPLOYEE GOALS ARE CONGRUENT

Why are goals and action plans, such as those established by Ludwig Inc., adopted by managers? How and why does achievement of these actions become a personal matter for these employees? The answers lie with employee participation during business planning.

Those expected to lead a change are more likely to do so if they have had a role in planning it. Participation encourages employees to offer planning ideas and to adopt the resulting goals and action plans as their own. This is the concept of "buy-in." When it occurs, the individual sets her performance expectations by adopting those of the company. These shared goals become benchmarks to measure success and permit planned and actual activity to be compared during employee performance evaluations.

Stellar Communications
Leadership Evaluation

ATTRIBUTES	5 – Outstanding 4 – Exceeds expectations 3 – Meets expectations 2 – Falls short of expectations 1 – Far below expectations				
	EVALUATION				
	1	2	3	4	5
1. Leadership					
2. Support					
3. Guidance					
4. Counsel					
5. Equity/Fairness					
6. Mentoring					
7. Judgment					
KEY AREAS					
8. Clients/Scope of Service/Service Delivery					
9. Human Resources					
10. Profitability					
11. Market Position					
12. Key Contacts					

Comments (if any): _____

_____

_____

_____

_____

Figure 24.3

Stellar Communications management examines goal achievement progress by assessing both company and employee performance. They use feedback to determine if new action plans are required to realign the two. Successful management of change relies heavily on the link between planning and evaluation. When employees fail at change, they are offered rehabilitation plans. Those who continuously refuse change are encouraged to look elsewhere for happiness. Performance reviews must also accommodate employee aspirations. Career goals are extremely important for the morale and growth of an individual. And it's important for the company to achieve the maximum potential from everyone. When evaluations are complete, a personal plan for the upcoming year should exist for each employee, and it should be congruent with corporate goals.

Commitment to this plan occurs when interviewer and interviewee sign the performance evaluation. Daily, weekly, or monthly completion dates are assigned to each action. Zender Corp. demonstrates the point well.

Zender Corp. was founded in 1920 by Louis Zender, a German immigrant. As master tailor, Louis manufactured men's suits for 31 years, until his death in 1951, when he left the $2 million enterprise to his son, Harold.

Louis built the company on strength of product quality — the best marketing and sales strategy. Products were of such high quality that they sold themselves.

After World War II, Louis's competition grew to five suit manufacturers who used aggressive advertising to enter the Zender-dominated market. Zender's sales began to decline.

In 1953, sales fell 5 percent, worrying Harold enough to call a special meeting of key management staff. Six hours of discussion resulted in consensus to move company focus away from production and toward marketing and sales. Sales plans were agreed to over the next two days, with responsibilities for action completion shared among the four senior managers. Each signed the final plan, signaling support for its implementation. Harold's first action was to hire a sales manager by May 28, and shortly afterward, he enrolled in night courses in marketing, to start on June 7.

The management team's change in direction increased sales by 7 percent in just 11 months. When Harold asked managers for help, they brought forward suggestions, which he in turn adopted. This encouraged their buy-in, and employee and corporate goals became one. A unified management team of five was a stronger force to turn around company fortunes.

While Harold Zender links employee to corporate goals by participation management, others accomplish similar results by satisfying more basic employee needs. Quality Roofing demonstrates the difference well.

> Quality Roofing, with sales of $2.3 million, employs part-time workers to resurface residential roofs. It differentiates itself from 22 competitors by guaranteeing completion of roof repairs in 1.8 days, and in just one day in moist weather. Contracts are usually fixed price, based on the 1.8-day goal. Every hour worked beyond the 1.8 days is not recoverable from customers.
>
> Quality also differentiates itself by advertising cleanliness of the customer's yard upon completion. This addresses a common customer complaint in the roofing industry about scraps of shingles, tarpaper, and plastic left behind when the job is done. Part-time workers are difficult to manage because their primary goal is a basic need for a paycheck. Quality's primary goal is speed, quality, and neatness of work. It's clear that in this case, personal and corporate goals are not compatible.
>
> Annual triage concluded employees must share the company's values if the desired market share is to be achieved. Two action plans were developed to offer incentives to employees. Crew members completing roofing jobs in under 1.8 days or 1 day in moist weather will receive a $50 bonus. Once a week, Quality's president will visit every completed site for yard inspection. The crew leaving the cleanest yard will receive an additional $50 per person reward.

Quality's linkage of corporate to employee goals is a basic bonus reward system. The method, although effective for Quality Roofing, will work only in instances where money is the primary need and motivator for the employees. More skilled employees often look for nonmonetary rewards, such as praise, days off, and company-paid conference trips to cement the connection between corporate and individual goals.

BITE 13: REWARD EMPLOYEES FOR GOALS ACHIEVED

Successful companies praise outstanding performers. Those who feel appreciated are more likely to work harder and smarter. More responsibility is often more readily accepted when accompanied by management's gratitude and praise. Despite this, how many managers consistently praise strong performers? Surprisingly few. Even though it costs little, many leaders are afraid employees will relax their performance if praised. Others fear they will be sending mixed signals should they have to reprimand that employee in the future.

Leaders having difficulty praising superior performers should talk to their soul mates. Overcoming this reluctance can be critical to minimizing staff turnover, low morale, and inefficiency. An ideal example comes to us from The Blue Shell Restaurant.

The Blue Shell is a 500-seat restaurant with approximately $8.2 million in annual revenue. It's owned and managed by Alex Desernoff. On average, Alex employs 40 people, primarily on a permanent part-time basis. Approximately half the employees, including waiters, waitresses, maître d's, bussers, and cloakroom attendants, appear before the public each day.

During annual triage, Alex compared The Blue Shell's size and sales volume to that of his primary competitors. To gather competitive intelligence, he paid for his cousin and wife's dinner at another restaurant. Armed with a checklist from Alex, the cousin observed more friendly and attentive staff than he experienced at The Blue Shell. Quality of food preparation was similar and prices comparable. Alex repeated the experiment at other competitor restaurants. All had more attentive staff.

He talked extensively about the problem with soul mate Earl Chekoff, also a restaurateur. Earl outlined a waiter incentive program implemented in his own restaurant. Alex listened carefully as Earl described how his once unresponsive staff was now driven solely by customer satisfaction.

The system is simple. Points are assigned those who achieve outstanding customer satisfaction. Points are deducted for complaints received. Performance ratings are attained through customer satisfaction surveys and customer feedback, which is sought as patrons leave the restaurant. Positive comments earn employees 10 points, 3 points are deducted for mediocrity, while negative feedback brings a 5-point deduction. Points are tallied to produce a total for each employee.

Employee, shift, and overall restaurant performance is tracked for

30-day periods. Every employee who scores a net total of 100 points or more receives a $100 bonus.

Since Earl's employees always work the same shift, it's possible to track shift performance over the same 30-day period. To encourage a consistent positive team attitude, he rewards shift members an additional $100 if net shift scores exceed 1,500 points. Earl wants a uniform positive attitude from all shift staff, not just a few. He has learned that success comes from both team and individual excellence.

Taking the system a step further, Earl encourages competition among shifts for the highest number of points accumulated during a three-month period. Winning shifts enjoy banquets in their honor while the lowest scoring shift waits on them — all in the spirit of fun competition.

Alex studied Earl's successful reward system in detail. When he discussed the plan with senior staff at The Blue Shell they became enthusiastic and a reward system was adopted as the primary goal for the year.

A year later when all results were tabulated, Alex happily observed the following:

- ▲ Overall staff morale had increased substantially, with competitive fun among shifts for accumulated points and bonuses.
- ▲ Chronic poor performers resigned from shift teams when peer pressure for superior customer satisfaction became unbearable.
- ▲ Repeat customers increased an average 15 percent.
- ▲ Food waste, and glass and dish breakage declined by 14 percent.

What a payback! Alex experienced positive gains in repeat customers, profit, and morale, and he didn't even have to fire his poor performers. Kudos to soul mates. A suggestion from someone in the same business brought tremendous profit improvement to Alex who, unlike Guido of Guido's Pizza, was not afraid to accept peer advice.

Samson Travel offers another case study showing the value of employee rewards.

Roy Samson owns and manages a small travel agency with two agents and sales of $1.8 million.

Consulting with soul mate John Snow, Roy determined that for corporate goals to be met, each agent must commit to $700,000 revenue generation each year. Roy intended to manage the balance of the sales budget until revenue supported a third agent.

During triage, John suggested that agents who exceeded the $700,000 mark should be well rewarded. To encourage participation, Roy and John asked the agents what reward would create the greatest incentive. The response was unanimous — a two-week holiday anywhere in the world. By agreeing to their ideal reward, Alex ensured his agents would make every effort to meet the corporate goal.

Three bites are practiced here. Soul mate John Snow provides guidance as the sounding board. Corporate and personal goals are linked when agents select their own reward. And finally, agents are rewarded for goal achievement.

BITE 14: ENCOURAGE REHABILITATION OF POOR PERFORMERS

Lesser performers must be given a chance for rehabilitation, but not in just any form. For successful rehabilitation, it's critical that the employee be involved from the planning stages. Employee participation achieves two goals. As we've already noted, people are more likely to improve if they have a say in how it will happen. If the employee agrees to the plan in advance, it's difficult for him to argue lack of fairness if he fails to improve.

Successful companies discuss rehabilitation plans openly, providing employees with the opportunity to suggest steps to be taken. Let's see how Lewis Printing handles the whole concept of rehabilitation plans.

Aldo Lewis, president of Lewis Printing, operates his custom printing shop with 10 employees who collectively accomplish sales of $5,600,000 annually.

Foreman Fred Uso manages the business while Aldo closes sales. In recent months, Aldo received complaints from shop employees about Fred's attitude. He had been barely civil to staff and had concerned himself with matters other than people. Productivity began to fall and customer complaints increased.

Prior to annual performance evaluations, Aldo customarily spends an hour writing notes on each employee's performance for the year. When he came to Fred, he decided the issue of attitude was too important to overlook. In their initial interview, Fred broke down when Aldo confronted him with his performance record. Unhappiness at home had made him inattentive and short-tempered. For two hours the two chatted about separating home and work, so unhappiness in one would not contaminate the other.

Following the initial meeting, Aldo considered a possible staff plan for Fred, being careful to be supportive, not critical. Rehabilitation focused on improving attentiveness, productivity, and time management. Aldo believed camaraderie in the shop would help increase company productivity. He also felt staff social functions might encourage improved morale.

During their second meeting, Aldo and Fred discussed positive aspects of the simple three-point rehabilitation plan outlined in Figure 25.3. Fred made only small adjustments to the plan before signing it and committing himself to taking the outlined steps to improve his attitude.

Lewis Printing
Staff Plan

Name:	Fred USO	Individual Criteria Ratings	Rating / 10
Job:	Print Shop Foreman	Dependability	8
Years of Service	7	Job Knowledge	9
		Attitude	4
Date of Review	18 March, 2002	Productivity	5
		Overall Rating	6.5

Preliminary Comments

Fred seems unhappy, as reflected by his attitude and productivity on the job.

Figure 25.3

Lewis Printing
Staff Plan

Rehabilitation Plans

1. Take productivity and time management course by June 30.

2. Hold two staff parties this year.

3. Focus on positive work attitude each day.

Aldo Lewis	**Fred Uso**
Aldo Lewis, Interviewer	Fred Uso, Interviewee

Figure 25.3 (cont.)

We learn a lot from Aldo's approach. The preliminary meeting was purely reconnaissance. He was simply trying to determine the true cause of Fred's poor performance. Only with this knowledge could he consider an appropriate rehabilitation plan. Out of concern for Fred's feelings, Aldo didn't dwell on the unhappiness Fred was experiencing at home. Instead, he focused on improving Fred's skills as well as his contribution to the atmosphere at work.

Not all rehabilitation is this gentle. Some situations require numerous meetings as superiors search for the most effective leadership style. In some cases, only a tough style achieves the desired results, as displayed by Everett Manufacturing Inc.

Everett, a manufacturer of airplane parts for major defense corporations, operates two production lines, physically parallel to one another. One line is managed by Bob Stone, the other by Bert Chandler.

Bob frequently spends time socially with his 12 employees, meeting them for a beer after work. Everyone feels comfortable with Bob in social settings, treating him more as an equal than a boss. On the job though, no one forgets who is boss. When a crew member is asked to rework a part, he does so without question. Everyone knows Bob only makes demands when it's absolutely necessary. He's a straight shooter.

Only once, two years ago, did Bob have difficulty with his shift. Brad Murphy wasn't pulling his weight on the production line, taking frequent breaks and calling in sick more often than the others. Brad had a rough demeanor, sounding like a bully even during the simplest of conversations. He didn't like Bob, and Bob didn't like him. They both knew it.

One day Bob saw Brad jam a small piece of metal into a sensitive gearbox essential to line operations. The line was shut down for two hours while maintenance pulled the box apart and sent a man to an outside machine shop for replacement parts.

Bob called Brad into his office, closed the door and laid the accusation of sabotage. Brad denied fault, forcing Bob's hand. Instead of firing him then and there, Bob took a day to think about it. He reviewed Brad's work history, even looking at performance evaluations prepared by his predecessor as line manager who was known as a tough evaluator of people. Brad scored high in all evaluations, too high to just fire him without first thinking of rehabilitation.

When Bob talked to Bert about the case, Bert's first reaction was to fire Brad. Although Bob often found Bert too quick with such decisions, he respected his opinion. After a lengthy discussion, they decided to transfer Brad to Bert's shift, to offer him a second chance.

Two months later during his regular meeting with Bert, Bob heard only positive reports about Brad's performance. He couldn't believe they were discussing the same employee. When pressed to reveal his magic for managing Brad, Bert said it was simple. The day Brad transferred to his shift, he called him into his office. There, he told Brad he had no use for his type, that his advice to Bob had been to fire him without notice, and that that's exactly what would happen if he tried the same behavior again.

Bert made it clear he didn't tolerate poor shift attendance. If Brad missed one day of work without a note from the company doctor, Bert would dock him two days' pay. If he missed two days of work without the note, he would not be allowed back on the premises. When Brad threatened to complain to the shop steward, Bert welcomed the threat, waving the sabotage report. Bert hasn't had a performance problem with Brad since.

What does Everett Manufacturing teach us? For starters, this is a most unusual rehabilitation plan. An employee deliberately sabotages a production line and is transferred to a supervisor who rehabilitates with threats. Not the theme of this book so far. But Everett was specifically selected to demonstrate that no matter what human resource theory might say, the goal is to generate desired behavior. You're dealing with people and they come in all shapes and with all kinds of attitudes. The trick to successful leadership is knowing how to motivate them. One size of leadership style does not fit all. In fact, in many cases it's the leader who has to change to accommodate his employees.

Bob Stone's inability to manage Brad Murphy doesn't mean he's a poor manager. He manages others quite successfully with his benevolent approach and has a high group performance rating from senior management. Tough guy Murphy couldn't respect Bob's benevolent approach to people. But bully him and you have an employee who understands management. Performance improves accordingly. The case also suggests gruff managers like Bert Chandler have a place in business management, though they should probably not be role models. Chandler made a point to understand Murphy and what management style would encourage him to adopt a better attitude. A military style became the most effective option. It's a style that should never be discarded completely simply because a leader finds it distasteful.

The Everett case also demonstrates what happens when leadership strengths become weaknesses, and weaknesses become strengths. Bob's strength for motivating people became a weakness in the Murphy case. It fell to Chandler's intimidation to handle the unique situation.

BITE 15: EXAMINE COMPETENCE AFTER SIGNIFICANT BUSINESS CHANGES

When you plan to maintain core competence, you assume it will remain at a static level. But what if management wishes to enter a new line of business, acquire another company, or sell an existing division? Required competence levels are likely to change. Re-evaluation of core competence should be performed to ensure a balance for existing operations. Change existing operations and you'll often change your requirements for core competence.

Significant changes in operations demand fresh leadership triage, even if the annual one has just concluded. All planning returns to the beginning stage. Management time has new demands placed on it and often shifts from existing to new operations, which means less time can be devoted to the completion of old action plans. But that doesn't mean that old action plans aren't still important. Let's look at Global Foods Inc. for the example here.

When Shirley Casman's father died, she became the third generation Casman to manage Global Foods. The wholesale giant services five cities with six warehouses and 500 employees. With Shirley as president and chair of the family board of directors, the company employs five other Casmans — one brother and four cousins. Brother Al is vice president of food purchasing and distribution — the heart of the business. One cousin, Gerry, is the finance man, while the other cousins share management of the six warehouses.

The business has always been profitable. Volume is the key to profit in food wholesaling, and with sales growing marginally each year, six Casman families earn a more than respectable living from the business.

Shirley's father, Arnold, was more ambitious than his health would permit. When alive and managing, Arnold grumbled about the margins retail chains earned on the food Global delivered. He even threatened to buy his own chain in retaliation. Even though he died before his dream came true, his grumbling was not in vain. Shirley had listened well and began discussions with a potential retail suitor just 18 months after her father's death.

An acquisition team was formed, including Shirley, Gerry, the company's lawyer, and its external accountant, Sam Lacy, who also had become Shirley's corporate soul mate following her father's death. Arnold had trusted Sam and this made him a natural ally for Shirley.

The acquisition team pored over every document offered by Alma Foods Limited, the potential acquisition retail chain. It asked for every piece of paper created by Alma during its 15 years of existence. Every irregularity was investigated by Global's most diligent employees. Gerry's controller dissected numbers, raising questions about purchases for Al to answer. Cousins managing Global warehouses spent two weeks at Alma retail locations, studying the history of stock movement — that is, inventory turnover and shrinkage such as wastage and theft.

Sam reviewed payment records of customers and provisions for doubtful accounts. He was to ensure Global did not pay too much for goodwill. He was determined that every issue would be thought through and he urged Shirley to prepare an acquisition digestion plan for blending the two operations. Shirley insisted it could be completed later; there was much to do now just to determine if there would be a purchase.

Legal documents prepared by Alma's lawyers were torn apart by Global's counsel. Frequent meetings ensured information was shared and considered by all team members to permit complete analysis.

Shirley, to this point, is a fabulous student of manageable bites. All acquisition functions are planned in detail, with specific actions, responsibilities, and completion dates. Alma's efforts to shorten the process were, quite appropriately, resisted by Shirley. The purchase closed on time and as planned. But further examination reveals one critical oversight.

Following the transaction closing, Al spent most of his time at Alma. Inventory reporting was not to his liking, the tolerance for error at Alma being somewhat more liberal than that which was permitted at Global.

Gerry encountered difficulty amalgamating the two accounting systems and had to totally redesign Alma's to consolidate results.

With so much time spent blending Alma into operations, management of Global fell into disarray. Purchasing drifted out of control with overstocking of certain perishables. Losses were incurred. Shrinkages increased. Because of his time spent at Alma, Gerry didn't complete revised financial projections for the bank, leaving that relationship strained with a new line of credit yet to be approved. Disorganization gave way to crisis management — a company out of control.

First quarter financial results were disastrous and company banker Jim Placer requested a meeting with Shirley so she could explain material performance variances. She brought along soul mate Sam Lacy, who confidently explained how purchase planning included a managerial digestion period. Prepurchase planning for digestion, eloquently described by Sam in the discussion with Jim Placer, sounded so good to Shirley she implemented it — eight months after she should have! She wished she had listened to Sam when he first recommended it.

Even though Shirley demonstrated manageable bite principles during acquisition, she failed to provide for post-acquisition planning — an oversight that cost her dearly. Shirley did not ensure the presence of sufficient core competence to manage the combined business. The demands of the Alma purchase had a negative effect on management at Global. The absence of key leaders demanded some internal promotions and some hiring to maintain Global's smooth operation. But in the rush to buy Alma, it didn't happen. In fact, while Shirley was looking for problems in Alma, she was creating her own at Global!

Shirley is a very bright leader, above average in fact. If her oversight frightens you, it should. Knowing core competence limitations determines the boundaries of what you can expect of employees — and of yourself.

BITE 16: APPOINT A LEADER FOR CORE COMPETENCE

People are of critical importance to any business, so it behooves any company to appoint a leader for core competence. This person is respon- sible for constantly assessing employee strengths and weaknesses, ensuring success is rewarded, and marshalling rehabilitation plans for poor performers. The role is critical for ensuring goal and performance congru- ency between company and individual.

For larger businesses, appointment of a core competence leader is a digestible decision. Owners of small businesses will argue it is not econom- ical when revenues and workloads do not justify a separate position. But the small size of a business does not eliminate the need for core compe- tence leadership. The duty may be one of many for owners of small businesses, but it must fall to someone in every business.

If responsibility for core competence is not assigned, it will not be assumed. And if it is not assumed, it will not be maintained. Account- ability for competency is the issue here. Alex Desernoff at The Blue Shell Restaurant assumed leadership when he developed his reward system. Art Thatcher of Igloo Ice Cream led core competence change when he promoted his strongest staff member to manager. Likewise, Frank Stellar of Stellar Communications assumed it by conducting performance evalua- tions. This need is further emphasized by the example of Zip Courier Ltd.

Zip Courier Ltd. owns and manages a fleet of 55 courier vehicles. Owner and operations manager Luc Simon shares management responsibility with his wife, Lily.

Lily operates the dispatch system, taking orders for courier deliveries. Luc ensures vehicles, financial affairs, and planning are all in good order.

Lily's responsibility to take customer orders makes her the first point of customer contact. She knows if customers are happy or displeased with Zip's service. Although never formally assigned the responsibility, it seemed natural for her to track customer satisfaction by car and driver number.

When Lily receives a complaint, she advises the driver in question and asks for improved performance. When more than one complaint is received, she asks the driver to report to dispatch for an interview. When the problem is with the driver, she encourages rehabilitation. Drivers who refuse rehabilitation are terminated in all cases.

Lily Simon doesn't know it, but she is Zip's leader of core competence. She ensures customer service quality and identifies poor performers for rehabilitation or dismissal. Even though Zip Courier Limited is a small business, Lily's role as leader is critical to company success.

Similarly, Avrum Wentzell became African Trading Inc.'s leader of core competence by identifying training necessary to meet average sales of $300,000 per person. Financial success in that case is specifically linked to sales training — the core competence to be maintained at African Trading Inc.

There are two major resource categories in any corporate organization — people and finance. A third exists for natural resource industries: the physical supply of oil, gas, water, timber, fish, or minerals. People, also known as core competence, is the single most important category of these three. The brightest and best-trained people will find solutions to shortages of financial and natural resources. Finance and resources are nothing, though, without the brightest and best-trained people to handle them. Not only is core competence the most valuable resource, it is the most difficult to maintain and the most complex to understand. But it can be tackled effectively — in manageable bites.

IV

Secrets to Revenue Growth

"Most people don't see the light
without feeling a little heat first."
— *ANONYMOUS*

Although soul mates, goals, action plans, and core competence are all part of leading by manageable bites, the process isn't complete without carefully examining all operating functions. Profit is the primary reason for being in business. It's every leader's benchmark for success and the measurement tool for every decision. All goals focus directly or indirectly on profit improvement. Successful leaders instinctively reduce every decision to a very basic equation, shown in Figure 26.4.

Basic Equation

$$\text{Revenue} - \text{Expenses} = \text{Profit}$$

Figure 26.4

Simply stated, profit increases come from revenue growth, expense reductions, or a combination of the two. The implementation of goals with the general aim of maximizing profit can be complicated. In the interests of simplicity, it's always better to categorize goals and actions into one of the two camps — those that increase revenue and those that reduce expenses. This chapter deals with the former. Generating revenue growth requires a thorough understanding of the market environment of both your competitors and your customers. Ideally, the process goes like this: sound data collection provides the basis for an analysis of market behavior. This, in turn, gives you the knowledge to allocate your resources wisely in pursuing market opportunities. Figure 27.4 demonstrates the primary path to revenue growth — that is, specific sales plans are developed from available resources and market intelligence.

Secrets to Revenue Growth

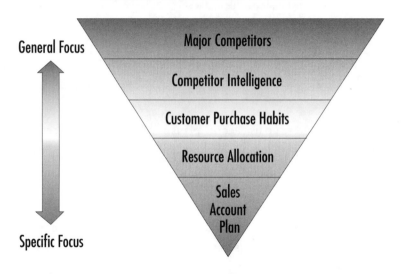

Figure 27.4

BITE 17: KNOW YOUR MAJOR COMPETITORS

Leaders define marketplace size by the sum of all sales of all businesses selling similar products or services into similar markets. For example, if six hotels, each posting annual revenue of $5 million, dominate the only beach resort on an island, the size of the market is $30 million. Although not perfect, especially for dissimilar products with similar purposes, this definition can serve as a practical rule of thumb. It may not catch smaller, more obscure competitors, but it will capture the major ones who set the pace of competition.

Knowing competitors well is a critical manageable bite. Your competition provides you with benchmarks for assessing your own company's product innovation, sales techniques, and operating performance. If you aren't outperforming them, comparisons should generate goals and actions to improve your company's performance. Competitor successes and failures are inexpensive lessons to you, as long as you observe and analyze them before you take risks. Competitor performance assessments can reveal marketplace opportunities for your company or show where your company needs to improve. For example, when competitors' customer service is poor and their sales decline, they create an opportunity for you to increase sales volume. On the other hand, if your revenue is declining relative to that of competitors, corrective action becomes necessary.

Identifying competitors isn't difficult. If you are at all aggressive, you bump into the major ones every day. Customers are also a good source of knowledge of competitor product and management problems. After years in business, experienced leaders should have a wealth of competitive information. New leaders have a bigger challenge.

No matter what your business, you can't compete without knowing your competitors. They'll know you and strive to be one step ahead, forcing you to spend time reacting to their successes rather than planning your own. The value of obtaining basic competitive information is illustrated in the story of Sea Dog Rentals.

Since Charlie Lacombe was a teenage surfer, he dreamed of owning his own water resort rental business. Boats of all sizes, power or sail, would form his fleet, which served sport-starved vacationers. Now 28, Charlie and three friends are planning to incorporate Sea Dog Rentals, fulfilling his boyhood dream.

Charlie's dad, Frank, a natural soul mate, managed his own business for 30 years. When the boys came to him not knowing where to start, Frank handed them the yellow pages. The boys looked bewildered. Dad explained. "Before committing to a sport rental business, you'd better study those already in the business," was his advice.

Flipping to the sea sport rental section of the phone book, they found a number of companies, perhaps indicating a saturated market. But

Frank calmed them. When no one's in the business, he advised, there is either a terrific opportunity or no market at all.

The next step was to determine which competitors were dominant and why. Each partner assumed responsibility for interviewing one resort company, armed with a questionnaire prepared with Frank's help. Sea Dog's questionnaire is illustrated in Figure 28.4.

The responses to the questionnaire, and many additional questions, would become Sea Dog's competitor intelligence and influence every decision about goals and actions for the new business.

Whether yours is a service-, manufacturing-, or resource-based business, it's not possible to sustain long-term corporate health without a strategy for growing the revenue base and defending your company from competitor attacks. Through Sea Dog's research, Charlie Lacombe learned that every competitor success and failure can be studied to determine:

- customer satisfaction;
- successful advertising strategies;
- sales force strengths and weaknesses;
- product quality;
- pricing policies;
- potential new products; and
- warranty and customer return policies.

Gathering intelligence is not a one-time event. Intelligence has to be maintained and monitored to consistently support your decision-making process. Over time, trends become apparent. These are important because they reflect competitors' behavior and reactions to competitive pressure. Without constantly updated intelligence, you do not know when to counter competitor strengths or take advantage of their weaknesses. This makes achieving stable revenue growth much more difficult. Hanover Auto Sales emphasizes the point:

Seth Hanover has been selling automobiles since he was 16. He never finished high school, leaving early to support his mother and two younger brothers when his father died.

Sea Dog Rentals
Competitive Questionnaire

1. Do you receive guest requests for sea sport rentals?   YES   NO

   If YES, how often?

2. Do you refer guests to existing rental operations?   YES   NO

   If YES, who? Why?

3. Which are the five sea sport rental companies you feel comfortable recommending to your guests?	4. If you perceived one weakness in each of these companies, what would it be?
1.	1.
2.	2.
3.	3.
4.	4.
5.	5.

5. What are the three most important factors making you feel comfortable recommending these companies to guests?

   1.

   2.

   3.

6. Would you consider referring business to a new company?   YES   NO

   Why or why not?

Figure 28.4

Even though Seth never acquired a secondary education, he possesses extraordinary sales skills, an ability to sell a car to even the most reluctant buyer.

Seth has two competitors — Alvin Motors and Big City Fine Cars. Together, the three companies account for 63 percent of all the cars sold within 50 miles of downtown. Competition among the three is so intense at times that selling just one car more than the other companies becomes more important than profit.

All three are accustomed to holding summer sales, usually in late August when new models are launched. One summer, Hanover lagged behind in unit sales volume, falling to third place behind his two competitors. A perplexed Seth spent considerable time thinking about how to turn around his company's fortunes. One day, to relax, he accepted an invitation to play golf with a friend who was in the newspaper business.

On the fourth green, Seth's friend asked if Seth had prepared his full-page advertisement for this year's August car sale. Seth, amused by the question, did not react. His sales manager was just finishing Hanover's ad for the August 20 paper. His golf partner said he thought the sale began on the 13th. Alvin and Big City had already committed advertising to his newspaper for the August 10, 11, and 12!

Seth could hardly contain himself during the balance of the game. Evidently, his two competitors were conspiring to shut him out of this year's sale. After the game, he returned to the office and called an emergency management meeting to discuss the matter. Seth and his team were determined not to be blindsided by their competitors and decided to hold their sale from August 9 to 12. Advertising had to be submitted by August 7 at the latest. With only two weeks remaining, timing was tight, but everyone agreed to work through the weekend to ensure that both the cars and the showroom were superbly decorated.

When Hanover's advertising hit the newspapers on August 7, Seth received angry calls from the presidents of Alvin Motors and Big City Fine Cars.

Hanover is one of many cases that illustrates the need for competitor intelligence. Alex Desernoff of The Blue Shell Restaurant is another example of a leader who successfully gathered competitor intelligence. For

Alex, it was his cousin's assessment of strengths and weaknesses of other restaurants that allowed him to tweak his own for greater success. The construction contracting business provides more excellent examples of the value of competitor intelligence.

In this often ultracompetitive environment, monitoring competitor bids helps companies determine how to tender future contracts to increase acceptance rates, and gives them a way to gauge whether a competitor is gaining or losing money. Summertime Pools provides an example.

Summertime Pools installs and services above- and in-ground swimming pools for the residential housing market. President Bill Watkins spends considerable time gathering market and competitor intelligence to manage his business. Data is not published, so intelligence accuracy is always in question. Multiple-year trends reveal patterns in contract bidding success and gross margin estimates within an accuracy tolerance that satisfies Bill.

Bill monitors four competitors. He uses information from city building permits, industry sales data, and direct competition for contracts to estimate the number of contracts bid by each company. Similar sources provide reasonable estimates of competitor bid success. Gross margin performance is estimated from discussions with homeowners. Although gross margin is the weakest estimate, Bill makes certain assumptions based on industry knowledge, standards, and experience with his own operations.

As shown in Figure 29.4, Summertime's competitor analysis tracks the number of contracts sent bids over several months. At first glance, L & M Pools is more aggressive, bidding 95 contracts, 12 more than its nearest competitor, City Pools. If this was the only performance criterion tracked by Bill, L & M Pools would appear to be the most successful. Bids submitted, though, are an indication only of market activity, not of contract success. Bill is more interested in the ratio of successful bids to those submitted.

More contracts have been awarded to National Pool Service than to any other major market player. At 46 successful bids, National is eight contracts ahead of L & M. Comparing ratios of successful bids to total submitted, National is successful 66.7 percent of the time compared with Summertime's 43.8 percent. Bill's estimates of gross margin also put National in first place.

Summertime Pools
Competitor Intelligence

Market Players	Number of Contracts Bid	Successful Bids	Bid Success Rate %	Estimated Gross Margin %
City Pools	83	35	42.2	38.6
National Pool Service	69	46	66.7	39.0
L & M Pools	95	38	40.0	33.1
Summertime Pools	80	35	43.8	38.2
Average	82	39	47.6	37.2

Figure 29.4

So, what does Bill Watkins learn from his analysis? Well, Summertime doesn't place first in any competitive criteria. Others outperform it in every category. National Pool Service bids fewer contracts but scores a higher bid success rate and gross margin percentage. It bids only on contracts it believes it can win. Selective bidding means more time to research and prepare individual bids to impress potential customers. Gross margins improve when costs aren't incurred by bidding on every contract — a policy followed by L & M Pools.

After his analysis, Bill applied this intelligence to annual goal setting and decided to bid only on contracts with a high probability of customer acceptance, as assessed by his salespeople. By not chasing every contract, one estimator position was eliminated, reducing the cost of sales and thus increasing the gross margin.

BITE 18: STUDY PURCHASING HABITS OF TARGET MARKETS

Successful leaders never assume products that are well accepted in one market will be as well accepted in another. Cultural differences, for example, play important roles. Fast food is slow to catch on in France, where fine dining is a serious daily ritual. Similarly, well-prepared food is not as popular at noontime in North America. As a result, hamburger chains analyze the two markets quite differently.

A culture's aesthetic preferences also come into play. Brightly colored product packaging and advertising are successful in some countries but not in others, so informed designers study cultural preferences before finalizing their market strategies. Leaders must know these market idiosyncrasies well. What may seem like a slight misjudgment can result in product failure. Months of planning, testing, and designing are lost as a consequence, at great cost, in terms of both money already spent and potential future earnings lost.

Product pricing, like cultural differences, affects consumer behavior. Customers have their own instincts for product worth. If pricing policies go against those instincts, products are often rejected outright. There are many examples. Electronic manufacturers love to sell televisions at $499.95 or $699.79. Why? Research tells them consumer resistance begins at $500.00 and $700.00 for certain models.

The automobile industry practices a different pricing strategy. Ford Taurus cars may be advertised at $21,600, but when you shop at the dealer, you find the model for you costs more than $25,000 — plus tax. The advertised price is true, but only for the very basic car — no stereo, air conditioning, electric windows, or leather. These are known as add-ons, options available at an extra cost. Despite customer grumbling, the marketing strategy works. We visit dealers expecting to pay one price, fall in love with a more expensive model, and come away having parted with more cash than we'd planned.

Advertising has a profound influence on purchasing behavior. Every day, subliminal messages help people choose Coke over Pepsi, Fords over Toyotas, one airline over another, vacation spots, cereals, televisions, stereos, and even burial plots. Well-researched and carefully designed advertising is a powerful tool when it catches our fancy. When it doesn't, our subconscious ignores the message and we're not motivated to buy. The line between successful and unsuccessful advertising campaigns is often very thin.

Product acceptance, then, is largely dependent on management's perception of the market buying profile. Intelligent product decisions about packaging, colors, advertising campaigns, and pricing policies cannot be made without understanding the purchasing habits of a target market. Let's look at how Sally's Dresses Inc. handles this step.

> Sally's Dresses Inc. is owned and managed by Sally Johnson. Operations include four stores: three in suburban shopping malls and one downtown. The east side shopping mall store is located in the heart of a large Spanish community, the west end store draws loyal clientele from the country, and the south end outlet caters to a number of middle class communities.
>
> Sally's greatest challenge is style selection in correct quantities for each of four buying seasons. With such a diverse clientele, it is impossible to take full advantage of the purchasing power of all four stores buying as one. Each has to be considered as a separate business.
>
> Before buying seasons, Sally circulates a questionnaire to gather preferred style and color intelligence for the next season. She hosts breakfast meetings with customers in each marketplace to discuss clothing tastes, resulting in very different buying lists for each store, as illustrated in Figure 30.4.

Sally's Dresses
Buying Summary

Store Location	Product Focus
East End	• Bright colors
	• Scarves
	• Informal daily wear
Downtown	• Business suits
	• Neutral colors
	• White blouses
West End	• Sportswear
	• Gardening wear
	• Durable products
South End	• Evening wear
	• Formal dresses
	• Sportswear

Figure 30.4

Sally faces a difficult challenge with such diverse customer purchasing habits. Substantial differences in culture and class affect the purchasing habits of Sally's clientele. It makes mass purchasing impossible and advertising a nightmare. But Sally knows her market well. She treats each store as a separate company with a localized purchasing and advertising focus. And as a result, she is successful!

BITE 19: BEWARE OF LUST FOR UNPROVEN MARKETS

Established markets represent today's revenues. They must be nurtured, and a company should set as many goals as necessary to maintain their stability. New markets are also important: they need to be explored in search of tomorrow's revenues. But beware. If your focus shifts completely from performing markets to unproven ones, your established markets will likely decay and competitors will move in for the kill. Damage to your revenue base compounds if the new markets do not blossom. Jim Bowes of Classic Shoes illustrates the danger.

Classic Shoes operates one shoe and leather store in central downtown. Owner-manager Jim Bowes gauges store success by monitoring two major competitors. Since opening 10 years ago, Classic has peaked at a 41 percent market share. Troubled by a recent decline in market share to 37 percent, Jim engaged a marketing consultant.

Four days later, the consultant produced a preliminary report concluding that Jim should shift merchandising practices away from traditional men's dress shoes toward a sports line. The advice represented a significant business change and Jim was quite concerned about its effect on profit. Hesitation caused him to speak to Al Lawson, neighbor and business soul mate.

Al stressed the risk associated with turning away from products that were so successful for 10 years — even though the consultant's report backed its recommendations with higher margin and profit expectations for sporting shoes. With his soul mate against the major change and a reputable consultant in favor, Jim was confused.

When he finished studying the report and its supporting analysis, Jim decided, on balance, to test the sport line. During the fall buying trip, he passed over traditional manufacturers in favor of sporting lines he felt would sell well in the city, stocking his shelves with medium- to high-priced sportswear.

Throughout the fall and winter seasons, Jim's share of the traditional shoe market virtually disappeared, while sales of sport shoes struggled to keep up. Revenues plummeted throughout the spring until the company's April 30 year-end revealed a loss of $62,000 — a decline of $140,000 from the previous year's profit of $78,000!

Where did Jim go wrong? First, the downtown market consists of businessmen, not sports aficionados. Professionals purchase traditional shoes in the area around their workplaces. Sportswear competitors usually set up in suburban malls, close to evening and weekend sports activity.

Stores with limited retail space can't introduce new lines without taking space away from old, possibly profitable, lines. This doesn't mean stores should never venture into new products. They should, and do, successfully, after gathering reliable competitor intelligence and marketplace purchasing habits. If Jim had analyzed his marketplace properly, he would have known why there were no sportswear competitors downtown. His decision would have been very different. Perhaps he would have maintained traditional lines downtown while exploring the possibility of opening a sportswear store in a suburban area.

There is another lesson here. Jim ignored his soul mate's advice. While it's not unusual for leaders to disregard soul mate advice against pet projects, it should be done with caution. Soul mates are not always right. Balancing their advice with your own view is a delicate matter. One rule is helpful: never ignore a soul mate's advice without first preparing a written analysis of the costs and benefits of each approach. Follow the logic of both points of view. Take your soul mate through it. Both of you will come to the right conclusion. The worst thing to do is to ignore a soul mate's advice without a well-researched, well-thought-out impact analysis. If you have no analysis, it's just your opinion against that of your soul mate. If a proper analysis proves your soul mate wrong, then pursue your dreams. If you selected a soul mate because you respect his or her judgment, it will take more than one disagreement to destroy that respect.

A-1 Window Washers offers a slightly different perspective on new markets and resource allocation.

Harley Crawford, president and general manager of A-1 Window Washers, cleaned high-rise commercial windows year round and residential windows during five months of the year.

Harley organized both commercial and residential contracts in two-man teams. Average high-rise contracts required two men for three days, while residential teams completed four contracts per day.

Soul mate Ben Shully advised Harley to transfer more resources from commercial to residential contracts. Ben's sketchy analysis focused on higher monthly gross margins for residential cleaning. For Ben, it made sense to apply all financial and human resources to the division yielding the greatest return.

Harley had trouble with Ben's advice. A-1 had been in the commercial window business for 15 years and enjoyed an excellent reputation. To move from commercial altogether to the more demanding residential market didn't seem right to Harley, even though Ben's advice was usually sound. He decided to check with his accountant, Linda Capshaw.

Linda studied all aspects of commercial and residential divisions before making a recommendation. During a three-hour discussion, she assembled as much relevant data as possible from Harley's books and recollection. When the information gathering was complete, they stepped back from detail to consider the overall impact of different courses of action.

Linda's analysis is cold and objective. With 10 full-time employees in commercial operations, Harley generates a net contribution of $20,400 a month, $244,800 annually. A-1 services 34 of 50 high-rise buildings in the area, representing 68 percent of the market. Commercial business is stable and profitable.

The residential division has some advantages. Windows are not cleaned during stormy and winter seasons so there's no need for full-time teams. And with 35 part-time university students working for just five months of the year, there is no employee benefits expense. Market price is $49 per house, with a $24 gross margin contribution. A 49 percent residential gross margin compares favorably to commercial's 46.2 percent. Linda points to residential's $33,600 monthly gross

A-1 Window Washers
Analysis of Market Contribution

	Commercial Windows	Residential Windows	
		Existing Business	Equivalent Business Required to Match Commercial
1. Full-time Employees	10	—	—
2. Part-time Employees	—	35	51
3. Monthly Customer Capacity	34	1,400	2,040
4. Average Bill to Customer	$1,300	$49	$49
5. Average Cost of Service	$700	$25	$25
6. Gross Margin	$600	$24	$24
7. Gross Margin %	46.2	49.0	49.0
8. No. of Months of Service Each Year	12	5	5
9. Monthly Contribution [Monthly Capacity (3) x Gross Margin (6)]	$20,400	$33,600	$48,960
10. Annual Contribution (8) x (9)	$244,800	$168,000	$244,800
11. Market Size	50	10,000	10,000
12. Market Share [(3) ÷ (11) x 100%]	68%	14%	20%

Figure 31.4

margin as Ben's motivation for encouraging all resources to be allocated to that division.

But she goes on. Because residential operates five months of the year, the division generates a contribution of only $168,000 annually, compared with commercial's $244,800. Market size is 10,000 houses compared with 50 office buildings; market share is 14 percent, to commercial's 68 percent.

Linda prepared an analysis of equivalent residential business required to match the commercial contribution. As Figure 31.4 demonstrates, to generate $244,800 net contribution from residential alone, Harle, would have to increase market share from 14 to 20 percent — from 1,400 to 2,040 homes for each five-month year. And that's just to meet the existing commercial contribution alone, not the combined $412,800 ($244,800 + $168,000) of commercial-residential business now being enjoyed. Many more homes would have to be serviced to reach the combined contribution.

If only residential business is pursued, operations would be closed and equipment mothballed at additional cost. To top it off, each spring, residential sales would have to be pursued vigorously just to maintain the same volume as last year. Commercial contracts, on the other hand, are normally on a three-year basis, reducing start-up risk each year.

When Harley and Linda finished their meeting, his course of action was clear. He would maintain the commercial contract division, while setting goals to increase the number of part-time residential teams over the next two years.

Even though Harley has an excellent soul mate in Ben Shully, his advice was not correct. The repercussions of allocating commercial resources to the more risky residential division were not properly analyzed until Linda became involved. Without her analysis of his soul mate's advice, Harley probably would be in the residential window washing business now, to the exclusion of commercial. Resources would be allocated to more risky markets at the expense of established and profitable ones.

BITE 20: ALLOCATE RESOURCES ONLY TO OPPORTUNITIES WITH POTENTIAL FOR OPTIMUM GOAL ACHIEVEMENT

Once you've allocated resources to established markets, you'll get a clear idea of what excess resources you have for new ventures. Only financial and human assets in excess of those required to maintain your traditional profitable revenue base are considered for potential new opportunities.

To make informed decisions, it is important to understand the nature of potential opportunities. If potential lies with the next generation of an existing product line, you may assume a relatively low risk in allocating resources to it. These opportunities deserve high priority. Conversely, if the potential opportunity is an entirely new product line, you are likely to take on a greater risk with it. These must be assigned a lower resource priority.

Resource analyses can be performed to assess potential risk, compatibility with existing products, profit potential, and the likelihood of market acceptance. The analysis is simply a way of rating potential opportunities to ensure resources are allocated in the best way possible. A case example is necessary here, so let's look at how Dillman Engineering Ltd. selects its revenue opportunities.

Dillman Engineering Ltd. offers a wide range of engineering consulting advice to both private and public sector clients worldwide. A medium-sized company with revenue of $118 million, its clients include not only domestic companies with construction activities in second world and third world countries, but governments of those countries as well. For planning purposes, clients are grouped first as domestic or foreign, then by country of activity, and finally by type of engineering advice purchased, as well as by Dillman's expectation for future consulting contracts with them.

In recent years, the number of domestic clients managing road construction in Africa has been on the rise. Governments there initiated an economic policy to build roads both as transportation improvements and a stimulus for employment. Demands for Dillman's staff now exceed available resources, forcing goal reexamination during annual triage. The dilemma facing Dillman is whether to hire eight additional engineers or accept less work.

Dillman knows the demand for additional engineers resulted from a temporary rise in revenue contract demands. Expected to last 18 months, the temporary demand does not seem to warrant additional hires. Some relief is in sight as well, as a result of rescheduling decisions by a number of clients. That leaves two projects yet to be staffed.

Dillman employs a proven model, demonstrated in Figure 32.4, to weigh the value of each project. First, the company asks managers and engineers to identify key business success criteria, those basic principles needing to be satisfied for their goals to be met. Dillman's senior staff were asked to list these criteria during the previous year's triage. What must be achieved for the company to grow? During lockup, criteria were discussed and the facilitator encouraged participants to negotiate away differences among them, and form common success criteria.

Weights were assigned to each key success criteria in relative magnitudes to reflect their level of importance to the company. Criteria and weights agreed upon by lockup participants included profit potential, assigned the weight of 10; available skills — 8; client relations — 10; stimulating work to do — 4; new design — 3; costs to be absorbed by the firm — 6; and risk of payment — 7.

Armed with project weightings, Dillman studies each project. A separate score is assigned for each criterion, in each project, to reflect the company leaders' forecast of the project's performance. Management then multiplies each criterion score by its corresponding weight of importance to arrive at a weighted score for each of each project. Total weighted scores are compared among projects competing for the same resources. For Dillman's existing resource shortages, management prepared the analysis shown in Figure 32.4.

High scores reflect high ratings. A profit score of 10 means an above average profit expectation from the assignment. Payment risk is low if a project is assigned a score of 7 out of a possible 7. A score of 6 for cost absorbed indicates the company expects to recover all expenses associated with the project. Available skills suggest the company currently employs the core competence necessary to complete the contract — and that that competence is available.

A client relations score of 10 indicates the importance of completing the contract and that failure to do so will affect future contracts expected to be awarded to the company by that particular client. A low score, conversely, suggests not accepting the contract will have little impact upon future profits or client relations. A high score concerning stimulating work means Dillman likes the nature of work and will apply itself to the project. New design scores reflect the effort necessary to invent the design. A high score means the design has been perfected on another assignment and there is lower design risk and overhead costs.

The South African highway project yielded a total weighted score of 233, a moderate score by Dillman standards. Profit expectations came in at 50, only half the potential mark. On the other hand, Dillman would incur only minimum payment and design risks. With only 50 marks out of a possible 100, the valuator did not think client relations was an important issue. South Africa was not a regular client and no future projects were known to be at risk.

Dillman Engineering
Resource Allocation Analysis

Project	Weights	Score	Weighted Score
South African Highway			
Project 122			
profit	10	5	50
available skills	8	6	48
client relations	10	5	50
stimulating work	4	4	16
new design	3	3	9
costs absorbed	6	3	18
payment risk	7	6	42
Total score			233
Ivory Coast Bridge			
Project 239			
profit	10	10	100
available skills	8	3	24
client relations	10	9	90
stimulating work	4	3	12
new design	3	1	3
cost absorbed	6	6	36
payment risk	7	7	49
Total score			314
Monaco Irrigation			
Project 502			
profit	10	4	40
available skills	8	8	64
client relations	10	1	10
stimulating work	4	4	16
new design	3	2	6
cost absorbed	6	1	6
payment risk	7	2	14
Total score			156

Figure 32.4

If there were no other choices, a score of 233 for the South African highway project would be attractive — at least more so than the Monaco irrigation project with a mark of 156. Monaco doesn't have the same profit potential, even with all the resources available to complete the contract immediately. Fortunately, no sensitive client relations are at stake if Dillman refuses to bid, reflected by the score of 1. Everyone wants to complete the stimulating and challenging work — the emotional weighting. Payment risk is high with progress billings not guaranteed by the World Bank. Overall, low profit compounded by high payment risk shows this contract to be a poor choice for limited resources.

The score of 314 for the Ivory Coast bridge project easily makes it the favorite. Profit is above average with little payment risk, and future work will be at stake if Dillman doesn't bid the project. Support for the South African and Monaco projects was based on the work being stimulating, not profitable. Personal stimulation came ahead of company success for those wanting to bid these contracts. But Dillman's objective resource allocation mechanism prevented it from choosing opportunities for personal rather than company gain.

Dillman's management tool may be applied to most resource allocation decisions. It's equally effective for a business with revenue of, say, $500,000 faced with a decision to purchase a $4,000 micro-computer, an $8,000 automobile, and office furnishings of $5,000 — but with only $9,000 to spend. When forced to rank importance, different weights will always be assigned to each choice — no matter what the decision. The rest is mathematics — a science that lends itself quite nicely to the removal of unwanted emotion often inherent in such decisions. To demonstrate the formula's versatility, let's study Carson Sports Shop Inc.

Carson Sports Shop Inc. operates a single retail outlet in a city of one million people. With sales of $8.5 million, it has been a profitable family enterprise for 12 years, specializing in sports equipment for hockey, skiing, football, and cycling. Owner-manager Joe Carson believes selecting the right inventory to satisfy equipment buyers is the most important success factor for his business. Profit is largely driven by how well these needs are predicted each year.

By Joe's own admission, he is not successful with every stock choice. An uninterested public left him with $175,000 worth of football equipment in 1982 and $148,000 of hockey gear in 1984. These are just two of Joe's expensive judgment calls.

Angered by his mistakes, Joe reviewed his approach to inventory selection during the spring of 1985. He agonized over sales statistics, effects of weather, popularity of styles, perceived quality, and seasonal patterns. To organize facts and make a sensible correlation between stock purchase and profit, Joe assigned the weight of one to the most successful products, five to the poorest performers. Numbers in between were allocated according to degrees of sales success. All products were evaluated in this manner to create classes of stock based on success.

A "one" stock item was a complete success, having arrived in time for customer demand, in the right quantities, color, label, and price range to ensure a sell-out within a season. "Two's" were also regarded as successful, but with a few left in stock for next season. "Three's" were less desirable still, and so on, until the "five's" which would include such items as the football and hockey gear failures of 1982 and 1984. When Carson applied his product grading scale, he discovered a pattern.

Customer buying behavior was traced to three main criteria: manufacturer labels, certain colors, and price sensitivity. Joe applied these customer motivation factors to inventory purchases to create a winning stock purchase formula for the 1986 season. When the season was completed, he analyzed the results. To his surprise the average number of items in categories one and two increased, threes declined, while fours and fives became nonexistent.

The formula to match Joe's stock selection with customer buying patterns became Carson's approach to allocating available revenue-building resources. By reducing the quantities of unsuccessful stock and allocating resources to more appealing inventory, sales increased with little additional investment.

Allocating available resources only to opportunities with optimum potential is so important to revenue growth, it deserves a third example. Marble Resources, a small oil and gas company, gives us an ideal case.

Marble Resources operates on a shoestring budget out of the basement of its president and principal shareholder, Jim Brown. Jim, a geologist by profession, searches maps and land areas looking for promising gas reserves. His long-time university friend, Hal Brooks, is a financial wizard and self-appointed vice president finance for Marble. Their wives are good friends, and help the entrepreneurs where possible with research, typing, filing, and other duties.

Jim's research revealed a tremendous reserve opportunity. If he could successfully negotiate the purchase of gas rights for this particular field, Marble Resources stood to net a million dollars a year, after related operating expenditures, for the next eight years. It was the break Jim had been waiting for.

A problem arose with financing though, shortly after the opportunity was identified. A shortage of funds would occur if gas well rights were purchased for $850,000. Marble could raise the investment capital but commitments remained for well-head expenses for another smaller investments. Hal insisted the company couldn't finance both existing commitments and the gas well opportunity.

The couples discussed potential solutions, including selling their houses to finance the two investments. The wives were against this option because of concern for their personal security. By the time they had discussed all options, the four had become emotional and still they had made no decision.

Jim turned to basic analysis to break the deadlock. Listing detailed commercial arguments for and against financing the gas well purchase or funding existing operations, he discovered a common ribbon of logic. He defined stable revenue as $650,000 per annum. At this level, the company would break even. Revenue in excess of $650,000 would be profit — a more appropriate guide for his decision.

Revenue and cash flow expectations were then analyzed from both an existing oil well and the proposed gas wells. The company owned 18.986 percent of the oil well. The well had sufficient production history and proven untapped resources to virtually guarantee Marble's expected $783,000 revenue stream for the next five years — an anticipated profit of $133,000 per year.

The gas well requires an initial investment risk of $850,000 to purchase, excluding operating commitments. Expected revenue to Marble is $1 million per year, representing a 12.927 percent interest in the field. When Jim studied their projections, he realized only 22 percent could come from proven well sites. The remainder was projected by the gas consortium to come from step-out wells yet to be drilled. Only $220,000 or 22 percent of expected revenue, was reasonably assured. The balance carried a high risk of realization.

Jim then compared his already-paid-for oil well revenue of $783,000 per year with a yet-to-be-purchased $220,000 income stream from the proposed gas well interest. Not only must Marble fund an investment price tag of $850,000, it would face a cash call demand from the consortium for 12.927 percent of the cost to drill each step-out gas well — a further risk of capital. For a company the size of Marble, in its start-up phase, the gas well investment was beyond risk tolerance.

What if the gas well was a tremendous success, adding handsomely to the wealth of the consortium, and Jim wasn't a member? The thought was unbearable. It would be better to have a smaller piece of a successful pie, to accommodate risk tolerance, than no piece at all. This led him to a compromise as he adjusted his expectations downward.

While analyzing operating obligations to oil partners, Jim felt Marble could risk $225,000 of investment capital without risking the entire company. Negotiations with the consortium resulted in an agreement for Marble to purchase a 3.778 percent interest in the gas field for $225,000.

Jim's resource allocation and risk tolerance analysis led him to preserve the $783,000 oil royalties first, then to pursue a 3.778 percent gas interest to yield an additional $65,000 of revenue the following year. Potential revenue from future step-out wells was there and total income of $848,000 from both fields balanced his tolerance for risk with his thirst for greater profits.

Dillman Engineering Ltd., Carson Sports Shop Inc., and Marble Resources each demonstrate the importance of allocating available resources to optimum opportunities. Although the businesses are very different, the challenge of financial and human resource allocation is the same. For stable revenue growth, leaders must use objective mechanisms to match available resources with potential opportunities. If these mechanisms are not used, the potential for mistakes and ill-fated decisions increases drastically.

BITE 21: IMPLEMENT ACCOUNT PLANS

Selling is a business activity that tests patience and discipline. Fraught with rejection and customer demands for satisfaction, it can put severe strains on personal make-up. So much so that many leaders wonder why career selling is so appealing. Yet, when you suggest a better life elsewhere, the successful salesperson won't hear of it. Why? Because nothing can replace the thrill of closing a sale. Targeting customers, devising sales plans, plotting strategies, and identifying products and services that the customer will want to buy becomes a rush. It is likened to wild game hunters preparing for the kill.

Salespeople live for the "cold call," the first-time customer contact. Successful sellers characterize them as introductions, not sales calls. In fact, they avoid selling at all during first meetings. Why? Prospects are expecting a pitch, and because they don't know the salesperson, it will never be easier for them to say no. And as successful salespeople know, a no is extremely difficult to turn into a yes later on.

So, as a salesperson, your first call is social only, a reconnaissance mission to learn customer interests, both business and personal. Make notes about the style, personal make-up, and interests of the prospect. Let a month go by. Then call again — perhaps for lunch. Tour his operations. Learn about his successes and failures — but don't try to sell!

During these first few contacts, you are simply obtaining customer intelligence, determining what the customer might be interested in buying. This increases your chance of making a sale in two ways. First, your knowledge of a prospect's operation better enables you to identify and then meet his needs. And as his familiarity with you increases, his resistance to purchase declines. By showing interest in his business, you are demonstrating that you're not just out for a fast sale. Instead, you build a relationship. He becomes more comfortable. And then you sell!

You may call on prospects many times before asking for an order. You'll know when the time is right. You'll have enough intelligence to match your product with his needs, your confidence will be at its highest, his resistance at its lowest. Attempting to sell before this point increases chances of failure dramatically. Leison Auto Parts offers an excellent example of relationship selling.

> Leison Auto Parts has been selling after-market auto parts to large auto service operations for fifteen years. Its most successful key account sales-man, Fred May, sells 40 percent more sales volume than does his closest rival. Leison's president encourages Fred to pass success secrets on to other sales staff, to foster a stronger team sales performance. He asks Fred to hold seminars on customer relationship building for the other salespeople.
>
> To teach his strategy for success, Fred walked the rest of the sales staff through his sales plan for his next cold call. With Jack Motors as his potential customer, he showed them his approach to making the sale as outlined in Figure 33.4.
>
> Fred explained each call meticulously, stressing how each successive contact is dependent upon the success of the previous one. In Fred's approach, each call has a small manageable goal — a golf game or a plant tour — that will take the relationship a rung higher. At the top of the ladder, of course, is the desired sale. He won't talk about Leison products until the fourth contact. Only then will he have sufficient intel-ligence to match product solutions with Jack Motors' problems.

Leison Auto Parts
Sales Plan for Jack Motors

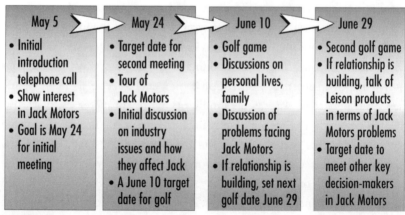

May 5	May 24	June 10	June 29
• Initial introduction telephone call • Show interest in Jack Motors • Goal is May 24 for initial meeting	• Target date for second meeting • Tour of Jack Motors • Initial discussion on industry issues and how they affect Jack • A June 10 target date for golf	• Golf game • Discussions on personal lives, family • Discussion of problems facing Jack Motors • If relationship is building, set next golf date June 29	• Second golf game • If relationship is building, talk of Leison products in terms of Jack Motors problems • Target date to meet other key decision-makers in Jack Motors

Figure 33.4

Fred May's approach to personalized sales plans makes him the most successful Leison salesperson. He plans each account in the same manner — even for repeat customers. It's just as important to maintain existing relationships as it is to create new ones.

Not everyone has the skill and personal make-up to sell as well as Fred. Many salespeople develop problems when implementing plans. Steven Astor's experience at Peoples' Drugs helps make the point.

Les Whitby, president of Peoples' Drugs, employs 31 people to achieve $28.2 million in sales. As outlined in Figure 34.4, Peoples' includes one retail drug store, a wholesale division selling to other drug and retail outlets, and an institutional sales division for hospitals, armed forces, and detention centers. Derek Lamb, manager of store sales, is responsible for $6.8 million retail sales, Steven Astor sells $18.4 million in wholesale, and Carolyn Green achieves approximately $3 million of institutional sales.

Steven services 42 wholesale accounts — some every three days, others weekly, monthly, and bimonthly. Regular and reliable scheduling of sales calls is critical to his success.

Ten of Steven's accounts are difficult to manage. Grumpy store owners and slow account payers demand extra time and delicate people skills. One account in particular, Johnson Pharmacy, creates particular hardship. Lewis Johnson yells at suppliers to keep them on their toes and discourage liberties with pricing. Steven finds Lewis so unnerving he searches for any excuse to avoid the account. If he has six calls to make in a day and Johnson Pharmacy is one, he will schedule it last and try very hard to consume the day with the first five.

Peoples' Drugs
Partial Organization Chart

Figure 34.4

At sales meetings, Steven always discusses Johnson as his most difficult account and seeks advice from others.

After two and a half months of procrastinating, Steven was summoned by Peoples' president Les Whitby. He had just received a call from Johnson complaining about the lack of service from Peoples'. A representative hadn't been on his premises for months. Steven attempted to explain the situation to Whitby, but the boss was unsympathetic. He ordered Steven to make the call immediately or not come in tomorrow.

En route, Steven didn't know whether to be angry or frightened. As he got closer to Johnson, he decided on anger. He told Johnson to sit down and listen to why every supplier in the drug industry avoided him. Treating every supplier as if it had cheated him created animosity, he informed Johnson, and when they avoided him, he just became angrier. He himself wouldn't be there if it weren't for the threat of losing his job. The account was so unpleasant, Steven told him, he didn't care if Johnson called Whitby a second time.

Johnson looked puzzled, as if not realizing the harm his behavior had caused. When he collected himself, he muttered something about starting their relationship over.

50 Steps to Business Success doesn't recommend yelling at customers as an effective sales technique. Situations do arise, however, where forceful behavior is the most appropriate alternative. Steven Astor had reached that point with Lewis Johnson. When pushed to the limit, he decided his job wasn't worth it. The relationship between him and Johnson simply had to change. By standing up to Johnson, Steven earned his respect and helped him understand how poorly he treated his suppliers. Together, they rebuilt the relationship. Today, Steven no longer looks for excuses to avoid Johnson.

The self-imposed stress of working in sales often manifests itself in avoidance behavior like Steven's. Some people load schedules with tasks they like to do — anything to avoid the pressure of a sales call. Others call numerous internal sales meetings to discuss the same plans over and over, to the point where they believe they're selling just by calling a meeting. Then there are those who develop contact lists every time they feel pressure to make a call. Still others focus on selling to industries rather than to single accounts.

People with these symptoms suffer sales panic. If you are one of these people, take a deep breath and grab a clean sheet of paper. For each of your sales accounts, list the precise actions you must take to achieve the outcome you desire. Plan dates for sales calls — perhaps a month apart, and as many as you think necessary to achieve your goal. Specify what information you require from second and subsequent calls. Leave the first call for social purposes, with perhaps a brief description of your achievements and interests. Remember, don't sell before your confidence is high and customer resistance is low.

The panic stricken may also lack the discipline to follow through with selling activities after they've managed the first call. Common experiences include:

- salespeople who begin with great enthusiasm — making one, maybe two, sales calls to potential customers — then losing interest. This is the Power Surge Syndrome, named for its strong start and poor finish.
- those who try to implement sales plans alone when they really need the support and skills of other staff to achieve them. Knowing when to bring in the cavalry is critical to successful implementation.
- those who oversell and end up talking the customer out of buying. Knowing when to stop talking is frequently a difficult lesson for the panic stricken.

Detailed sales plans alleviate these afflictions because they provide a road map, and this, in turn, breeds confidence. Sales plans should also include the all-important step of consulting your soul mate. As in all bites, the soul mate's input is an essential ingredient to sales success.

V
Product Intuition Is
Worth a Thousand Hours

Product intuition represents the ability to produce the right product, at the right time, and at the right price and quality to meet customer needs. Get all the criteria right and you ride the crest of product success. Get the criteria wrong and you spend enormous amounts of time and money mitigating losses. Products fail if companies lack the patience to link them to customer satisfaction. It's fatal to rush products to store shelves prematurely, before customer demand is assured.

The age-old debate used to be whether a company should be customer satisfaction or product development oriented. That debate is over: the customer won. Products are no longer designed and produced to satisfy the technological dreams of research departments. Customers have made it clear. They don't want better mousetraps. They want traps that work, at the right price, color, and size, and only with options to meet their needs — nothing more and nothing less.

Product-driven companies build new products with more options and functions than necessary to meet customer satisfaction. Development costs must be recouped through revenue, and overdeveloped products are usually priced less competitively. Customers won't pay for a sledgehammer if a mallet will do.

Customer-Driven Activity

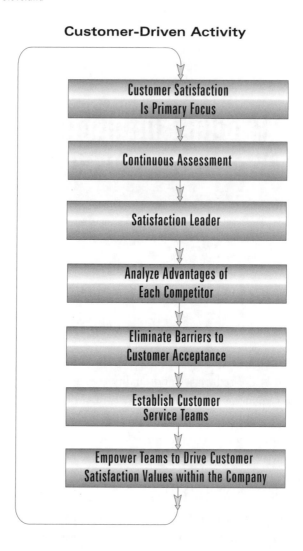

Figure 35.5

Customer satisfaction is the only consistent product design criterion. Businesses won't survive unless they organize every process around it. Every decision regarding products, expenditures, investments, and management is made with customer needs in mind. More than anything else, this single element differentiates successful organizations from mediocre ones.

While product-driven companies innovate in a vacuum, customer-driven companies continuously study shifts in customer needs. Results are compared against their own product advantages and those of competitors. Any barriers to customer product acceptance are addressed through planning during triage.

Customer service teams identify and continuously monitor customer needs. These needs form the basis of what the team perceives to be the customers' values when assessing products for purchase. The team encourages everyone in the company to satisfy those values, and measures employee performance on that basis. This continuous assessment of customer needs and values also offers valuable intelligence for the design and creation of new products.

Customer satisfaction leaders facilitate this process. Service teams ensure the results are implemented. This system for closely monitoring customer needs is critical for all businesses, large and small.

The components of the customer satisfaction focus are illustrated in Figure 35.5.

BITE 22: CONTINUOUSLY ASSESS CUSTOMER SATISFACTION

Leaders who don't employ objective customer needs analyses are gambling by using complacency as a strategy. At best, they'll maintain existing sales volumes. At worst, aggressive competitors will gain ground. Only a poor customer needs analysis is worse than complacency because it risks not only time and money, but also a potential mismatch between product development and customer needs.

⋏ It's possible to maintain customer satisfaction without thoroughly assessing customer needs; however, luck has never been a reliable strategy.

-> And once customer respect is lost, it's very difficult to win back. Leaders who suffer this humiliation never forget it. They learn the hard way that the only route to customer respect lies in continual analysis of customer activities, markets, and products.

When marketing and sales leaders gather information about the level of satisfaction of their customers, they study both existing and next-generation product requirements. They assess service and warranty performance intelligence as it applies to new product development. Service and warranty leaders are often closest to customers, making them a valuable source of satisfaction intelligence. They represent the first line of fire when customers demand attention, so they are also often the first to become aware of product innovations that could better meet customer needs in the future.

Intelligence must be concerned with both product improvement and new product development. If only current needs are assessed, future satisfaction may be at risk. Conversely, if leaders look only at future product needs, problems with current products may be overlooked. To maintain a healthy business, customer satisfaction assessments must always include strategies for both the near and distant future. The timing of customer intelligence is everything. Significant lead times are required to design, develop, and deliver products. Even with reliable intelligence, markets can change quickly. For this reason, new product development is often the most frightening aspect of leadership. If customer needs are assessed incorrectly, you lose. If products are designed incorrectly, you lose. If the right products are chosen and designed appropriately, but timing doesn't match customer needs, you still lose. If you did have any doubts about the need for continuous customer satisfaction analysis, you shouldn't have them anymore.

It's important in any customer satisfaction analysis to answer such questions as, What are the foreseeable technical and service demands of the customer? What product advantage will be demanded during the next five years? Ten years? What is the timing of new product needs? What lead-time, planning, and resources are necessary to meet these needs? To answer these questions, leaders must have a clear understanding of customer business cycles as well as of their own plans for development, growth, and profitability. And they have to keep in mind the primary objective of enhancing customer loyalty. Brendeen Manufacturing Inc. found an interesting way to link product intelligence with customer loyalty.

Brendeen Manufacturing Inc. builds parts for large automobile manufacturers throughout the world. Brendeen's success comes from its ability to anticipate changes in engine design and adjust its parts designs accordingly. The company's most lucrative market is in engine parts not sensitive to style and performance differences that are built for popular automobile models. Neither manufacturers nor the public care if different models have a similar carburetor part.

Customers view Brendeen as a volume producer of nonstrategic model parts at prices lower than it costs to build them in-house.

Brendeen's challenge is anticipating engine design changes and the resulting effect on parts. There is greater risk if one manufacturer completes major design changes before others, forcing Brendeen to produce "one off" parts for a single customer. In this case, the company does not enjoy the same economies of scale that it does on mass-produced industry parts.

With the level of design secrecy that exists in the automotive indus-try, it isn't easy to accurately assess customer needs. The manufacturers' reluctance to discuss future designs led Brendeen to create a new intelli-gence system to link customer and company interests.

Customer intelligence is assessed each year to get an idea of the activ-ity at each automobile manufacturer. Through surveys, Brendeen gathers data on expected changes in the customer organizations, engine performance, satisfaction with Brendeen's parts, known engine design evolution, and futuristic models.

The validity of survey answers is tested when Brendeen invites the customer's key production and design personnel to become members of in-house product teams. The company avoids competitive problems among customers by having a different product team for each manufac-turer, permitting each the opportunity to influence supplier quality.

Each year Brendeen hosts a formal dinner to reward each customer for its participation. Awards are presented for the most helpful design suggestions.

Brendeen's policy of integrating customer personnel with its own prod-uct design people is brilliant! Not only does it provide intelligence from customers, but it also creates a positive atmosphere in which customer relationships can develop. Customers are loyal to suppliers who are prepared to accept product suggestions. Brendeen also employs customer surveys designed to provide technical input to product team discussions, integrating customer feedback into product design.

Jasmine Inns offers a second example of customer satisfaction assessments.

Jasmine Inns owns and manages three motor lodges with combined annual sales of $20.8 million. Owner Sheila Jasmine firmly believes business success is tied directly to customer satisfaction. Competition among hotels is intense with little customer loyalty. Customers switch hotels over one ill-prepared meal, a less than friendly bellhop, or a lengthy line-up at the front desk. Pressure is tremendous to ensure all employees focus exclusively on guest comfort.

Sheila monitors guest comfort in three ways. Guest satisfaction surveys appear in every room for each guest to complete and drop at the front desk. Not every guest takes time to answer the questionnaire, so Sheila ensures a senior clerk on duty asks each guest if his or her stay was comfortable. Suggestions for comfort improvement are always encouraged. Within 30 days of each checkout, a letter is sent thanking the guest for his or her patronage and again encouraging suggestions for improvement. In Sheila's experience, 18 percent of hotel guests complete the questionnaire, clerks talk to 22 percent during checkout, and 8 percent respond to letters sent within 30 days of checkout. In total, Sheila's three-way approach to testing customer satisfaction reaches a full 48 percent of all hotel guests.

Sheila's staff monitors the patterns and trends arising from guest comments and suggestions. These then become topics for biweekly staff meetings. Guest comments frequently result in menu changes, decorating decisions, and training courses for guest-handling skills.

Jasmine's approach to customer satisfaction creates a rolling trend analysis to identify common suggestions and complaints. One-time comments are generally dismissed. Most comments in this category are frivolous. Sheila's 48 percent rate of customer feedback permits a representative assessment of client needs over time.

Simeon House provides yet another example.

Simeon House manufactures and distributes women's clothing, principally sweaters. Owner-manager Jack Simeon inherited the business from his father 13 years ago when sales were $14 million. Jack's strategies have since grown the business to $46 million.

Jack has implemented many successful strategies, but he credits his design satisfaction team for having the most influence over company success. The team constantly interacts with five major customers, obtaining intelligence on quality, popular colors, and design suggestions. Simeon's design team hosts an annual customer day — a full day of work and fun with key representatives from each customer group. It's a popular reward for customer loyalty.

In focus groups held in the morning, customer and company representatives discuss future product designs and taste changes. The afternoon is for relaxation. Activities include golf and tennis. Simeon is careful to match one staff member with each customer group. The day is completed with a gala dinner and the presentation of customer awards.

Customer satisfaction is assessed, intelligence for future products gathered, relationships enhanced, and appreciation shown to customers — all in one day!

BITE 23: APPOINT A LEADER FOR CUSTOMER SATISFACTION

The importance of customer satisfaction extends far beyond product development. Response time, product delivery, and after-sales service also affect customer relationships. Employees have varying levels of awareness of customer needs, which makes customer satisfaction a challenge for any company. But it can't be left to chance. Customer satisfaction requires a leader strong enough to influence consistent delivery to all customers — a Sheila Jasmine, for example. Without a strong leader, customer satisfaction almost inevitably declines. For this reason, every business must designate a leader of customer satisfaction — someone who is granted authority and accepts responsibility to continuously build customer relationships in a positive way.

Small businesses are not exempt, even though their limited resources may be stretched to the limit. In many small businesses, owner-managers are part of every business activity. They sell, design products, manage employees, and probably update accounting records at night. But until the business grows, they must also function as leaders of customer satisfaction. It seems appropriate to now discuss Zepher Agencies.

Zepher Agencies sells general property insurance. Owner-manager Len Zepher began the business 16 years ago from his home office. As customer volume grew, he rented space in a small shopping center and hired a clerk to process insurance documents.

During year eight, Len's son, Ron, showed an interest in the business. The volume of insurance could not support two families, so Ron initially worked only two days a week, assuming responsibility for insurance documents and maintaining office files.

Len spent more time developing new business and servicing clientele. The result was a 20 percent increase in yearly sales volume. The increase gradually created a full-time demand for Ron. Ron enjoyed managing the office and servicing existing customers as Len added new ones to the fold. Today, Len and Ron have 300 customers with insurance coverage in excess of $600 million.

Although Len may not have realized it, he was leader of customer satisfaction the day he opened his doors. This function was critical to grow the revenue base. Ron's later entry into the business presented Len with the opportunity to become a full-time customer satisfaction leader. Today he employs six people. If he hadn't managed customer satisfaction, insurance volumes may have declined, or at best, stagnated.

SuperSound Electronics provides another excellent case.

SuperSound Electronics consists of three retail stores selling stereos, televisions, compact discs, and other audio-related products. Owner Elliott March built the business to a $4.8 million sales volume by ensuring customer satisfaction. Placing considerable emphasis on sales training, he ensures each salesperson is well coached in customer satisfaction.

Elliott's business card encourages customers to call him directly if they are not satisfied with merchandise or service. Salespeople know poor performance will likely be reported directly to Elliott.

Figure 36.5 is a partial organization chart illustrating the importance of customer satisfaction at SuperSound Electronics. Elliott, by assuming the responsibility of customer satisfaction leader, demonstrates his seriousness about satisfaction. Since each salesperson reports directly to him, Elliot

SuperSound Electronics
Partial Organization Chart

Manager, Customer Satisfaction
Elliot March

| Southside Store | Meadowview Store | King's Heights Store |
| 8 Salespeople | 6 Salespeople | 7 Salespeople |

Figure 36.5

can ensure his customer satisfaction values permeate the company. Reporting to the president reminds each salesperson that customer satisfaction has an immediate impact on job security. Even though SuperSound is small, Elliott, by placing himself between customers and salespeople, successfully administers core competence training, adoption of customer values, and continuous customer needs assessment. SuperSound is an excellent example of manageable bites in a resource-poor small business.

BITE 24: ANALYZE COMPETITOR ADVANTAGES

Competitor advantages are the areas where your competition holds a permanent upper hand. The advantages may be such things as favorable locations, purchasing power strength, or brand-name recognition. They are the tangible and intangible assets that account, at least in part, for the continued success of your competitors.

Competitor advantages are obstructions to your goal achievement. To level the competitive playing field, you have to be better than they are in other ways. To that end, successful leaders structure their approach to customer satisfaction with competitors' advantages in mind.

Competitive analysis can take whatever form is most useful to company decision-makers. Typically, leaders gather industry data to identify competitor advantages and to determine goals necessary to regain or maintain the competitive edge. Irving's Furniture Inc. offers an attractive example.

Irving's Furniture
Analysis of Competitor Advantages

	Competitors				
	Newfurn Inc.	Balmoral's	National	Clifford's	Irving's
Location	Lakeview Mall	Pleasant St.	Westland Mall	Eagle Ave.	Prince St.
Square Footage	20,000	12,000	17,700	12,800	15,000
Population Draw	23,000	15,600	26,000	10,000	25,000
Sales	$2.3M	$1.0M	$2.0M	$1.6M	$2.1M
Advertising Budget	$250,000	$50,000	$125,000	$85,000	$175,000
Sales/ Population	$100	$64	$77	$160	$84
Ranking	2	5	4	1	3
Sales/ Advertising $	9.2	20.0	16.0	18.8	12.0
Ranking	5	1	3	2	4
Sales/ Square Foot	$115	$83	$113	$125	$140
Ranking	3	5	4	2	1

Figure 37.5

Irving Cruthers, president and only shareholder of Irving's Furniture Inc., spends one day a year updating competitor-advantage intelligence. Accurate and current competitor data is critical for assessing merchandise, pricing strategy, advertising decisions, locations, and store layout.

Irving compares his company's market penetration, efficiency of advertising dollars spent, and sales per square foot of display space with competitors' figures. Square footage and population numbers are published in municipal records. Sales and advertising budgets can be obtained from a credit investigation firm.

Irving draws a number of conclusions from the analysis shown in Figure 37.5. Clifford's generates the highest average sales per population, reflecting the store's strategy to sell expensive living room and bedroom furniture to wealthy clientele. Clifford's is also in an enviable second position with respect to efficiency of advertising dollars — generating 18.8 sales dollars for every advertising dollar spent, only slightly behind the most efficient — Balmoral's.

Space efficiency is measured in sales per square foot. Here, Irving's performs best with $140 per square foot, while Clifford's manages second place with $125.

Irving's scores poorly in sales per population and advertising dollar efficiency — ranking third and fourth respectively. Clifford's never ranks below second place and is the best overall performer. As a result, Clifford's becomes the benchmark for Irving's. The business advantages of the strongest competitor become improvement targets for the rest.

To surpass Clifford's $160 sales per population, Irving studied his inventory mix and considered its appeal to different disposable income levels in the market. He concluded that his lower-valued inventory needed to be enriched, that is, made slightly more upscale. Irving used published industry data to study Clifford's inventory selection. He found Clifford's product mix to be more expensive, clearly designed to serve a wealthy clientele. Irving was careful to consider the level of affluence of his own customers when making product decisions.

Irving listed Clifford's major products with their approximate purchase and sale prices. He then compared each product with compatible ones with Irving's market. Furniture too expensive for Irving's population base was eliminated.

The products selected were ranked in order of Clifford's estimated sales volume. With less space than Clifford, Irving can select only products with a high probability of sale within 45 days. The same process was applied to advertising choices. Using competitor and customer intelligence, Irving systematically allocated advertising dollars to radio, newspaper, and television. Thus, Irving completed a revamped strategy. His analysis of Clifford's competitive advantages allowed him to implement a plan to neutralize those advantages.

10 Minute Coffee Break also emphasizes the importance of analyzing competitor advantages.

Lucy Drucker owns and operates four coffee shops in as many down-town office buildings, under the name 10 Minute Coffee Break. Sales totaling $1,900,000 come from building populations during morning and afternoon coffee breaks.

Lucy's primary competition is Coffee Anyone?, three coffee counters owned and operated by Darren Black, also in downtown office build-ings. Darren opened his shops when the buildings were first constructed, even before tenants had been located. He struggled financially for a number of months until each building became fully leased.

Lucy opened her coffee shops in fully leased, mature buildings after studying the coffee break patterns of tenants. She met profit goals set during triage for two and a half years while Darren struggled to break even.

Darren, aware of Lucy's success, approached owners of her buildings four times, offering to purchase exclusive coffee counter rights. If accepted, Darren's proposals would have caused Lucy's contracts to be canceled. The owners refused each time.

Refusing to give up, Darren approached his building owners, suggest-ing they lobby tenants in Lucy's buildings to move as leases came due. The landlord followed Darren's proposals, offering incentives to tenants willing to relocate. Five large tenants, with combined populations of 1,500 people, were persuaded to move. These people now buy coffee at Coffee Anyone?, not 10 Minute Coffee Break! Lucy's profits declined as Darren's improved. Her competitive advantages were now reversed.

Lucy didn't stand idly by. Wanting to avoid a landlord war, she chose an alternative weapon — her customers. She built relationships with customers now located in Darren's buildings. She wrote personal notes, thanking each patron for their loyalty over the years.

As time passed, customers became disenchanted with the service at Coffee Anyone? They missed Lucy's personal touch. She encouraged them to lobby landlords to tender coffee locations for her, and the land-lords eventually bowed to their tenants' wishes. Lucy, with the help of a soul mate, prepared successful tenders for each building. Lucy was now back in, and Darren was out.

Rivalry between Lucy and Darren is obviously very intense. Each continuously assesses the other's advantages and sets strategies to gain competitive ground. Notice the shift in competitive edge. At first, 10 Minute Coffee Break had the primary clientele, ensuring a reasonable profit. Darren failed to buy his way into Lucy's buildings, but succeeded in influencing his own landlord. Profits shifted from 10 Minute Coffee Break to Coffee Anyone?, but Lucy didn't stand idly by. She applied the ultimate weapon against her competitor — customer satisfaction. Darren failed to meet his customers' need for personal relationships. Customer power wins.

BITE 25: ELIMINATE COMPANY-CREATED BARRIERS TO MARKET

Achieving revenue goals is difficult enough without leaders creating barriers for themselves. One-week lead times for product delivery, for example, may be convenient for in-house managers, but it's definitely a barrier to customer satisfaction if customers want delivery in two days. If competitors also take a week to deliver, customers are forced to settle for dissatisfaction — but only until a better performer comes along! When that happens, they will flock to the competitor with enough determination to break the one-week delivery cycle.

Continuous customer satisfaction assessments should identify all obstacles to achieving satisfaction. Benchmarks representing the highest level of service must be used to examine every step between product creation and customer satisfaction. There is a simple technique for accomplishing this: simply list all criteria necessary to please customers, then score your performance against those criteria. The process is similar to Dillman Engineering's resource allocation process. Areas for improvement become obvious when customer and competitor intelligence is studied.

Determining why noncustomers do not buy can be difficult. Successful leaders often use customer surveys to identify obstacles. Then, they eliminate those obstacles with one goal in mind: making it easy for customers to buy. Let's look at Pearl Divers Inc.

Pearl Divers Inc., a small diving school and equipment rental operation in the South Seas, caters to tourists vacationing at five resorts located along a heavenly island beach strip. The company employs five people, each with a 20 percent ownership interest. President Wally Ural and his wife Nancy manage the rental shop and accept bookings for scuba lessons taught by the other three owners, Sandy Parker, Julia Collins, and Catherine Dempsey. The shop location is perfect, set on sand dunes halfway between resort buildings and the beach.

Sandy, Julia, and Catherine provided one-hour lessons to scuba enthusiasts, starting at 9:45 a.m. each weekday with bookings accepted for no later than 5:30 p.m. Since operations began four years ago, they continuously tried to improve morning bookings, without success. Wally complained that business isn't strong until 3:30 in the afternoon. Capacity at that time is limited, with no room to increase lesson revenue. The result is mediocre income for the five owners.

Wally's soul mate, Larry Berry, is a resort owner down the beach. The two lunch once a month just to talk business. Wally's inability to increase low lesson-volume was the topic of one month's lunch with Larry.

Wally explained that Pearl Divers had not only increased advertising, it had also reallocated it among newspapers and tourist magazines with greater circulation. The five had also voted to reduce the price of scuba lessons from $25.00 per hour to $19.95, hoping to attract greater volume.

When Larry considered Wally's problem, he looked at lesson times and discovered that island and water tours also departed between 9:30 and 11:30 a.m. Lesson times competed with other entertainment, which had to be booked a day in advance. Offering lessons during the same time period made it difficult for tourists to buy Wally's product. When cruise and land tours finished in the early afternoon, the demand for scuba lessons increased dramatically. Larry suggested experimenting with lesson times, so Wally tried scheduling the first morning lessons for 7:30 a.m. to 9:15 a.m. People could choose scuba lessons first, then take island tours. Wally's change resulted in a 22 percent increase in lesson volume.

Now feeling confident, Wally approached local tour operators to propose they combine marketing efforts. He suggested they try special "above and under water tours" promotion programs — a one-hour glass-bottom boat tour followed by a one-hour scuba lesson. The promotion appealed to tourists and within a week, Wally had hired two additional part-time scuba instructors to satisfy new lesson demand.

Wally's first thought was to blame lesson price as the barrier to revenue achievement. But his soul mate helped him second-guess this thinking and see that the problem was with business hours.

How do you know when to think "outside the box" to solve problems? Well, if goals remain unachieved for more than a year, you should examine the failure carefully. Is the goal unreasonable or are you failing at implementation? Unreasonable goals should be modified. If it's the implementation that's the problem, talk to your soul mate and examine your leadership.

Wally Ural's instincts were to follow the advice of his soul mate. A willingness to question all previous thinking led Wally to accept changes in lesson times. This does not mean ideas of others should never be challenged or dismissed. Objectivity is the key. When excellent ideas can compete honestly, choices are depersonalized. Let's look at Figure 38.5 to see what lessons Wally learned while lunching with Larry.

Pearl Divers
Analysis With versus Without Soul Mate

Pre–Soul Mate	Post–Soul Mate
• Consumers are motivated only by price.	• Holiday consumers want to do as much desired activity as time permits.
• People choose among competing products based on personal criteria.	• People wish to experience all activity unavailable at home.
• There is natural resistance to spending money.	• Holiday consumers are focused on vacation satisfaction and have less resistance to spending money.

Figure 38.5

The left-hand column of Figure 38.5 reflects Wally's traditional thinking — his long-held beliefs. But holiday consumers throw logic out the window, wanting to reward themselves with carefree time. Most live year-round by the principles listed in the left-hand column. They take holidays to experience the principles listed in the right-hand column.

Identifying obstacles to customer satisfaction is of such importance that it demands a further illustration. Another look at Brendeen Manufacturing Inc. will do nicely.

Brendeen Manufacturing Inc. prepares a matrix analysis each time it updates customer intelligence and competitor data, summarizing the most recent intelligence for annual triage. Figure 39.5 illustrates this process.

Brendeen's analysis shows competitor performance trailing only slightly, requiring 26 to 30 hours to respond to orders compared with Brendeen's 23 to 28 hours. The difference isn't great enough to give Brendeen a competitive advantage. Intelligence indicates that a competitor has assigned a team to shorten its delivery time to 20 hours. If the competitor is successful, Brendeen must reduce its delivery time to 18 or 19 hours.

In the failure rate, Brendeen compares favorably, failing one of every 3,200 units. Again, the competitor has appointed a task force to improve performance and reduce cost per unit from $1.98 to $1.90.

Since it's difficult to discuss customer and competitor intelligence without considering product delivery, Brendeen helps us once again.

Product teams at Brendeen include production managers, sales and marketing personnel, customer representatives, and employees involved in new product development. Each meeting has a preset agenda, with items separated under two major headings: product quality for existing products and new product design. To rate existing products, Brendeen asks customer representatives to report satisfaction levels and any technical issues that need to be resolved.

On one occasion, a customer complained of metal filings in carburetors. Generated from wear, filings retarded carburetor performance during tests. The effect on engine performance was a slight hesitation during acceleration.

The usual meeting agenda was set aside to resolve the matter. Product design representatives proposed a change in material compounds and suggested that parts be dipped in an acid-based solution prior to shipment. Within two weeks, a solution was developed, tested, and perfected to restore customer satisfaction.

Customer loyalty was enhanced when Brendeen reacted quickly. Customer representation on the team helped detect a problem that may not have been uncovered at all. The cost to Brendeen would have been customer dissatisfaction and, perhaps, lost sales.

Brendeen Manufacturing
Customer Satisfaction Analysis

Perceived Customer Needs	Perceived Success	Perceived Success of Brendeen's Closest Competitor
Carburetor parts must be delivered within 24 hours of ordering.	Delivered on average between 23 and 28 hours.	Delivers on average between 26 and 30 hours of customer order.
Part failure rates cannot exceed 1 in 2,700 units.	Average part failure rate is 1 in 3,200 units.	Average part failure rate is 1 in 2,725 units.
Unit price must be below customer cost to make at $2.22 per unit.	Average per unit price $1.92.	Average per unit price $1.98.
Company representative must visit monthly during third week, to discuss revised ordering, product quality, and other relationship matters.	Regularly, on time.	Regularly, on time.
Vendor invoices five days before month end.	Regularly, on time.	Regularly, on time.
Vendors must have a company representative on the production floor within 40 minutes of part failure to begin investigation.	Meets customer satisfaction.	Meets customer satisfaction.

Figure 39.5

BITE 26: ESTABLISH CUSTOMER SERVICE TEAMS

Brendeen's product teams devises technical support plans from the company's production, marketing, and new product development divisions as well as from customers themselves. But why stop there? Why not apply the same theory to every aspect of customer relations? Consider a single team to develop action plans, gather competitor and customer intelligence, allocate resources, and develop personalized sales plans for each major customer. This customer service team would concern itself with all matters of customer satisfaction.

Customer service teams (CSTs) are not a new concept. In an increasingly competitive business world, they have become necessary for survival. They not only encourage relationship harmony, but they also force customer issues to be a company's primary focus.

Teams may consist of anywhere from one person to usually no more than five people. Large teams are ineffective because they find it difficult to schedule meeting times and settle on productive agendas. In general, smaller is better, as long as every division of the company is represented. CSTs can be created to fit any business, big or small. Corner retail stores may have a one-person customer service representative for an entire neighborhood retail base. A small business with, say, $4 million in sales, 32 employees, and eight key customers might have two or three CSTs, each consisting of perhaps three people. CSTs may expand and contract in terms of skills to meet client needs. They meet frequently — usually monthly and no less than quarterly — and set such agenda items as:

- customer problems and concerns;
- relationships with key decision-makers;
- resolution of relationship issues;
- customer intelligence;
- competitor intelligence;
- long-term sales targets;
- account profitability;
- existing product performance;
- potential new products;
- quality satisfaction; and
- determination of products and services adding no value to customer.

CST members ask: "What keeps the customer awake at night?" The answers are inventoried to help identify and develop cost-effective solutions. Cost/benefit analyses are applied to each solution to measure its potential value to the customer. This information is then passed on to customer decision-makers. By the time the customer hears of the solution, a solid case has been made for its adoption.

The very existence of CSTs is a competitive advantage. CSTs demonstrate an investment in and a concern for customer well-being. You are not just interested in a quick sale. What matters is relationship building.

CST meetings should be held at the customer's premises whenever possible. This makes the team visible. If you can, follow Brendeen's example of inviting a customer to join the team. At a minimum, consider having a customer make guest appearances. When the customer feels that your team is her team, her loyalty will grow.

Every aspect of social, business, and professional interaction between CST members and customers is designed to increase loyalty. Members become more responsive to customer needs, setting higher, longer-term sales targets, and in the process, outperforming companies with traditional sales forces. Appleby Appliance Repairs demonstrates the value of CSTs.

Jim Appleby has owned and managed a small-appliance repair business from three locations for 20 years. Appleby's key customers include the five largest retail chain stores that sell household appliances. Each store provides a three-year warranty on products. None wish to be in the repair business, so contracting this aspect of customer service to Jim Appleby is an economic marriage of convenience.

When appliances fail, customers are encouraged to contact Appleby directly. Retail stores assess satisfaction by contacting customers after Appleby has serviced the product.

Jim's problem is that he has two customers for every appliance — the store that contracts him and the customer who must be satisfied. Customers sometime complain to stores just to negotiate extra service. This is a source of annoyance to Jim. His soul mate advised him to form customer service teams to minimize these complaints.

Jim formed one customer service team for the major chains. He debated having one team for each, but the issues for all of them were so similar, he knew one team could do the job. The team consisted of two repairmen, two members from management, and one from public relations. The first meeting focused on the team's mandate and the information it required to fill that mandate. The following resolutions were adopted:

▲ design detailed customer satisfaction surveys for public input;

▲ design detailed customer satisfaction surveys for chain store input;

▲ assign a team member to gather intelligence on number of complaints, service response time by Appleby and its competitors, rates charged by competitors, and advanced design and repair information for next season's products;

▲ hold at least one customer service team meeting per quarter with each chain store to discuss service matters and present customer satisfaction survey responses;

▲ target the elimination of two of five competitors currently contracting with each chain; and

▲ double revenue in five years.

When three months had passed, Jim noticed a change. His staff had become focused on team goals. Chain stores had reacted positively to the attention. Since no competitor had taken the same initiative, Appleby Appliance established itself as the competitive leader.

Appleby's customer service team gradually changed company culture from a technical to a market focus. The new team spirit at the company also inspired ambitious goals for long-term revenue growth to be fed by a reduction in customer complaints.

BITE 27: EMPOWER CUSTOMER SERVICE TEAMS TO DRIVE CUSTOMER SATISFACTION

Customer service teams are of little use if they have no authority to drive internal change. Team self-respect declines if responsibility to grow revenue is assigned without the authority to implement the plans necessary to do so. To be successful, CSTs need to be empowered. Let's follow the Appleby case a little further.

During the next 18 months, Appleby's customer service team focused on reducing response time for repair calls. Part of the plan involved installing computer software to measure time between repair call and repairman arrival at a customer's premises. Times were reduced from 1.3 to 0.8 hours in 18 months. Efficiency not only improved satisfaction survey responses, it reduced the need for additional repairmen as volume increased.

Complaints received by chains historically averaged 10 per month. Jim challenged repairmen to reduce the average to one complaint per month. The goal was achieved 19 months after forming the customer service team. More important, the next strongest competitor receives 6 complaints per month.

Twenty-one months after its creation, the team received notices from two chain stores advising it that contracts currently held by competitors were maturing. If Appleby could match competitor rates, the contracts would be awarded to Appleby thanks to its superior customer service.

Change occurred when Jim transferred responsibility and authority to the service team. If he hadn't, the team would be nothing more than a committee. No team satisfaction means poor customer satisfaction. A team will perform well only when its members believe team strength is more important than individual performance. For that strength to emerge, the team must be empowered. Sage Manufacturing Ltd. demonstrates what happens when teams are not empowered.

Sage Manufacturing Ltd. manufactures computer software and achieves sales of $589 million. President Les Isnor manages 682 employees with a dictatorial leadership style.

Soul mate Jeff Lonside has advised Les on numerous occasions to create customer service teams for key corporate clients. Les, not convinced of the value of customer teams, reluctantly agreed to the partial measure of an advisory committee. The committee members selected were the six key decision-makers and Les encouraged them to offer suggestions for him to consider. Suggestions he thought worthy would be implemented.

During the second meeting, members unanimously agreed to invite a customer representative to spend six months in Sage's design group. The design group would gain insight into customer direction and future software product needs. When the team presented this recommendation to Les, he dismissed it immediately, citing the risk of software theft.

The committee was demoralized. There was little value to making suggestions. In the months that followed, meeting attendance declined and few suggestions made their way to Les.

By refusing to give authority to the committee, Les rendered it impotent. Members could not achieve personal satisfaction when recommendations were immediately dismissed. Employees' respect for Les Isnor declined.

Sage Manufacturing hasn't learned that meeting customer satisfaction requires effort from all employees — in marketing, sales, production, new product design, and general management. Processes that are not linked to customer values leave satisfaction to chance.

Leaders are often uncomfortable transferring authority to customer service teams. Authority is the traditional reward for climbing corporate ladders, and can be difficult to relinquish. But these same leaders are faced with a changing business world. More and more frequently, success comes from the actions of a team, not a single individual. It isn't easy, though, to alter something as engrained in business culture as the concept of reward for individual initiative. The truth is that every successful business requires both energetic individuals and effective teams. And both must be rewarded. The challenge is finding an equitable method to do so. Companies that can find a good balance will first experience employee and customer loyalty, then revenue and profit growth.

Leaders may be uncomfortable inviting customer representatives to participate on internal teams. Perhaps leaders fear that customers will learn company weaknesses. In the search for success, this fear must be overcome by the competitive need to link customer satisfaction with business process improvement.

VI

Secrets to Expense Reduction

"Net — the biggest word in the language of business."
— *HERBERT CASSON*

Finance is the engine that determines the size and speed of a company's goal achievement. Accounting is simply the language of finance. It provides the means of expressing transactions in financial terms, and hence, it is an integral part of every company's core competence. Small companies often purchase financial skills from external professionals, while larger companies tend to build their own in-house expertise. In either case, top-notch financial skills are critical to business success. They allow businesses to analyze and measure progress toward goals.

Successful companies set goals with specific financial measurements in mind. This helps to create a sense of accountability. When goals and standards of measurement are widely known within the company, peer pressure to meet and surpass them challenges employees who have that sense of accountability.

Goal performance that is not measured is less likely to be satisfactorily achieved. Without it, no benchmarks exist to highlight success or failure and to encourage corrective action when success lags. Goals expressed in financial terms can more easily be compared to actual performance. Corrective action can be implemented when a company is not living up to its own expectations. Over time, this process generates continuous improvement. Figure 40.6 illustrates the flow of focus from initial triage to continuous process improvement.

Triage Focus

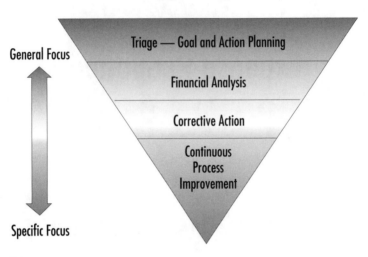

Figure 40.6

A company's finances are constantly changing. Funds are consumed by daily commitments, then replenished by profit, debt, or equity. That instability often denies businesses the luxury of matching available financial resources with expenditures committed. Leaders must continuously monitor available resources and prioritize expenditures to ensure they stay in balance. Few companies have the financial resources to implement all desired expenditures. Leaders have to make choices.

Forecasting is one of the best tools business leaders have to make successful choices. A financial forecast uses all available information about a company to predict its profit and loss, cash flow, and financial position over a given period of time. Once a forecast is prepared, leaders have something with which to compare actual performance to get a sense of how things are going financially. If actual performance lags far behind the forecast, corrective actions are recommended. Even the forecast may be examined for flaws such as poorly predicted variables or business variables that have been missed altogether. If finances are ahead of forecast, goals can be stretched a bit to continually challenge the company to reach its full potential. The cycle between forecast and either goal stretching or corrective action is shown in Figure 41.6.

Financial Analysis Cycle

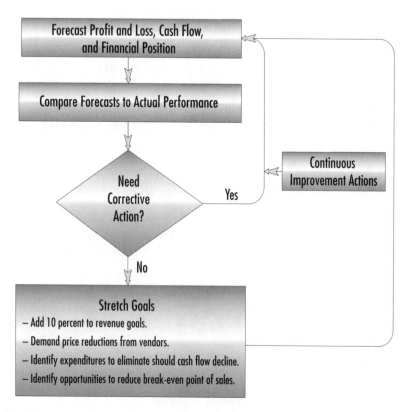

Figure 41.6

Forecasts can have one potential negative effect; they can cloister free thought about business goals. If employees know resource limitations, they may not feel free to think larger than what those current resources may support. For this reason, possible goals should always be explored before forecasts are prepared. Goals can be reexamined later for reasonableness, once forecasts are complete. It's also important that goals be constantly challenged and stretched throughout the year. Stretching goals pushes an organization toward success.

BITE 28: PREPARE FINANCIAL FORECASTS ANNUALLY

During annual triage, goals and action plans are translated into the language of profit and loss, cash flow, and financial position projections for each business period. Preliminary projections are reality checks to match initial goals and actions with the human and financial resources available to achieve them. Amendments are always necessary to achieve optimum matching. Goal expectations and available resources are adjusted up and down until they are accepted as the blueprint for the next period performance. This blueprint becomes the company's financial forecast. Once leaders accept forecasts, they commit themselves to achieving the next period's performance. This process is illustrated in Figure 42.6.

Reconciling Available Resources with Goals Prioritized

Business Goals at Triage

Financial Projections — Are goals achieveable?
Are resources optimally allocated?

Goals are adjusted to optimize resources.
Resources are adjusted to optimize goals.

Financial projections are amended and adopted.

Figure 42.6

Let's see what happens in companies where financial forecasts do not exist.

Duckworth Rentals Inc. was a short-term automobile rental agency. Lionel Duckworth, its president for 10 years, continually struggled to meet payroll and automotive purchase commitments while operating within a line of credit restricted by the bank. He frequently held checks back from mailing to avoid exceeding his bank line of credit, which was closely watched by his bank manager. Monthly financial statements were always prepared late and frequently not available for the bank until the last week of the following month — a concern for the banker. Suspicion about Lionel's management abilities motivated the banker to monitor his line of credit.

Each month the banker met with Lionel to discuss performance. When financial statements finally arrived, they were always worse than Lionel had indicated. The relationship deteriorated as the banker became more convinced that Lionel was not capable of managing his business.

After 18 months of continuous relationship decline, the banker demanded a meeting between Lionel and the bank's vice president. He announced the bank would no longer support the business. It had lost all confidence in Duckworth Rentals Inc.

Lionel pleaded with the bank to give him more time to improve the business. When the four-hour meeting concluded, the bank agreed to support Duckworth for three more months, conditional upon implementation of proper financial reporting systems, including projections and comparative analysis. Lionel had to manage the company more professionally to minimize loan risk for the bank. If financial controls were not implemented in three months, a receiver of Duckworth's assets would be appointed.

Businesspeople in Lionel's position are always very upset with banks. Reality has to set in before they realize proper financial systems are critical for managing any business, with or without bankers. Without annual financial projections and comparative analysis, how could Lionel possibly know what his outstanding commitments and available cash flow were? Were sales increasing or decreasing? What was the timing of payment for the balance of accounts payable? These are only a few questions a leader must answer to effectively manage cash flow, profit, and financial position. Without forecasts, no financial goals are in clear focus.

Leadership is about confidence, as illustrated in Figure 43.6. The confidence of employees, customers, bankers, and shareholders means they believe you have the appropriate vision for the company and the determination to optimally match resources to goals to achieve that vision. Tools such as financial projections, or forecasts, enhance confidence in leadership.

The Confidence to Achieve Goals

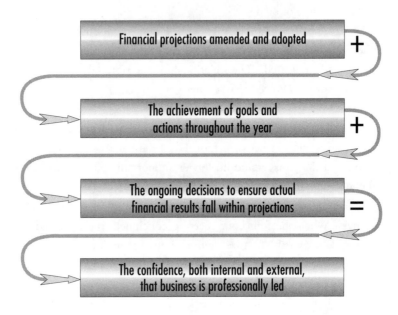

Financial projections amended and adopted **+**

The achievement of goals and actions throughout the year **+**

The ongoing decisions to ensure actual financial results fall within projections **=**

The confidence, both internal and external, that business is professionally led

Figure 43.6

BITE 29: COMPARE ACTUAL PERFORMANCE TO FORECASTS ON A MONTHLY BASIS

Forecasts anticipate goal achievement. Actual results are prepared in the same format as forecasts to facilitate comparison and the creation of the three leg analysis, illustrated in Figure 44.6, to establish trends over time.

The first leg is actual financial performance for the period. That's the amount of profit or loss. The second leg compares actual profit and loss to forecasts to answer the question, How well did the company perform compared with the plan? Line-by-line comparisons of sales, expenses, profit, assets, liabilities, and cash flow will reveal variances and their effect on overall financial position.

The Three Leg Analysis to Establish Trends over Time

Trend Analysis Over Time

Actual Performance

Comparative Percentage Analysis

Comparative Forecast Performance

Figure 44.6

The third leg of the analysis calculates percentage comparisons in each financial component. For profit and loss, for example, sales are assigned the base of 100 percent, while costs, gross profit, and overhead expenditures are expressed in terms of a percentage of those sales. When percentages are calculated for both forecast and actual profit and loss, comparisons often lead to further investigation. For example, significant variances in percentage between forecast and actual gross profit should encourage leaders to investigate inadequate bidding processes, pricing errors, or costing problems. Similarly, significant variances in predicted and actual overhead expenditures may reveal poor controls over discretionary commitments. A typical question arising from this analysis might be something like, Why were actual expenses 86 percent of sales compared with a forecast of 81 percent? The third leg of the analysis locates the origin of poor performance so management can take corrective action.

These trends may indicate flaws in forecasting or in actual performance. Those flaws become clear only when a number of successive years reveal cyclical patterns. They usually require three or more years of comparison to be identified.

To discover how the three leg analysis applies, let's see how Duckworth Rentals Inc. reacted to the banker's ultimatum.

When Lionel calmed down after his bank meeting, he called in the financial systems experts recommended by his soul mate. Two and a half weeks later, the analyst proposed a specific software package to record transactions and analyze profit and loss. The cost of installation would be $75,000, a sum the bank agreed to finance if Lionel installed the system immediately.

While the system was being installed and Duckworth's employees trained, Lionel projected monthly profit and loss statements for system entry. During the first month of the system's operation, a number of errors occurred, which was normal for newly installed systems. The second month produced fewer errors, with none coming in the third. Once results tested favorably, Lionel and the consultant decided to discontinue his old, manual system.

As demonstrated by Figure 45.6, segregating comparative monthly profit data revealed certain idiosyncrasies. Net income for the first quarter is $129,000; $126,000 was made in the third month. The first month generated a small profit of $16,000, only to be virtually eliminated by a $13,000 loss during month two. Month three's superior performance is attributed to a business convention that increased demand for rental cars that month.

Through analyzing the data, Lionel can see that once sales pass break-even levels, there is a significant positive effect on profit. Once overhead for the month is paid, every dollar goes to the bottom line. The longer a vehicle is rented, the greater the percentage of gross profit. The analysis also confirms that convention business is more profitable than daily rentals.

A review of expenses and profit as a percentage of sales for the quarter indicates no significant overall variations. In month three, though, the 49.4 percent gross profit is significantly higher than the 35.2 percent projected, demonstrating the impact of the convention. Daily rentals during months one and two show poor performance when compared with projected expectations.

Comparative profit and loss analysis provides only partial information for managing a business. It isn't designed to reveal the timing difference between revenue and expense recognition and the actual flow of cash. The two vary depending upon the nature of the business and its cash cycle. Companies selling products on account record sales at date of delivery, but

Duckworth Rentals
Comparative Profit and Loss Performance for the Quarter (in $000s)

	Month 1				Month 2				Month 3				Total Quarter			
	%	Projected	%	Actual	Projected	%	Actual	%	Projected	%	Actual	%	Projected	%	Actual	%
Revenue	100.	$404	100.	$359	$404	100.	$356	100.	$404	100.	$539	100.	$1,212	100.	$1,254	100.
Direct Expenses	64.8	262	70.2	252	262	64.8	269	75.6	262	50.6	273	64.8	786	63.3	794	64.8
Gross Profit	35.2	142	29.8	107	142	35.2	87	24.4	142	49.4	266	35.2	426	36.7	460	35.2
Discretionary Overhead Expenses	11.6	47	12.0	43	47	11.6	52	14.6	47	17.3	93	11.7	141	15.0	188	11.7
Fixed Overhead Expenses	11.9	48	13.4	48	48	11.9	48	13.5	48	8.7	47	11.8	144	11.4	143	11.8
Net Income	11.7	$47	4.4	$16	$47	11.7	($13)	(3.7)	$47	23.4	$126	11.7	$141	10.3	$129	11.7

Figure 45.6

cash is received sometime later. Similarly, accounts payable for goods received now will be paid in future. Let's return to Duckworth to see what other information Lionel's new system produces.

> At first, Lionel resisted recommendations to include comparative cash flow analysis in his new system. Later, after being persuaded by his consultant to use it, he discovered the analysis generated such valuable information as:
>
> ▲ timing effects of goals and actions on monthly cash flow;
> ▲ when cash flow requirements peaked, which also determined line of credit requirements;
> ▲ requirements to reduce discretionary expenditures; and
> ▲ flexibility, if any, to expand action plans.
>
> Lionel learned much from his cash flow analysis, illustrated in Figure 46.6. Actual performance for the quarter shows a net decrease in cash of $29,000, reducing the already tiny cash balance of $40,000 to $11,000. Individual monthly performance demonstrates dramatic swings in net cash, ranging from a net depletion of $7,000 in month one to $16,000 in month two. The volatility makes cash flow management critical for Duckworth.
>
> Monthly percentage analysis depicts dismal performance. Discretionary overhead expenditures for month one are 21.4 percent of cash receipts, compared with a budget of 8.4 percent. Fixed overhead costs are also significantly higher than forecast. In month two, direct expenses consumed more cash than budgeted when 79 percent of actual cash is spent compared with the 49.1 percent budgeted. The same occurs in month three. The consultant believes the monthly forecast cash results were just badly timed, as the quarter's total cash receipts are relatively on target. With the quarter forecast to generate $248,000, the $29,000 decrease suggests control problems exist over expenditures.

To complete the financial picture, Duckworth's new system also generated comparative balance sheets, as illustrated in Figure 47.6. Projected asset, liability, and shareholder accounts compared with actual accounts

Duckworth Rentals
Comparative Cash Flow Performance for the Quarter (in $000s)

	Month 1				Month 2				Month 3				Total Quarter			
	Projected	%	Actual	%	Projected	%	Actual	%	Projected	%	Actual	%	Projected	%	Actual	%
Cash Receipts	$265	100.0	$112	100.0	$265	100.0	$623	100.0	$265	100.0	$62	100.0	$795	100.0	$797	100.0
Less: Direct Expenses	130	49.1	33	29.5	130	79.0	492	49.1	130	58.1	36	49.1	390	70.4	561	49.1
Discretionary Overhead	22	8.4	24	21.4	22	14.6	91	8.7	23	33.9	21	8.4	67	17.0	136	8.4
Fixed Overhead	30	11.3	62	55.4	30	9.0	56	11.3	30	17.7	11	11.3	90	16.2	129	11.3
Net Change in Cash	83	31.2	(7)	(6.3)	83	(2.6)	(16)	30.9	82	(9.7)	(6)	31.2	248	(3.6)	(29)	31.2
Opening Cash Balance	40		40		123		33		206		17		40		40	
Closing Cash Balance	$123		$33		$206		$17		$288		$11		$288		$11	

Figure 46.6

Duckworth Rentals
Comparative Balance Sheet Performance for the Quarter (in $000s)

Assets					Liabilities and Shareholders' Equity				
	%	Projected	%	Actual		%	Projected	%	Actual
Cash	2.2	$288	0.1	$11	**Liabilities**				
Accounts Receivable	9.4	1,230	9.8	1,260	Accounts Payable	11.1	$1,448	13.1	$1,686
Fleet Inventory	86.2	11,230	87.7	11,230	Fleet Financing	71.3	9,300	69.1	8,850
Other Assets	2.2	290	2.4	310	Subtotal	82.4	10,748	82.2	10,536
Total	100.0	$13,038	100.0	$12,811	**Shareholders' Equity**				
					Common Stock	3.9	500	3.9	500
					Retained Earnings	13.7	1,790	13.9	1,775
					Subtotal	17.6	2,290	17.8	2,275
					Total	100.0	$13,038	100.0	$12,811

Figure 47.6

provides a useful end-of-period snapshot of Duckworth's financial state, taking into account not only changes in profit and cash flow but also financing activities with creditors and equity stakeholders. It is the company's final scorecard for the period.

The three financial statements must be reviewed together because each statement is an integral part of the other two. Increases and decreases in profit lead to increases and decreases in cash flow — and eventually a positive or negative effect on balance sheets. A leader's focus zooms in on individual months for specifics, then back to quarter ends for global period performance.

Duckworth is in a capital-intensive business that constantly requires financing to replace automobiles. Total debt hovers around 82 percent of assets, with shareholder ownership accounting for the balance.

Let's look at accounts receivable levels. Projected receivables of $1,230,000 for the quarter, compared to actual of $1,260,000, appear reasonable when profit and loss and cash flow statements are reviewed. During the previous month, however, actual sales were below projected levels. If accounts were being collected on time, cash flow from accounts receivable should be less the following month. Negative sales variances one month should generate negative cash receipts the next, if all else is equal. There were also fewer sales on account. This should mean less, rather than more, accounts receivable at the end of the current month. An investigation reveals four slow-paying clients that account for the difference. Lionel now must toughen his collection procedures.

Once a shoddy manager, Lionel Duckworth is now a disciple of the benefits of financial analysis. Not only does he manage profit, cash flow, and assets better, he has a more supportive banker. Both are one manageable bite closer to peace of mind.

BITE 30: IDENTIFY CORRECTIVE ACTIONS

Goals are not always achieved on the first attempt. Even when goals are met on the first try, financial analysis is still necessary to identify business processes in need of improvement. Regardless of whether goals are achieved or not, leaders should be constantly striving to improve their companies, asking questions such as, How can the company perform better? How can I anticipate poor performance far enough in advance to initiate corrective action? Even in good times, the desire for continuous improvement is an essential mentality.

Duckworth's revenue for the quarter is projected to be $1,212,000. Targeting this amount will not yield success. Targets must be higher than expected to allow for inevitable slippage of customer commitments. The company should press for, say, $1.5 million if it hopes to achieve the $1,212,000 goal.

Duckworth is also concerned with efficient use of its expense dollars. Management must be challenged to ferret out and eliminate any wasteful spending.

Profit analysis brought the margin effect of convention contracts to Lionel's attention. He saw that when sales passed break-even levels, his profit rose at an increased rate. This drove him to redirect advertising and sales efforts toward volume sales. Advertising had always been general, primarily in newspapers and magazines. Results were mediocre. When convention groups became the promotion target, sales and profit increased substantially. Lionel's analysis led to different promotion goals and action plans.

Cash flow analysis raised more complex corrective issues. Forecast monthly cash receipts of $265,000 did not anticipate convention business. Corrective actions for advertising will likely increase group sales. Initial cash flow projections will become obsolete.

Revised projections matched the commitment for expenditures with estimated timing of receipts. Lionel scheduled payments to coincide with periods of cash flow surplus. He persuaded the bank to accept principal payments quarterly, instead of monthly, to match available cash with debt reduction obligations.

Balance sheet reviews focus attention on reducing dependence on borrowed money to replace automobiles. Corrective action plans led to replacing 20 percent of the fleet every 20 months. Previously, Lionel replaced 30 percent of the fleet annually. This policy change reduced depreciation expense, cash outflow, and debt. That solution probably wouldn't have been discovered without financial analysis.

Corrective action must be realistic and achievable, challenging but not crippling to the organization. Too aggressive goals won't be met if company resources are stretched too far. Lazy goals, on the other hand, don't exercise core competence abilities. They lead to poor performance. Balance is difficult. Goals aimed at the sun often hit the horizon. Those aimed at the horizon fall shorter still. Lionel was aiming far short of the horizon, but now his focus is higher.

National Advertising Ltd. offers a second example of corrective action plans.

National Advertising Ltd. is owned and managed by James St. John. Boasting 52 retail clients, National designs and implements advertising programs for businesses selling products and services to the general public. Sales for the current year approach $8.9 million, while sales for the previous three were $6.1 million, $7.4 million, and $7.8 million, respectively. Net income after tax for the current year is $505,000, while the previous three stood at $539,000, $509,000, and $493,000, respectively.

Four-year trends in sales growth look good, but income after tax has declined. Analysis reflected unusual margin variances between large and small groups of clients. Annual triage had focused on growth of small- and medium-sized clients. National accordingly grew its small client base from 23 to 36 in just 18 months. Larger international companies attract greater competition.

Gross margin analysis revealed more time being spent on small clients than on large ones. Small clients are less sophisticated in advertising matters and require more interaction from account managers to be effectively serviced. Large international clients, on the other hand, could replicate advertising programs in different parts of the world and were satisfied with less interaction with National's account managers. Gross margins from smaller accounts averaged 23 percent, while those from international clients approached 34 percent. Although sales grew steadily each year, net profit declined as growth came from small and medium clients with thinner margins. James must now implement corrective action to restore healthier profits.

James called a general management meeting with five senior account managers. They studied ways to reduce account time and apply similar strategies to similar clients. When the meeting was completed, they agreed to five corrective goals:

▲ organize clients by industry;
▲ devise similar advertising strategies for accounts within the same industry to replicate advertising programs;
▲ hold client seminars to increase knowledge and reduce number of individual client meetings; and
▲ apply higher billing rates to custom, one-time advertising programs for small clients.

James St. John would have continued to earn profits at a declining rate had he not dissected his company's financial performance. The resulting corrective actions made profit fortunes for National.

Languard Industries Inc. offers another example for developing corrective action.

Languard Industries manufactures and sells novelty toys at prices ranging from $2 to $20. Products include boats, planes, games, and miscellaneous novelties. Lower-end retail chains and convenience stores make up the target market.

President Cecil Languard is unhappy with his product contribution margins. The controller's analysis, illustrated in Figure 48.6, shows a reasonable contribution margin from boats and miscellaneous novelties, but only 9 percent from games and 0 percent from planes. Preliminary projections indicate similar expectations for the future. Triage focused on corrective actions to improve margins.

Cecil's team of five senior managers investigated every revenue and expense item in the forecast. Cecil himself facilitated the meeting and recorded agreed-upon decisions. They agreed to vigorously pursue the corrective actions indicated in Figure 49.6.

Languard Industries
Forecast Profit and Loss (in $ millions)

	Boats	% of total = 28	Planes	% of total = 19	Games	% of total = 34	Misc.	% of total = 19	Total	100%
Sales	$9	100%	$6	100%	$11	100%	$6	100%	$32	100%
Cost of Sales	7	78	6	100	10	91	4	67	27	84
Contribution Margin	$2	22	—		$1	9	$2	33	$5	16

Figure 48.6

Languard Industries
Corrective Action Plans

- Increase prices of miscellaneous novelty items by 10 percentage points.
- Increase prices of planes by 15 percent.
- Reduce distribution staff by six people.
- Photocopy on both sides of paper.
- Combine company meeting schedules with customer sales calls.
- Downgrade management cars from Cadillacs to Chevrolets.
- Refocus advertising expenditures to target markets.
- Subcontract redundant space to third parties.

Figure 49.6

Cecil estimated that successful implementation of these actions would increase contributions from novelty planes by 8 percent, boats by 10 percent, games by 6 percent, and miscellaneous novelties by 11 percent. Together with proposed expense reductions, Languard would achieve an 18 percent increase in net profit! Cecil's team identified improvement actions, one bite at a time.

BITE 31: STRETCH YOUR REVENUE GOALS

Goals need to be stretched, then tested, through a process sometimes referred to as "what ifs?" Through this process, leaders ask a range of questions such as, What effect would a 10 percent increase in sales have on cash flow? Is it achievable? What would be the effect of a 5 percent decline in employee headcount? Depending on the answers, goals may be adjusted up or down.

Historic performance is never satisfactory to leaders who want to grow revenues. Salespeople need to be challenged with higher expectations. When realistic and achievable goals are established, leaders need to add 10 percent to projections. That premium is arbitrary, not scientific. Some may think a higher or lower premium is appropriate. The appropriate stretch percentage becomes evident during triage. Duckworth Rentals Inc. has served us well so far. Let's see what Lionel does in the area of stretching and testing goals.

When financial analysis is complete and action plans fine-tuned, Lionel is encouraged to check goals for maximum expected actions.

He applies a unique analytical test he calls the triple 10 percent. The test asks three questions: What happens to my bottom line if I increase sales prices by 10 percent, sales volume by 10 percent, and reduce cost by 10 percent? The compound effect of 10 percent changes in sale prices, volume, and cost of delivery become interesting.

Price increases are estimated to yield $25,000 per quarter — all making its way to net income. A 10 percent increase in volume would generate a $45,000 gross profit, becoming marginally higher with the 10 percent price increase. A 10 percent reduction in direct expenses brings about $15,000 savings. When all the numbers are added up, the triple 10 percent change increases quarterly net income by $85,000, or 66 percent!

Lionel now has to determine whether the triple effect is reasonable and attainable, given company resources. Even a 1 percent improvement in each category could potentially increase quarterly profit by 15 percent.

Mountain Water Inc. provides another example of goal stretching.

Mountain Water Inc. bottles spring water for commercial and household use. Jonathan Mountain successfully built the business from a first-year sales volume of $823,000 to $6.6 million in just four years. Public concern about the quality of drinking water has led to growing demand each year.

As Jonathan prepares for triage, he asks the sales force of five to provide preliminary sales targets. Initial targets reflected sales expectations of $6.8 million, a major disappointment for Jonathan.

At his regular monthly meeting with soul mate Les Tate, Jonathan talked about the maturity of his business. With expected growth of only 3 percent next year, the rapid growth years may be behind him. He wondered if the business is entering its mature phase. Les strongly disagreed, arguing that the salespeople were simply afraid to set aggressive targets. They would avoid failure if they set lower expectations and then exceeded them.

Jonathan agreed and chaired a second sales meeting to negotiate a $1 million increase in sales targets. The higher sales goal may not be achieved, but it encourages a greater effort that may not occur without it.

Jonathan Mountain learned through soul mate Les Tate that goals must be tested and challenged — not simply accepted as prepared. Pushing targets to higher, yet reasonable, heights creates a bias for maximizing success.

BITE 32: DEMAND PRICE REDUCTIONS FROM VENDORS

Goal stretching should always test vendor pricing sensitivity. Payments to vendors, if not the largest consumption of cash, rank second to payroll. Such significant expenditure categories warrant special focus for cash preservation and expense reduction.

Substantial purchases mean you're a valuable customer to vendors. Leaders often overlook this simple fact and the potential asset buried within accounts payable. Vendors cherish your business and may be prepared to reduce their margins to retain it. Take advantage. Ask vendors for at least a 1 percent price reduction — better yet, be bold enough to ask for more. You'll be surprised how much you are valued. Again, let's look at what happened with Duckworth.

> Lionel was advised by consultants to write all major suppliers to ask for a 10 percent reduction in product prices before he finalized his financial projections. Responses ranged from outright refusal to his actually receiving the requested 10 percent reduction. In all, he realized an over-all weighted saving of approximately 7 percent of Duckworth's total annual purchases. Given volumes of approximately $800,000 per quarter, cash savings approached $56,000 for each three-month period!

BITE 33: IDENTIFY EXPENDITURES TO ELIMINATE

Testing cash flow forecasts is like driving an automobile in busy traffic: it must be done defensively, under the assumption that an accident will happen. Effective leaders always assume less cash is available than forecast. Expenditure levels and timing of commitments are forecast conservatively in case cash receipts fall short of expectation.

To make these conservative forecasts, expenditures must be segregated into fixed and discretionary camps. This is done for both financial and managerial reasons. Financially, discretionary expenses are the obvious place to look for reductions if preservation of cash flow becomes critical. Managerially, the segregation forces a careful analysis of the necessity of each expenditure. Which expenditures will be reduced, for example, if there is a 10 percent decline in cash flow? Such planning is essential because cash flow declines often come swiftly and without notice.

> Lionel's new financial system automatically separates expenditures into fixed and discretionary categories. By writing key suppliers to request a 10 percent price reduction, he has already established a 7 percent reduction in direct expenses. Discretionary overhead expenses, amounting to

$188,000 for the quarter, contain $27,000 of entertainment and travel, and $15,000 replacement costs for Lionel's vehicle. In the event cash flow does not meet expectations, he has set a goal to reduce entertainment and travel by $16,000 and to postpone replacing his own automobile until next year. This establishes an approximate $31,000 expense cushion, or 16 percent of total discretionary overhead expenses, should cash flow become tight.

BITE 34: REDUCE OPERATIONAL BREAKEVEN

It's not enough to be content with existing levels of operational breakeven. You know your competitors are relentlessly pursuing opportunities to reduce theirs, and you had better do the same. Intense competition will force you to do it sooner or later, so it is better to plan it before that crisis comes about.

Leaders continuously search for ways to reduce expenditures. In doing so, they also strive to reduce the corresponding break-even level of sales. Are there new ways to reduce printing costs? Courier expenses? Photocopy charges? How about photocopying on both sides of the paper? How many times do we handle the product before delivery to the customer? Are we advertising in the right media? These are just a few questions leaders must ask in pursuit of a lower breakeven. Coogan's Hardware provides an excellent example.

Coogan's Hardware owns and operates 15 hardware stores serviced by two warehouse operations. Larry Coogan is known for his drive to reduce the break-even level of the company. So intent is he on lowering overall company expenditures that he offered a trip for two to Europe annually for the employee who offers the best idea for the greatest permanent expense reduction.

During the past five years, Larry has received many innovative ideas from his employees. Thanks to them, Larry has combined two warehouse operations, reduced inventory handling by 20 percent, lowered telephone expenditures by 30 percent, and reduced permanent staff in favor of part-time workers. Added together, the suggestions have brought $859,000 in permanent expense reductions! Coogan would have to sell an additional $2 million of products to yield the same impact on net profit. Sales required for the company to break even are now significantly less, but more importantly, the cost savings significantly increased profit.

Larry Coogan was prepared to pay staff to encourage innovative ideas for cost savings. His investment paid substantial dividends. Let's return to Duckworth Rentals Inc. to see what Lionel does to reduce the break-even level of sales.

Several months after implementing his new financial system and analytical approach, Lionel turned his attention to ways of lowering breakeven. He asked his vice president of finance to search for opportunities.

The resulting analysis identified the premise leases as an opportunity for renegotiation. Leases were up for renewal in a year. Any negotiated benefit could be long term.

He wrote a letter to his landlords indicating that he was unhappy with the existing lease arrangements and that he was beginning to search for new premises now, a year before the lease was up.

Lionel's landlords felt it was in their best interest to give Duckworth a more favorable lease than lose a tenant. After months of negotiations, Lionel was successful in reducing annual lease expenses by $223,000, significantly improving profit margins.

Lionel Duckworth proved to his banker, and more importantly, to himself, that financial analysis is critical to goal achievement. Leaders do not have to be experts in finance, but they must use quality analysis to make profitable decisions. Forecasts of a company's profit and loss, cash flow, and balance sheet express what a company expects to result from those decisions. These forecasts become the standard for actual performance measurement. Financial analysis, in turn, becomes the tool to analyze that performance and find hidden strategies for expenditure reductions and increased profits. And it all happens one manageable bite at a time.

VII

- **Barriers to**
- **Profitable Growth**
-
-

"The art of being wise is the art of knowing what to overlook."
— *WILLIAM JAMES, 1842–1912*

Profitable growth comes in two major types: acquired and organic. Acquired growth occurs through acquisition of, or merger with, another entity having strategic value. It is usually expensive growth, because cash or shareholdings are exchanged for products, sales, territorial rights, or distribution channels. The challenge is to blend two organizations with different cultural backgrounds quickly enough to benefit from potential economies of scale. Though often expensive, acquired growth offers instant revenue growth.

Organic growth is natural growth. It is most effective when it is planned and implemented with consistent discipline. Measured by volume increases, it should produce a regular, yearly growth in employees, locations, or products.

If sales become the only focus for growth, profit will suffer. It is not unusual to find growth and profit goals in conflict — when sales targets are met at the expense of profit. The two must be carefully planned and balanced to achieve optimum profitable sales growth.

Competition between growth and profit can be studied during annual triage to avoid selecting one goal at the expense of another. Dillman Engineering Ltd. avoided this by ranking its available contracts to match limited resources. Its decisions may have been quite different without a process to select profitable sales growth.

Self-inflicted barriers to profitable growth are always a concern. It's one thing to battle a competitor if you have a competitive edge, but quite another if you spend $110 to win a $100 sale. This can happen when companies commit to goals one at a time. Goals must be compared with other goals to avoid working at cross-purposes. Companies such as Ludwig Inc. ensure goals are compatible by bringing senior managers together to finalize goals and action plans. Without this exercise, action compatibility can be a matter of chance.

BITE 35: ENSURE ACTION PLANS ARE COMPATIBLE

Triage brings about many action plans for such functions as general leadership, marketing, sales, core competence, customer service, production, service delivery, and finance. Strong leaders ensure that goals and the action plans developed to realize them do not compete with each other or cancel each other's positive effects. But the process of identifying competing action plans can be difficult. Let's look at Beacon Electric Company Ltd. and how it identifies competing action plans.

Beacon Electric Company Ltd., a small power generator, earns revenues of $25 million. Business activities span four counties, two of which account for 80 percent of company revenues. Company president Eric Stemer is pushing sales growth through penetration into the two larger-volume counties. In these markets, Beacon competes with two other electrical companies.

Company earnings have approximated $5 million annually for three years. This year's triage results in profit-increase goals totalling $1 million, to come primarily from counties three and four. Management believes the goal is attainable as long as certain changes are made to core competence, including adding a new production leader and hiring additional technical support staff. Also, sales personnel have become complacent, forcing performance improvement plans in that area.

At the same time that he wants to increase profits, Eric is concerned with increasing customer complaints of power surges and outages within certain company grids. A technical study to determine outage causes will cost an estimated $1 million.

Draft goals and action plans were circulated among senior management. Before attending the planning lockup, Eric requested that his vice presidents synchronize their goals and action plans. The schematic of goal compatibility they prepared is shown in Figure 50.7.

Eric studied the diagram, noting the overlapping rings as areas of conflict. Planning to achieve sales growth in the adjacent counties at the same time as adding competence and reducing customer dissatisfaction would make increasing net income by $1 million a challenge! Goal conflict would be a problem.

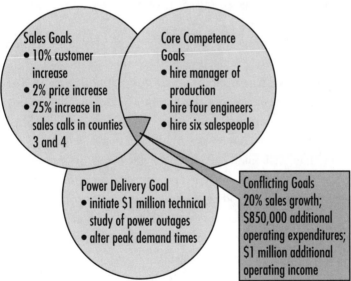

Beacon Electric Company
Compatible Goals Analysis

Sales Goals
• 10% customer increase
• 2% price increase
• 25% increase in sales calls in counties 3 and 4

Core Competence Goals
• hire manager of production
• hire four engineers
• hire six salespeople

Power Delivery Goal
• initiate $1 million technical study of power outages
• alter peak demand times

Conflicting Goals
20% sales growth;
$850,000 additional operating expenditures;
$1 million additional operating income

Figure 50.7

Eric decided these goals might be achievable if implementation was graduated over the year. For example, advertising could be directed at counties three and four during the first month while the search for sales competence gets started. The production manager would be needed to handle the anticipated growth. For the first 11 months, the vice president of production could manage existing and emerging production matters. Human Resources could begin the search for a manager in month 10 with a target commencement date partway through the following year. The investigation into customer complaints needed to be completed first anyway, to define the necessary qualifications of the proposed manager. Preliminary cost estimates for the study of power outages were high. Outages are localized into one core grid, not spread across total markets, demanding less fieldwork. Bids will be sought from competing engineering firms for a study of lesser magnitude.

If Beacon had pursued all goals at once, results would have been very different. A broader-scoped engineering study, at greater expense, would prove unsatisfactory when it failed to focus on localized problem grids. The production manager would be engaged some six to eight months prior to need, while a shortage of salesmen would result in a missed window of opportunity.

Eventually, sales growth became the priority goal with resolution of power outages closely behind. Longer lead time for market penetration postpones the immediate need for additional technical support. The more narrowly focused production investigation would, in all likelihood, eliminate 80 percent of customer complaints when problems identified were resolved. Other production areas would be examined later.

Beacon didn't eliminate action plans identified at triage. It merely altered the timing of their implementation to prevent premature expenditure commitments from eroding profit. Projected 20 percent sales increases approach $5 million and require $850,000 in expenditures to be phased in together. Competing goals would most likely result in profits less than $5 million, far from the $6 million target.

Dunphy's Convenience Stores did not have the same foresight as Beacon Electric. Let's see what happens when there is no mechanism to resolve dysfunctional action plans.

Dunphy's Convenience Stores owns and operates six corner retail outlets, carefully placed throughout suburban neighborhoods. Ned Dunphy, the single shareholder, is anxious to increase his number of stores to 10.

Senior management consists of Ned and Sid Farrell, a loyal employee for fifteen years. Annual triage and planning usually takes place in Ned's recreation room where, once a year, the two men meet to discuss new store openings, merchandise turnover, products in poor demand, and financial arrangements with the bank.

Last year, Ned convinced Sid they must open two new stores. Since average store sales were $526,000 per year, two additional stores were sure to add $1 million in new sales. New stores in the past have reached breakeven in year one, with second- and third-year profits approaching $50,000 to $100,000, before management fees and taxes. Ned's goal is to earn $50,000 in year two and $100,000 in year three from each new store. After six store openings, his finely tuned implementation procedures provided confidence to proceed.

During month one, Ned contracted construction for each store. Each location was constructed quickly and, within 90 days, Ned and Sid found themselves deciding merchandise and floor layout.

Two weeks before store opening, the community developer expressed concern about declining housing sales. Uncertain job markets had shaken the confidence of first-time homebuyers. People seemed content to remain in apartments until the uncertainty declined. This did not come as good news to Ned.

When the new stores opened, demand was very slow. They were moderately busy after four months, but business didn't approach Ned's expectations. Instead of breaking even in year one, he lost $50,000 in one store and $22,000 in the other. Year two saw moderate improvements with losses of $25,000 and $5,000 respectively — far below the $50,000 to $100,000 net income per store Ned had expected.

Ned assumed that his experience with the first six stores would automatically reoccur. Lust for sales prevented him from making an objective assessment of the neighborhood. Ned's other stores had opened in more mature neighborhoods with well-established residents. Mature neighborhoods spend more than young neighborhoods. More stores does not automatically mean increased profits. When neighborhood barriers to profitable growth are not identified, losses are incurred.

Action plan incompatibility can happen in many situations. The importance of identifying and eliminating incompatibility cannot be over-emphasized. Presto Weight Loss Products Inc. offers another good case for examination.

> Louis Mendelsohn, president and chief executive officer of Presto Weight Loss Products Inc., manufactures dietary products — food, dessert, and treats. Food consists of prepared frozen meals, and dessert lines include cookies, cakes, sherbets, and pies. Treats are candy and ice cream with artificial sweeteners and low calorie and fat content.
>
> Jim Thorpe, manager of treats, is pushing sales of ice cream. It has the highest contribution margins — between 43 percent and 49 percent — of any product Presto produces. Given fixed capacity, the more ice cream manufactured and sold over lower-margined candy, the greater the contribution to overall company profit.
>
> Jim transferred $50,000 to ice cream advertising to encourage marketing promotion.
>
> Roger Knotting, manager of the dessert line, believes a direct relation exists between food and dessert sales. Customers purchasing dietary frozen food dinners often purchase cakes or cookies too. Recent sales of cakes, cookies, and pies, with profit contributions of 19 percent to 29 percent, increased at the expense of sherbet and yogurt, which provide profit contributions of 20 percent to 38 percent, resulting in a negative effect on profit.
>
> During triage, Roger met with Louis and John Bach, manager of the food division. Actions emerged for joint marketing of certain food and dessert dishes designed to increase the volume of high-margin dessert products.
>
> Compatible sales and marketing actions resulted in actual revenue of $523,000, exceeding forecast of $419,000 by $104,000 — at 24 percent margins! Profit was $44,000 greater than last year and $30,000 greater than planned as indicated in Figure 51.7.
>
> Jim Thorpe was less happy with his results, illustrated in Figure 52.7. Not only had sales not increased to $906,000, they had declined below last year's level to $693,000. Profit dropped by $67,000 to $304,000, $122,000 less than planned. Margin percentages dropped to 44 percent from 46 percent last year, and did not meet the 47 percent forecast.
>
> After studying each division's results, Louis called a divisional leader

meeting. The vice president of finance presented combined profit analysis while each leader discussed variances between actual and forecast performance.

Presto Weight Loss Products, Dessert Division Summary Profit Contribution (in $000s)

	Last Year	Projected	Current Year
Revenue	$410	$419	$523
Direct Expenses	328	323	397
Division Contribution	$ 82	$ 96	$126
Contribution Percentage	20%	23%	24%

Figure 51.7

Presto Weight Loss Products, Treats Division Summary Profit Contribution (in $000s)

	Last Year	Projected	Current Year
Revenue	$800	$906	$693
Direct Expenses	429	480	389
Division Contribution	$371	$426	$304
Contribution Percentage	46%	47%	44%

Figure 52.7

Presto Weight Loss Products, Dessert and Treats Summary Profit Contribution (in $000s)

	Treats	Dessert	Total Dessert and Treats
Actual Profit Contribution	$304	$126	$430
Forecast Profit Contribution	426	96	522
Nonfood Profit Contribution	$(122)	$ 30	$(92)

Figure 53.7

Although pleased with Roger's improved performance, Louis felt his achievement had come at the expense of planned ice cream actions, as indicated in Figure 53.7.

Customers often chose ice cream as a dessert, not as a treat. The company always accounted for it as a treat and set sales strategies based on that determination. Marketing lower-profit dairy desserts with food encouraged customers to move away from ice cream as a dessert. Sales increased in Roger's division at the expense of higher-margined products in Jim's, the vice president of finance summarized.

With competing goals, the leaders cost the company at least $92,000 in profit. Conflicting action plans are now part of the triage agenda.

Roger had no idea his marketing plan detracted from company profit. Current year triage substantially reduced company profits because two well-meaning action plans were not compatible.

Dwight Bay Seafoods Ltd. also helps us understand the need for action compatibility.

Dwight Bay Seafoods Ltd. is known for high-quality seafood products. The company procures them daily from fishermen. Owner Shirley Bassinger buys only Grade A groundfish and shellfish for her seven retail stores and two wholesale operations.

Shirley started Dwight Bay Seafoods 15 years ago when demand for fresh, Grade A seafood was increasing. Sales grew steadily until Dwight Bay had a 78 percent share of the market. Growth has come primarily from retail, driven by public desire for better quality seafood than is generally available in food stores.

When Shirley completed annual triage planning and viewed Figure 54.7, she concluded wholesale to be an underdeveloped business. Resulting action plans focused on wholesale volume growth to food chains.

As Shirley implemented action plans, monthly reports showed definite improvement in wholesale sales. To her surprise, demand for retail sales declined. Soul mate Seth Kreiger suggested Shirley prepare a contribution analysis of sales by division to provide background for their next meeting. Shirley asked vice president of finance, Darryl Fredericks, to prepare the analysis in Figure 55.7.

When Seth reviewed the analysis provided by Darryl Fredericks, he realized Shirley planned to grow wholesale without considering the impact on retail sales.

The primary reason for Dwight Bay's success is Grade A seafood. General food store chains sell Grade B. The public shopped at Shirley's for this reason. By selling Grade A quality wholesale, she is placing Grade A stock on the shelves of retail store competitors!

Action plans to grow wholesale effectively destroyed the competitive niche of her retail stores. General chains now have Dwight Bay quality seafood and there is no need for the public to shop at Shirley's retail stores.

Dwight Bay Seafoods
Contribution Analysis by Division, Before Implementation of Current Year Action Plans (in $ millions)

	Retail Sales	Wholesale Sales	Combined Sales
Sales	$2.4	$.50	$2.90
Cost of Sales	1.0	.28	1.28
Gross Margin	$1.4	$.22	$1.62
Percent	58.3	44.0	55.9

Figure 54.7

Dwight Bay Seafoods
Contribution Analysis by Division, After Implementation of Current Year Action Plans (in $ millions)

	Retail Sales	Wholesale Sales	Combined Sales
Sales	$1.9	$1.1	$3.0
Cost of Sales	0.9	.616	1.516
Gross Margin	$1.0	$ .484	$1.484
Percent	52.6	44.0	49.5

Figure 55.7

What do we learn from Shirley? Her goal to increase sales was accomplished when combined sales grew from $2.9 million to $3 million — growth accomplished at the expense of profit. Gross margin on retail sales averaged 58.3%, while those for wholesale approximated 44%. As whole-sale business increased, weighted average margins declined from 55.9% to 49.5%. Strategies were for growth, but not profitable growth. Goals were incompatible.

BITE 36: ELIMINATE PRODUCTS WITH POOR PROFIT CONTRIBUTIONS

Financial reporting often calculates profit and loss by location, with attention to product performance. Geographical results may hide poor performing products by combining extraordinary product contributions with those generating losses. Overall financial results may still appear satisfactory but optimum performance is not achieved.

Product profitability reporting removes the shield strong performers provide for weak ones. Once it is removed, poor product performers can be identified for profit improvement or discontinuance. Energy and resources can then be directed to products with the greatest potential. The same may be said for company divisions. Profit analysis must be completed for both.

Most organizations subsidize a product or location at least once as an investment in future sales. What's important is identifying and monitoring the cost of that decision. Investments failing to be profitable within a reasonable period of time should be discontinued so that attention can be redirected to more profitable pursuits. Reasonable periods of time are defined during triage. Let's look at The Banachek Bus Corporation.

The Banachek Bus Corporation offers continuous passenger bus service among six cities, maintaining its own terminals in three. The remaining locations operate on leased premises adjacent to train stations.

The company was founded by Karl Banachek 25 years ago, with the construction of the Crystal Bay downtown depot. Later, Karl constructed similar but smaller depots in neighboring Blue Falls and Juniper.

When Karl's son, Steven, assumed the role of president 12 years ago, he led the company to expansion. Population growth in west end Crystal Bay caused him to lease a branch location. Heavy media advertising directed toward people of Crystal Bay West brought passenger volume. Last year's profit and loss summary shown in Figure 56.7 reflects this success.

A meticulous leader by nature, Steven never feels his operation performs to the optimum. Confiding regularly with his soul mate, businessman Ralph Lewis from Juniper City, he wrings his hands over the likelihood of poor profit performance next year. Meeting for poker every fourth Saturday, Ralph frequently talks of his quest to build an empire of medium-sized retail companies.

At the last poker night, Steven revealed his anxieties about the future. Seeing his friend quite troubled, Ralph offered to spend a few days reviewing the bussing operations with him. Steven jumped at the offer.

Ten days later, Ralph arrived, prepared to spend four days studying scheduling, occupancy, and financial and employee performance. He spent the first day familiarizing himself with operations details, meeting staff, and reviewing books and records. Ralph spent the second day by himself, analyzing contributions and operational statistics. A couple of observations intrigued him.

The Crystal Bay City West location was smaller than City Center, yet it contributed margins in excess of $1.8 million and a passenger-occupancy of 90 percent. Other locations hovered between 60 percent and 72 percent occupancy. The city center location incurred a loss of $91,000 last year while other locations profited handsomely.

Ralph looked at each business process behind every revenue and expense line of the summary contribution statement. Crystal Bay West expenses duplicated City Center's. And the leased premises cost $5 per square foot more than average rental space in the area.

Like a true soul mate, Ralph grilled Steven about the logic behind having two locations in the one city. How many passengers in the west would you lose if you combined Crystal Bay's two operations at the City Center depot? What are the exit costs of the City West lease? How much would expenses at City Center increase to accommodate the extra volume from City West?

Ralph considered the cost-savings of going to one location. It would mean one location for heat, light, and power; one refueling station; one cleaning crew; one manager; and less time wasted shuttling between two locations. In total, Ralph believed direct costs would decline by more

Banachek Bus Corporation
Summary Statement of Profit and Loss by Location (in $000s)

	Crystal Bay City Center	Crystal Bay City West	Total Crystal Bay	Blue Falls	Juniper City	Total Company Locations
Population	980,000	250,000	1,230,000	930,000	250,000	2,410,000
Number of Buses	6	7	13	5	3	21
Passenger Capacity Utilization	60.0%	90.0%	78.1%	71.6%	68.9%	76.5%
Revenue	$2,693	$5,247	$7,940	$2,227	$1,578	$11,745
Direct Cost of Sales	2,164	3,396	5,560	1,345	981	7,886
Contribution Margin	529	1,851	2,380	882	597	3,859
Contribution Percentage	19.6%	35.3 %	30.0%	39.6%	37.8%	32.8%
Direct Overhead	620	963	1,583	469	309	2,361
Contribution	($91)	$888	$797	$413	$288	$1,498

Figure 56.7

than $500,000 per year if the two locations were combined.

Then he attacked direct overhead. If the City West lease was not renewed in three months, lease payments, common area costs (costs, for such things as parking, that are shared with other businesses), administration, and accounting would decrease, saving the company $645,000 per year. The decision to combine the two Crystal Bay operations was a foregone conclusion. But what about revenue?

How much passenger occupancy would be lost by moving to City Center? Steven didn't know. To answer the question with any confidence, he had to ask customers. What would they think of the change? To find out, Banachek developed questionnaires to circulate in neighborhoods with large numbers of passengers. Bus drivers were encouraged to ask passengers to answer the questionnaire while riding Banachek during the next two months. The survey suggested west end customer volume could decline by 8 percent. Ralph rounded that to 10 percent, to be conservative.

Banachek Bus Corporation
Comparative Analysis of Proposed
Crystal Bay Consolidation (in $000s)

	Contributions from Existing Operations	Contribution from Proposed Combined Locations
Revenue	$7,940	$7,415
Direct Expense	5,560	5,051
Contribution Margin	2,380	2,364
Direct Overhead Expenses	1,583	938
Crystal Bay Contribution	$ 797	$1,426

Figure 57.7

Steven couldn't believe the profit potential from combining the two locations evidenced by Figure 57.7. At first glance, he would have closed City Center and moved its business to City West. That decision would have been wrong. Summary profit and loss didn't reflect the unused capacity in each location. City Center was larger, and could better handle the increased traffic. Combining the two generated expense savings far outweighing the 8 percent to 10 percent passenger decline —

a loss Steven believed could be earned back with advertising and promotion.

The Banachek Bus Corporation scenario clearly demonstrates how summarized financial data can lead to erroneous conclusions. Steven, believing his contribution statement, would have closed City Center depot immediately, throwing away enormous profit potential. Only a detailed review of the business processes behind each location revealed that under-utilized capacity weighed heavily on City Center profits. City West profited by stealing passenger volume from City Center. Leaving related expenses behind, City Center looked like the poor performer. Poor performers are not always obvious. Analysis must be thorough enough to draw optimum profit conclusions.

It's difficult to discuss poor performing products without returning to Presto Weight Loss Products and next year's triage activities.

Louis Mendelsohn is determined to prevent incompatible action plans from recurring among food, dessert, and treat divisions. When lost profit in excess of $92,000 was communicated throughout the company, Louis asked each division leader to rank the company's 11 categories of products in descending order of profit contribution. The result is shown in Figure 58.7.

When Finance allocated certain portions of overhead expenditures, Louis became disturbed to learn products, with a contribution margin below 30 percent, generated a loss. Product contribution, never a previous topic for triage, now became an important agenda item.

Roger Knotting now focuses on reducing break-even cost of producing cakes, cookies, and pies, and examines the sensitivity of price increases. He has 12 months to move contribution margins to over 30 percent. Any products with less than 30 percent contributions after 12 months will be discontinued. Managers are now encouraged to increase high-margin product sales, whether manufactured in their division or not. Competition among the three managers resulted in the company eliminating products with contribution margins less than 30 percent and focusing on higher margin products.

Presto Weight Loss Products
Product Contribution

Product Category	Percentage Profit Contribution
Ice cream	47
Pasta dinner	41
Candy	40
Beef dinner	39
Chicken dinner	37
Turkey dinner	34
Sherbet and yogurt	33
Fish dinner	32
Pies	29
Cakes	27
Cookies	24

Figure 58.7

To demonstrate the universality of eliminating poor profit performers, let's look to Stay Clean Waste Disposal Inc.

Juan Santos owns and operates a garbage-pickup service with an $18 million municipal contract for weekly pickup, box recycling, removal of hazardous waste, and special holiday clearing days.

Although Juan never graduated from business school, he possesses an instinct for making business profitable. He knows an $18 million city garbage disposal contract can be profitable if managed well.

When two years of the five-year contract had expired, Juan's accountant approached him with a summary annual profit and loss statement showing only a break-even position for Stay Clean. Juan refused to believe the results. His staff worked hard, wasting no time with pickup and disposals. Gas and oil appeared to be in line with anticipated usage — and there were no serious repair costs for his 25-truck fleet. Why couldn't he make money?

Carlos, his accountant, asked about different service costs. Does it cost the same for garbage as it does for special holidays? What does it cost to pick up recycling boxes? Juan saw no cost difference among garbage, recycling, and special pickups. The same workers drove the same trucks each day. Usually when Juan failed to make money in the past, it was due to high truck repair costs.

Carlos argued extra pickups took more time, required additional wage costs, and caused more wear and tear on vehicles. He decided to investigate revenues and expenses associated with each extra service.

Juan analyzed only total results in Figure 59.7 — $18 million of revenue with $18 million of expenses. Carlos explained special contracts required overtime payments, pushing labor costs to twice what they were for recycling — with only two-thirds the revenue. In fact, special pickups cost Juan $1.5 million per year and eliminated any profit generated from normal garbage pickup and recycling. Juan would be better off subcontracting special pickups to small operators, eliminating the need for 3 of his 25 trucks.

Once Juan was convinced costs of all pickups were not equal, he focused on saving $1.5 million per year. Juan Santos identified his barrier to profit. Then, by subcontracting unprofitable contracts, he eliminated it.

Stay Clean Waste Disposal
Analysis of Service Product Contribution (in $ millions)

	Garbage	Recycling	Special Pickups	Total
Revenue	$13.0	$3.0	$2.0	$18.0
Expenses				
Trucking	8.0	1.0	1.0	10.0
Labor	2.0	1.0	2.0	5.0
Overhead	2.0	.5	.5	3.0
	12.0	2.5	3.5	18.0
Operating Income	$ 1.0	$ .5	$(1.5)	$ 0

Figure 59.7

Barriers to profit do not occur only with products. The Stunning Model Agency offers the proof.

Jennifer Lewis manages The Stunning Model Agency, employing 21 male and female models for work in television commercials. After four years of success, Stunning has reached sales of $4.8 million. Continuous growth gave Jennifer confidence to add five new models during the past year.

New hires are given considerable training in expression, etiquette, and grace of movement to compete with other modeling agencies.

In addition to preparation of profit and loss statements, Jennifer prepares sales and contribution analysis, by model, to show demand for each, fees they command, and certain trends between male and female candidates. This analysis helps her to identify corrective actions required in individual performance, and gives her market intelligence about what kind of models to seek.

Six months after engaging the five new hires, Jennifer noticed declines in contribution margins. Standard monthly sales of $19,000 per person, of which $8,000 was contribution margin, had declined to $17,000 per person, and a contribution of $6,000. Very concerned about these trends, Jennifer interviewed a number of clients to research reasons for the declining fortunes.

When research was completed, Jennifer learned her recently hired models were more temperamental than the others. They complained of long working hours under hot lights and disagreed with clients on presentation and expressions in commercials. In most cases, they were not asked to do follow-up commercials, reducing the time billed to clients to levels less than other models. Jennifer's weighted-average-per-model revenue declined along with contribution margins.

Jennifer Lewis's five new models were functioning just like poor products. With difficult personalities, they became barriers to sales growth for The Stunning Model Agency. Jennifer had no choice but to terminate them to avoid further declines.

Organizations with competing goals, such as experienced by Beacon Electric or stores opened in inappropriate neighborhoods such as Dunphy's Convenience Stores, must have tools and processes to seek out incompatible goals and poor performing products — both common barriers to profitable growth.

The forces of profitable growth determine whether it increases or declines. As Figure 60.7 depicts, triage actions with assigned responsibilities and completion dates are designed to push profitable growth — whether acquired or organic — upward. On the other hand, incompatible goals and poor product-performers push growth downward. With good information and analysis, both can be avoided. Remember, incompatible goals can have a more negative impact on profitable growth than can no goals at all. Like poor performers, they are self-inflicted barriers to profitable growth.

Forces of Profitable Growth

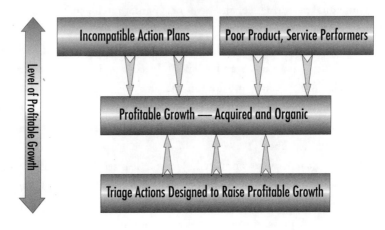

Figure 60.7

VIII

Change: Evolution or Revolution?

"Unless you interpret changes before they have occurred,
you will be decimated trying to follow them."
— *ROBERT J. NUROCK*

Business leaders expect change to occur more rapidly in the next 10 years than it has during the past 50. Faster change means less time to plan, execute, and accomplish goals, creating tremendous pressure to make decisions quickly and accurately. Leaders, now forced to change at ever-increasing rates, will barely have time to perfect new business processes before they must change them again. Past success will not guarantee future success.

Traditional leadership styles, approaches, and techniques were built from theories studied and tested over time. That was the old speed of change; the new world has greater fluidity. By the time one approach is accepted, another renders it obsolete. In this climate, survival truly depends upon your readiness for change.

Until the 1980s, change happened slowly enough that managerial approaches could be developed to drive day-to-day business activities. Approaches were in vogue long enough for leaders to perfect techniques. Employees worked fixed hours and had clear rules for productivity, benefits, and corporate behavior. Customers tolerated liberal product delivery times, back orders, and inefficiencies. Suppliers dictated terms to customers. Leaders predominantly acted like benevolent dictators, giving direction to their employees. Business life could be, and was, controlled, and employers and employees accepted the situation.

By the early 1990s, competitive pressures had forced the reexamination of all existing business processes. The business world entered an environment of permanent change. Leaders challenged old, accepted methods of doing business in the search for more productive ways. They dissected old methods of manufacturing goods and delivering services, seeking to eliminate redundant or non-value-added activities with the goal of permanent reduction of product and service costs. New efficiencies were implemented quickly for profitable growth. Everyone rushed to reduce costs and pass on price reductions to customers to achieve a competitive advantage. Self-preservation became synonymous with change. This environment accelerated with the pace of technology. The speed of computer development and its rapid acceptance in transacting business magnified change. Computer technologies became obsolete within 6 to 12 months of market introduction.

Computers made business information and data accessible to everyone. Once concentrated in the hands of leaders and senior management, it was now available at every desk. Change could now be initiated through network servers and intranets. Training could be delivered to all at work stations. The information explosion redistributed the power of knowledge throughout companies. Leaders began to encourage employees to initiate change to their own responsibilities. Empowerment became a popular managerial debate. Organizations became less hierarchical when individuals were empowered to conduct their own day-to-day business activities. Fewer management levels were now required, leading to further opportunities for overhead reduction.

Today, prosperity no longer rests with a handful of senior executives who expend enormous energy pushing continuous change through organizations not motivated to accept it. Successful leaders have seen first-hand the fatal pitfall of that formula — that employees told to change are more likely to resist it. Left in the hands of a few, continuous change will fail in the face of continuous resistance. But employees who themselves initiate change are more likely to embrace it and work hard to make it happen. In the increasingly competitive world of business, employee participation is crucial for success.

Organizations dedicated to change now present guidelines, rather than rules, to employees. Guidelines offer encouragement rather than strict control. This environment has the pleasant side effect of developing stronger leadership judgment below senior levels. Employees become stronger decision-makers, better prepared for their next promotions and more ready to cope with change.

Readiness for change should be recharged at annual triage to ensure its consistency throughout the year. Successful companies prepare for change with action plans or through company initiatives like Appleby Appliance Repairs' customer service teams.

Jim Appleby at one time managed operations personally by issuing repair instructions to individual repairmen, then measuring their efficiency by calculating the time taken to complete each repair. Directives were in the form of work orders. Repairmen were never asked for creative ideas, nor did they offer them. It was not part of the management culture.

Then, Appleby formed a customer service team, with two repairmen as members. Suddenly involved in the management of the company, the repairmen responded well and productivity increased. The customer service team became the vehicle for change readiness by applauding repairmen for their ideas to improve repair cycle times each month. Employees, once order-takers, now work under customer service guidelines. Because they now have responsibility to contribute to change, they are more receptive to it. All Jim has to do is add agenda items for teams to consider and new initiatives come from an already receptive employee group!

BITE 37: ANALYZE YOUR READINESS FOR CHANGE

How receptive are your employees to improving the way they conduct day-to-day tasks? Is change met with resistance, or is it accepted as a natural part of the conditions in which all employees are expected to perform?

The answers to these questions will tell you a lot about your company's readiness for change. Bringing about change in a company always forces modification of employee behavior. Consequently, any analysis of readiness must assume human behavior will increase the complexity of change. For example, considering technical and process changes without anticipating people's reactions to those changes usually results in greater resistance. In certain environments, highly technical changes will be accepted based on well-researched technological study. Other changes may bring implementation resentment if technical managers fail to plan for employee acceptance. Employees have feelings and attitudes toward change, and these are often magnified by miscommunication.

Figure 61.8 shows the analysis of an organization's readiness for change. This involves studying competitive matters such as product evolution, research and development, ability to satisfy future customers' needs, and leadership's willingness to make change a personal quest. A balanced assessment of your existing position and that of the rest of the industry can tell you your current state. You can't embark on a change until you have determined the starting point.

Analysis of an Organization's Readiness for Change

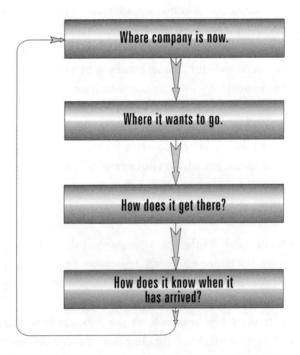

Figure 61.8

A company's current state, though, is relevant only when management knows where it wants to go. In simple terms, you need a beginning and an end before you can develop a plan to link the two. For example, if your goal is to be one product generation ahead of the competition, change means faster product development to meet future customer needs. If your company is mired in a reactive culture, always waiting for customers to communicate needs, the change needed is to shift the business to a culture of foresight. But how do leaders know when a change has been success-fully completed? The gradual events of change often cause mutations from the original plans — the destination shifts as you move down the road toward it. No problem. Successful leaders simply fine-tune their approach and continue. But continuous fine-tuning may make finite changes seem more like continuous improvement. And that makes it difficult to know when change has finally been achieved.

If the company belongs to an industry that is changing more rapidly than others, the process becomes a never-ending loop. Let's look at a case study.

The Baker Chemical Company is a small manufacturer of lawn and garden chemicals with sales of $6.5 million and 35 employees. It is owned and managed by Jerry Baker, who started the business from his two-car garage seven years ago.

His wife, Linda, is secretary to the business and responsible for customer records and monthly billing. As business volume grew, Linda had gradually added staff to prepare invoices and process accounts payable and monthly customer statements. When she began to find it more difficult to prepare information on a timely basis, she inquired about alternative methods during a meeting with the external accountant, Sam Shafer. He was concerned about her lack of speed collecting receivables so he suggested a computerized billing process to integrate accounts payable and monthly financial statements. He felt a number of software packages could help Baker Chemical improve its financial position.

Linda was enthusiastic and when she blurted out her plans, she was disappointed with the lack of enthusiasm from her staff. Her five admin-istrative employees suggested every possible reason why computers wouldn't work. Tension grew between Linda and the workers in the weeks following her announcement and she became very frustrated. When manual financial-data preparation became slower and more inaccurate, Linda made another appointment with Sam Shafer.

After relaying the story to Sam, he offered to introduce her to his partner who specialized in change management. Linda agreed to meet the partner that afternoon.

Events at Baker Chemical are not unusual in companies not ready for change. When leaders are enthusiastic about the benefits of change but insensitive to the perceptions of employees, resistance occurs. Linda's staff resisted because computerization was perceived as a threat to their positions. They were employed for their manual record-keeping skills. Computers would surely replace them. Panic resulted. Fear manifested itself into alienation from Linda and poorer work performance.

So, how should Linda have handled management of change? If she had paused to analyze Baker's readiness for change, she would have asked herself a number of questions:

- What is the current speed and quality of information prepared by administrative staff?
- What are the most cost-effective and accurate computerized systems currently available to Baker Chemical?
- Which technology must be acquired to install the most appropriate system?
- What administrative skills are required to change?
- What training is available?
- What sensitivities to this change should I anticipate? How should I communicate my idea to ensure employee acceptance?

If Linda had considered these questions before announcing the change, she would have been more cautious. Before telling her employees, she would have assessed the company's current state, decided what she wanted to accomplish, and determined how she could bring technology and skill to the change process. By considering these questions, she would have become aware of staff sensitivity to computerized accounting.

A second example comes from the American Pen Company.

The American Pen Company manufactures ball-point pens under the leadership of president Gino Lazaro. Last year, sales approached $143 million when the company successfully became the sole supplier of a drugstore chain.

Gino, constantly in search of efficiencies, engaged a consulting firm to review plant operations. Packaging, design, manufacturing, and shipping departments were to be analyzed in search of higher productivity.

Early consultant reports described the current state of efficiencies in each department, highlighting duplication of paper, accounting personnel, and multiple inventory counts as being costly to American Pen while adding little to accounting controls or quality. Analysis revealed that five people were employed for non-value-added tasks.

Gino accepted the findings and intended to implement the changes within three months. Advisors cautioned him that implementation would be a delicate matter. If changes were announced early, employees would likely feel threatened and distrusting of him. Advisers recommended that he involve each department in the design of implementation plans.

Gino met with each department separately, indicating company desire to find new, more efficient ways to carry out departmental functions. Who better to involve in finding solutions than those affected by them? He offered all employees a bonus of 10 percent of the permanent savings achieved as a result of their suggested changes.

Without referring to the consultant's report, he guided departmental managers gently toward elimination of task duplications as a source for their bonuses. Gino was both surprised and delighted with the similarities in findings between employees and the consultant. The same duplications were identified!

Unlike Linda, Gino considered the impact of changes on morale and productivity. By involving employees in the process, Gino's change became their change — with a bonus as a reward.

BITE 38: ENSURE EACH INITIATIVE HAS AN AGENT

Linda Baker became the agent of change for Baker Chemical not just because administrative staff reported to her. She had the interest, enthusiasm, and determination to move the company to computerized accounting. Anyone who wants to be an agent of change must have these characteristics to be successful. More important, an agent must be respected by those who are expected to accept the change. A change agent who lacks enthusiasm or personal credibility will fail. Poor agents cause the change itself to lose credibility. The change will require more effort and expenditure, even if the most well-respected leader is brought in as a substitute change agent. If the change is important enough to implement, it is important enough to have the right agent. Take time to make the right agent selection. It will be the best investment you make in the change process. Change analysts determine a company's readiness for change. That's why Linda Baker's consultant provided her with a sample analysis questionnaire to complete before implementation.

In addition to an agent, each company change needs a sponsor. This is an individual or group promoting the change within a company, whereas the agent is responsible for successfully effecting the change. Linda was actually both the change sponsor and agent. So was Gino Lazaro at the American Pen Company. In many cases, responsibilities will rest with different people.

Baker Chemical Company
Analysis of Proposed Administrative Changes

1. Write a brief description of the change project.

2. List the steps and components of this project that are vital for this change to succeed.

3. What outcomes are expected as a result of this project?
   Technical Objectives:

Figure 62.8

Baker Chemical Company
Analysis of Proposed Administrative Changes

_____

_____

_____

Human Objectives: _____

_____

_____

_____

_____

4. What time, money, or other constraints are relevant to this project?
   Time Frame for Implementation: _____

_____

_____

_____

_____

Budget Constraints: _____

_____

_____

_____

Other Constraints: _____

_____

_____

_____

5. What is the primary reason (problem or opportunity) driving the decision to change?

_____

_____

_____

6. What sponsors will legitimize the change?

_____

_____

_____

Figure 62.8 (cont.)

Baker Chemical Company
Analysis of Proposed Administrative Changes

7. Why is this project important to the sponsor?

8. Why is this project important to the organization?

9. Who are the primary individuals who will be affected by the change?

10. How can those affected be made to see the desirability of this change?

11. How can those affected be made to see the accessibility of this change (in terms of such issues as financial cost, education, support, priorities, and time management)?

12. Do sponsors expect resistance or support from those affected or other key people when this change is implemented?

Figure 62.8 (cont.)

Baker Chemical Company
Analysis of Proposed Administrative Changes

13. What are your responsibilities as a change agent during this project?

_____

_____

_____

_____

Figure 62.8 (cont.)

Those affected by the change are people who must alter something about their knowledge, skill, behavior, or attitude for the change to be successful. Baker's affected people were Linda's five administrative staff.

Linda's answers to the change questions presented in Figure 62.8 led her to understand the importance of planned implementation. The questionnaire forced her to consider details of the changeover from manual accounting to a computer system and the staff training that would be required. Fear for job security caused her staff to resist the change. To ease their fears, Linda had to turn training into a selling feature to break their resistance. In the end, managing change was a lot more difficult than Linda had initially thought.

BITE 39: APPOINT A LEADER OF CHANGE

Change sponsors identify the need for change. They can come from anywhere in an organization. Mailroom clerks, for example, may identify better ways to sort and deliver correspondence and suggest that change to management. If the change is accepted, they help plan the implementation.

As illustrated in Figure 63.8, leaders of change facilitate the implementation process. They support the change plans and work with change agents and sponsors. Change agents, in turn, draw on the leader to guide execution of each plan. Leaders of change are similar to leaders of core competence, and just as essential to the long-term health of a company.

Larger companies usually have full-time leaders of change; smaller companies have more modest commitments. The smaller the company, the more likely the leader of change will be the president or owner. The importance of the role, however, remains the same, no matter what the size of the business. In the Baker Chemical case, Linda was sponsor, change agent, and, really, the corporate leader of change. If Baker Chemical was a $100 million business with 700 employees, Linda would probably have a full-time leader of change. This is a good time to visit the case of Blue Sea Foods Inc.

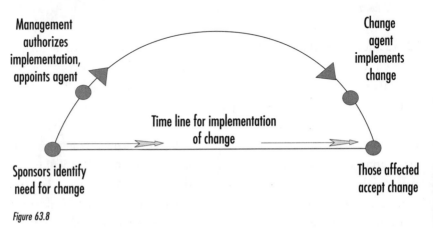

Leader of Change Facilitates Implementation

Management authorizes implementation, appoints agent

Change agent implements change

Time line for implementation of change

Sponsors identify need for change

Those affected accept change

Figure 63.8

Hank Xyler opened Blue Sea's first seafood restaurant in 1961 and managed to open one new store each year for the next 10 years. The next 20 years saw individual franchise owners build and operate 700 franchises throughout North America, Europe, and the Pacific Rim. Hank continued to own and operate 11 stores himself.

Large restaurant franchises face the challenge of maintaining consistent food and service quality among multiple owners. Hank felt the task was impossible, because there were always 10 percent to 15 percent of restaurants that maintained renegade food processes or poor service standards. Reports of poorly cooked fish and rude employees reached head office weekly, keeping in-house counsel busy writing letters to delinquent franchisees. Annual triage found Hank at an all-time low over his franchisees' resistance to quality standards. He refused to conclude the planning lockup until managers and advisors had solved the problem.

The vice president of franchising operations suggested the company hire a full-time leader of change. Hank and other senior managers argued that a new person should address quality control, not manage change. The vice president relentlessly defended his definition of the position. Maintaining quality standards is a symptom of a larger problem. That is, the company is just not strong enough in implementing change. Every change made to menus or approaches to service must be uniformly implemented across all 700 restaurants. Quality control becomes a concern when there is lack of compliance to standards. In the restaurant business, variety and continuous change are necessary to maintain customer loyalty.

Hank was convinced. To grow revenues and market share, uniformity of change was essential. Restaurants with renegade recipes and procedures would continue to detract from franchiser changes. He agreed to hire a leader of change.

Hank actually gave more responsibility to the leader than originally proposed. The leader was not only to devise and implement franchisee changes; he would audit changes on an anonymous basis, without notice. Franchisees not implementing change as prescribed would risk forfeiting their franchise rights. Power to revoke franchises ensured the leader of change had the attention and respect of restaurant operators. Last year, Hank's renegade stores amounted to 4 percent, down from 10 percent.

Ludwig Inc., our case for annual triage and planning, offers a different approach to change leadership, primarily because of its size. With computer technology changing so rapidly, Ludwig appointed Lee Wilson as full time vice president of change to encourage change sponsors and agents. Let's examine what he found.

Lee's triage, performed before planning lockup, identified numerous weaknesses in Ludwig's management and implementation of change. Mid and upper management lacked the skills to diagnose the need for change. They required training to:

▲ diagnose Ludwig's need and readiness for change;
▲ design and communicate change plans effectively;

▲ identify and relate to emotional reactions to change; and

▲ reduce and manage negative reactions to change.

Lee's primary goal was to train 60 upper management personnel in management of change by fiscal year end. The action plan suggested to accomplish this goal was to commit the 60 leaders in teams of 15 each to a one-week training course commencing March 15, June 15, September 15, or December 15 of the current fiscal year.

Lee increased awareness of Ludwig's specific needs for managing change. If successful in achieving his goals, he will create an organization more receptive to change.

Leaders of change, by their very existence, demonstrate an organization's commitment to change. Employees accept it as a continuous leadership process and, over time, resistance to change itself declines.

BITE 40: PREPARE RESOURCE PLANS TO IMPLEMENT CHANGE

Having a leader of change is important, but it is not enough to guarantee that changes are successfully implemented. A resource plan is also critical. Created and monitored by leaders of change, the resource plan feeds action plans into current year business plans. This yields four distinct advantages:

- Change implementation is introduced as a step within overall business planning.
- Change planning becomes accepted practice. The more normal change planning becomes, the more it is expected by those affected — leading to less resistance with time.
- Including change goals and action plans during annual triage forces a congruent approach to goal setting.
- Annual business planning, with milestone dates to monitor progress, provides a natural climate to follow up change implementation.

This is an excellent time to return to Baker Chemical Company to follow Linda's progress in implementing her proposed administrative changes.

Baker Chemical Company
Draft Change Implementation Plan

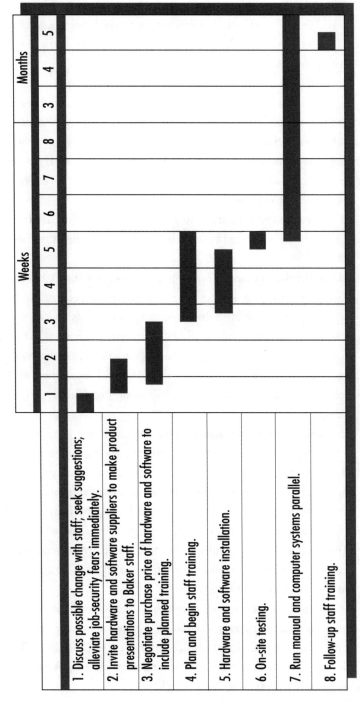

Figure 64.8

When Linda completed her proposed administrative change analysis, she returned to the change consultant to study implementation plans. Linda now felt knowledgeable enough to draft her change implementation plan.

Linda's plan in Figure 64.8 accommodates key success criteria necessary for change, planning for both technological and human resources. It alleviates fears of job termination by selling change as an opportunity for staff training, not termination. Notice the invitation for staff to contribute implementation ideas. That step helped Baker Chemical recover from its poor beginning to change.

To appreciate the benefits of implementation planning from the beginning, there is no better example than Hank Xyler's Blue Sea Foods Inc.

Hank's leader of change became Jim Thames. His first task was to attend leadership discussions concerning worldwide luncheon menu changes.

Hank's first initiative for luncheon menus was the inclusion of a seafood luncheon salad. Worldwide concern for fitness and health led food researchers to highlight salads as a sales opportunity. Customer surveys identified desired combinations and quantities of seafood, lettuce, and garnishments. Special dressing ingredients were still to be determined.

During the meeting, actions were assigned to the participants and Jim accepted the challenge to prepare preliminary implementation plans for the 700 restaurants. When the planning committee reunited, he presented his proposed implementation plan in the form of the time line in Figure 65.8. Recipe ingredients had first to be finalized — and no later than mid-May if sales targets were to be accomplished this year. There would be two months of testing in company-owned restaurants to improve quality and consistency of the salad itself and establish sales records to pass on to franchisees.

Detailed recipe instructions would be delivered to all franchisees prior to concluding two months of testing, permitting each restaurant time to test the salad and resolve any issues. In July, head office would deliver the results of sales and testing data and, if positive, encourage immediate adoption of the menu changes.

Blue Sea Foods

Proposed Implementation of Seafood Salad Luncheon

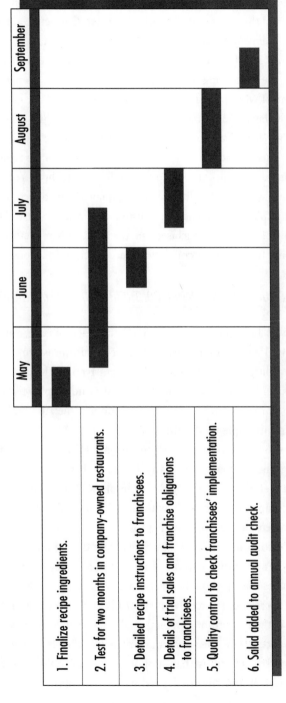

	May	June	July	August	September
1. Finalize recipe ingredients.					
2. Test for two months in company-owned restaurants.					
3. Detailed recipe instructions to franchisees.					
4. Details of trial sales and franchise obligations to franchisees.					
5. Quality control to check franchisees' implementation.					
6. Salad added to annual audit check.					

Figure 65.8

Jim proposed that preliminary implementation checks be conducted by quality control throughout the month of August. Corrective action plans could be implemented for those having difficulty. To ensure the salad was consistent in all franchises, the salad recipe would be added to audit checks for the upcoming year: starting in September, someone from quality control would eat a salad in each franchise.

Although the planning meeting resulted in minor adjustments to Jim Thames' plan, it was accepted in principle. With his inclusion of testing and audit checks, he had responded to Hank's recipe consistency concerns. Increased sales during testing reduced franchisee resistance to change. Hank was also delighted to see his quality control people helping franchisees implement the change. Tensions had always existed between quality control and the franchisees in the past. When quality control began helping franchisees become more successful, the tensions eased.

BITE 41: ENSURE SUBJECTS OF CHANGE CONTRIBUTE TO IMPLEMENTATION

Change initiatives fail when corporate goals and actions are not aligned with those of employees. Employees with career aspirations are focused on organizational politics, while organizations are driven by the economics of their market place. Find a way to connect the two and employees willingly contribute to organizational change. Fail to connect the two and you fail to achieve optimum implementation.

Figure 66.8 shows the pillars of organizational alignment. The foundation supporting these pillars has many levels. It begins with an understanding of each employee's personal career plans. With this knowledge, leaders match company triage goals with those of the employee. This is an attempt to align employee goals with those of the organization. Leaders obtain employee commitment to goal achievement during annual performance reviews. When employees accomplish these goals, they are rewarded in a way that matches their personal career objectives. If the employee's objective is to make more money, achievement of his goals means more money. If a promotion is the important personal goal, then that is the reward. The annual performance review then becomes a review of the employee's success and failure at personal actions that support corporate ones. The rewards reinforce the behavior and culture desired by the company.

Pillars of Organizational Alignment

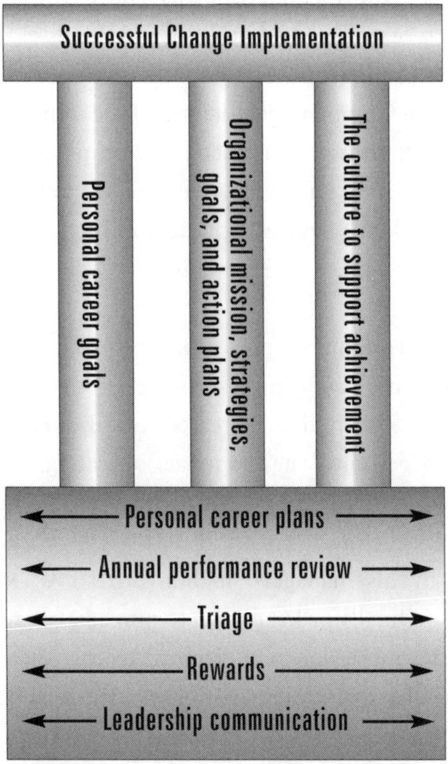

Successful Change Implementation

Personal career goals

Organizational mission, strategies, goals, and action plans

The culture to support achievement

←———— Personal career plans ————→
←———— Annual performance review ————→
←———————— Triage ————————→
←——————— Rewards ———————→
←——— Leadership communication ———→

Figure 66.8

Leadership communication is foundational to this alignment. The company vision, mission, strategies, goals, and actions must be communicated clearly, then communicated again, and then reinforced. Every employee should understand what the company wants to look like in five years and what he needs to change in his daily activity to bring the company closer to realizing its vision. Successful leaders communicate through memos, presentations, meetings, town halls, and with one-on-one encouragement. Using one or two of these approaches is not sufficient reinforcement. Leaders must use them all consistently — and repeatedly — until everyone's actions reflect the company's vision. Only then do you have a culture that supports successful change implementation.

Most of your employees are much smarter than their responsibilities permit them to demonstrate. They have creativity and energy that is often masked by hidden and political agendas. They may think speaking out about inefficiencies and problems will cause more trouble than it's worth, or displease leaders. State clearly that this is not the case. So let them think. Encourage them to think. Your success depends on it!

The American Pen Company demonstrated the importance of involving employees in the preparation of implementation plans. The alternative is an atmosphere of fear, like the one Linda Baker experienced when she first announced her plan. Engineering Software Inc. provides another case illustrating what not to do.

> Engineering Software Inc. employed 325 people in the design, creation, and production of engineering software products for a worldwide clientele. Sales of $863 million increased steadily on a weighted five-year average of 16.5 percent. One year, chief operating officer Simon Bates was challenged by declining profit, down to $21 million from $35 million two years before.
>
> Frustrated by his managers' inability to solve expense escalation problems, Simon finally ordered them to immediately reduce staff by 15. Faced with a short deadline to implement the change, managers selected the 15 staff members who were least busy at the time. Estimated savings from reduced salaries and benefits were $1.2 million.
>
> Three weeks after the employees were terminated, Simon received calls from important clients complaining that software products were not being completed according to agreements. When he investigated, he learned that 3 of the 15 people terminated were key to the completion of certain client contracts. Once again, he became enraged with his managers.

The interesting lesson from Simon's case is that Engineering Software reacted to short-term profit pressures by terminating the 15 people who were not currently busy. No analysis was conducted to determine which 15 people in the organization were poor performers. No plan existed to identify the current state of the company and determine where change should take it in future. Simon's managers reacted to orders without thinking. After all, they were never asked to think. Simon's dictatorial management style made following orders the path of least resistance: since they weren't part of change planning, his managers could not be held accountable for its implementation. Simon might have had a better result if he had asked his managers to identify 15 employees who added no value to the ongoing success of the company.

When Linda completed Baker Chemical's change planning, administrative staff formed the transition team. They were receptive to the new computer accounting system. Taking computer courses at company expense was presented as an investment in Baker staff, not remedial action for poor performers. At worst, better training would make them more employable if they chose to leave in future. Linda's willingness to pay for training eliminated her staff's fears of being replaced. Although technical problems occurred during the switch from manual to computerized accounting, the change was completed within six months. Linda transformed employee revolution into the evolution of better business processes.

Jim Thames accomplished the same result with Blue Sea's quality control staff. When he dispatched them into the field of franchisees, he was able to solicit ideas from those franchisees. He published good ideas from the field in his monthly franchise newsletter. Relations with franchisees improved. Barriers to change declined. The result was an organization more receptive to positive change.

IX
Process Improvement: Stimulate or Stagnate

"There's only one corner of the universe you can be certain of improving and that's your own self."
— *ALDOUS HUXLEY*

At the heart of *50 Steps to Business Success* is a fundamental culture of continuous improvement. This culture drives leaders to maintain a constant quest to improve the conduct of all aspects of business, from mission statements to the simplest action plans. Perfection is never reached; there are always better ways to deliver customer service and products. The issue is how to identify and implement these improvements. In the hands of only a few leaders, business improvement is a strenuous task at best, and more likely impossible. Leaders alone cannot be expected to identify the possibly hundreds of improvements to be made throughout an organization. That would be leadership gone mad. Instead, improvements must be identified at all job levels, on a continuous basis, and with a common direction — the company vision — in mind. Anything else would produce a disjointed, project-by-project effort and would not represent a culture of continuous improvement.

In the absence of continuous improvement culture, leaders must devote energy and time to improvement initiatives each time they perceive improvements are needed. A general improvement culture, on the other hand, stimulates improvement naturally from photocopy room to boardroom. Ideas percolate from all levels of the company so long as people are rewarded for positive suggestions and feel no job insecurity from their implementation. Businesses without such a culture stagnate and eventually fall behind industry standards. Competitive spirit never permeates the organization. Competitiveness declines. To maintain a healthy competitive edge, continuous improvement must be instinctive throughout the entire business.

The goal of improvement cultures is simple: Reduce expenditures through the elimination of unnecessary processes and procedures. These can be simple things, such as the elimination of unnecessary customer order approvals, or they may be larger issues, such as the number of people involved in decision making, excess documentation and paper flow, misdirected advertising, excess travel costs, and unnecessary product packaging waste.

Drivers of Process Improvement

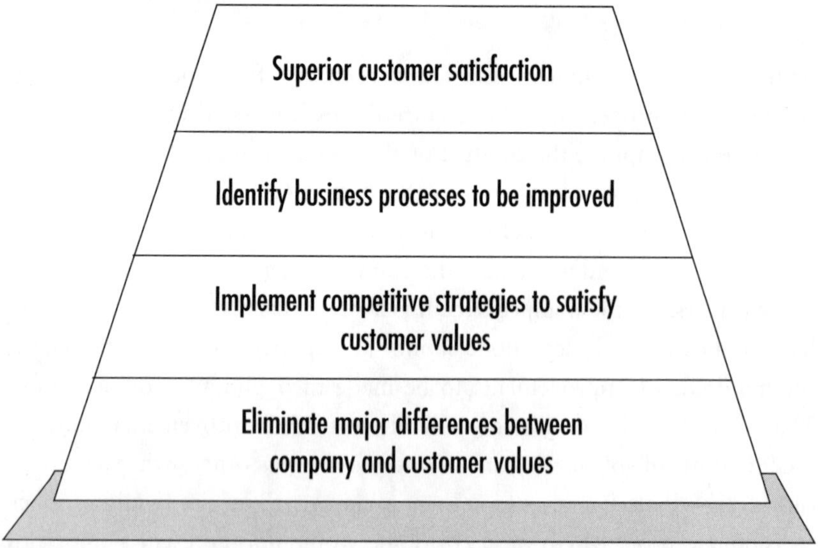

Superior customer satisfaction

Identify business processes to be improved

Implement competitive strategies to satisfy customer values

Eliminate major differences between company and customer values

Figure 67.9

It all begins with *50 Steps to Business Success*'s primary raison d'être: superior customer satisfaction as shown in Figure 67.9. Customers pay for and are entitled to receive satisfaction. The cases of Appleby Appliance Repairs, Leison Auto Parts, and Brendeen Manufacturing Inc. have all shown that nothing else matters. Please the customer and all other stakeholders follow suit. Leaders, employees, creditors, and shareholders enjoy greater success and feel more secure.

True belief in superior customer satisfaction means employees believe their jobs and personal success are tied to that satisfaction. That belief creates complete alignment of values between an organization and its customers. Customer values are determined first, and company values are then modeled after them. Superior customer satisfaction will not exist until your company action plans ensure supplier and customer values, attitudes, and beliefs coincide.

Once major value differences are eliminated, leaders focus on competitive strategies to achieve those values — the actual meeting of customer expectations. If customer expectation is for speedy product delivery, you deliver faster. If customers focus on research and development, you form a superior research department, and so on. If you deliver the best research and development when customers care more about speed of delivery, the values of the two organizations are dysfunctional. The supplier takes longer in order to achieve perfection while the customer wants a cheaper model, faster. Successful strategies build synchronized supplier-customer values.

Goals and action plans emanating from synchronized competitive strategies target processes that do not add value to customer satisfaction. These are processes to be improved or eliminated for customer satisfaction to achieve superiority. Unnecessary managerial approvals, for example, taking resources away from cost-effective product delivery, are ferreted out. Similarly, warranty service is synchronized with customer needs. Every value important to the customer is the target of continuous review and improvement each year, to keep one competitive step ahead of the industry. Stimulating constant process improvement discourages stagnation and mediocre performance.

BITE 42: ELIMINATE MAJOR DIFFERENCES
BETWEEN COMPANY AND CUSTOMER VALUES

Company values developed independently of customer needs are usually inwardly focused. Leaders in such organizations concern themselves with their own hierarchy, paper processing, and procedures within sales, marketing, production, finance, and human resources, rather than focusing on the customer. They engage in turf wars and tend to blame each other for poor performance rather than aim for improvements. More concerned with self-preservation than customer satisfaction, leaders and employees in these companies tend to waste time and incur expenses just trying to avoid accountability. Without change, companies with these cultures are doomed: at best, to mediocre performance, at worst, to business failure. In successful companies, only superior performance matters. An excellent example of matching company and customer values is provided by Dresham Dry Cleaners.

Dresham Dry Cleaners is a chain of 17 dry-cleaning outlets operating in four cities. Owner Lew Dresham believes the chain's customer service needs improvement. Stores were added as demand increased, but new employees were not adequately trained in public relations.

A significant increase in customer complaints from 6 of 17 locations caused Lew to revisit stakeholder values with store managers. When managers met for triage, Lew asked each to list their perceptions of customer, company, supplier, and shareholder values. They then debated each submission and agreed upon a common set of perceived values as outlined in Figure 68.9.

The rest of their time in triage was spent discussing how Dresham's values could meet stakeholder expectations. Most felt "customer satisfaction at all cost" meant courtesy and same-day service. Eight of 17 managers, though, admitted they didn't practice courtesy or same-day service with as much determination as they should. Front-desk clerks, they felt, completed their tasks adequately, but not with any warmth toward the customer. Three of 17 stores never provided same-day dry-cleaning. Pick-up was always for the following day or two days from the drop-off date.

Company values already matched safe-cleaning expectations. At times, clothing got damaged, but "customer satisfaction at all cost" meant replacement without question. All store managers agreed to improve two processes: to ensure same-day service for all clothing dropped off before 11 a.m., and to provide each salesclerk with a minimum of three hours courtesy training, prior to her first shift.

Dresham Dry Cleaners' Value Chain

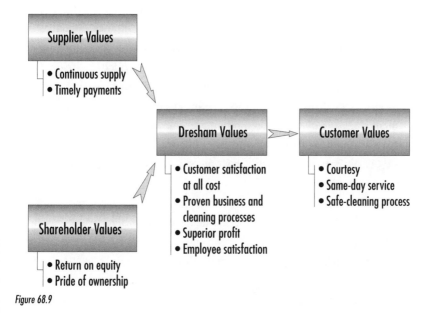

Figure 68.9

Lew insisted these process improvements be adopted as action plans for the coming year. Goals were also set for superior profit and employee satisfaction — synchronizing the values of all Dresham stakeholders.

When customer and company values are analyzed, it's also time to examine competitor performance. How successfully are competitors matching customer values? Intelligence-gathering during triage should provide a clear picture of your company's advantages and disadvantages.

Dresham felt same-day service and customer courtesy would distinguish their performance from that of competitors. At the time of triage, Dresham's performance was much the same as competitors'. When customer values were seriously studied, the opportunity to competitively distinguish Dresham's service became clear. It provided unique insights into competitive advantages.

Old Orchard Fruit and Vegetable offers a second case for matching company and customer values.

Old Orchard Fruit and Vegetable grows and harvests a number of fruits and vegetables from its 15,000-acre farm. Owner Sam Pullman built the business to sales of $80 million over its 22-year history. Other major farm operations grew over the years to compete with Old Orchard, making it difficult for Sam to achieve his $100 million sales goal.

He believed his goal could be met by reducing prices on volume vegetables — potatoes, carrots, and peas. He decided to lower these prices by 12 percent for the upcoming season. When the first seasonal month passed, his accountants produced comparative financial statements, season over season, showing a sales decline from $32 million to $26 million. Perplexed by the decline, Sam met with a number of distributors to ask why customers were not taking advantage of favorable prices.

The counsel of distributors made it clear. Consumers purchase vegetables in fixed quantities. Reducing or increasing prices has little effect on buying behavior. The consumer is primarily interested in the freshness, quality, and rich coloring of the produce.

By reducing prices without understanding customer values, Sam Pullman gave away profit. Synchronizing with customer values meant improving quality through better growing and harvesting processes, not reducing prices. In fact, Sam later improved the richness of his produce at very little cost, then increased prices by 16 percent — and wrestled market share away from his competitors!

BITE 43: DEVELOP COMPETITIVE STRATEGIES TO SATISFY CUSTOMER VALUES

Creating competitive strategies is not a static process. It's continuous. A competitive advantage now may not be so advantageous three months from now, after competitors have completed their own process improvements. Advantage is achieved by those who add the greatest customer value with the least resources — that is, those who deliver what customers want, when they want it, at the least cost. Dresham met these requirements with same-day dry-cleaning service and increased courtesy. If Dresham customers were concerned only with price, Dresham may have favored cheaper cleaning processes over same-day service. Let's return to Dresham to understand how it links competitive advantage to customer values.

Dresham Dry Cleaners
Competitive Advantage Review

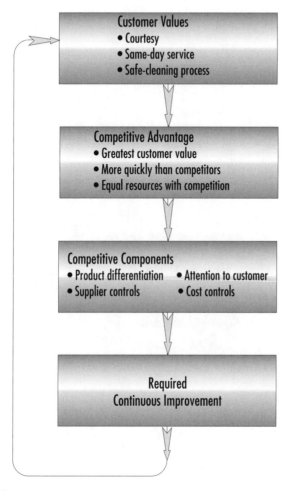

Customer Values
- Courtesy
- Same-day service
- Safe-cleaning process

Competitive Advantage
- Greatest customer value
- More quickly than competitors
- Equal resources with competition

Competitive Components
- Product differentiation   • Attention to customer
- Supplier controls   • Cost controls

**Required
Continuous Improvement**

Figure 69.9

Figures 69.9 and 70.9 depict how Dresham studies customer values before establishing its own — defining its competitive advantage in the process. Required continuous improvement is a set of actions necessary to develop that advantage. In this case, training salesclerks in courtesy, diplomacy, and customer handling is the requirement. Same-day cleaning delivers value more quickly than competitors. The combination of the two, at no additional cost, becomes Dresham's competitive advantage.

Dresham Dry Cleaners
Required Continuous Improvement

Process I:
More Pleasant Customer Service

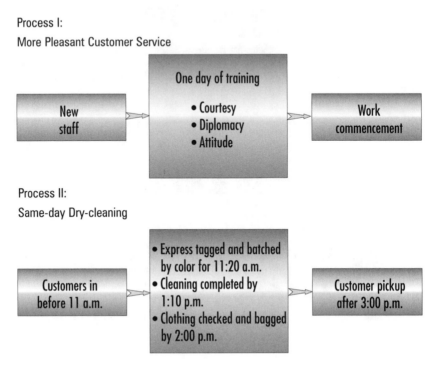

Process II:
Same-day Dry-cleaning

Figure 70.9

To achieve the required change, Lew created two defined processes. Process I depicted in Figure 70.9 became goals and actions for more pleasant customer service — a day's training course in courtesy, diplomacy, and attitude, to be given each month. New staff cannot commence work until they complete the course.

Process II considers all aspects of same-day dry-cleaning. Instead of batching randomly by color, causing delays and 24-hour turnaround, Dresham developed a new process of color tagging by desired completion times. Red became the express tag for 11:20 a.m. cleaning; green for 2:20 p.m.; blue for 3:50 p.m.; purple for the 6:00 p.m. run. Processing could now be controlled by customer pickup time as opposed to by internal production cycles.

Dresham mapped out each process to highlight opportunities to save time and to create new benchmarks to measure competitive performance. Houston Paper struggled with a slightly different competitive strategy issue from that of Dresham.

Houston Paper manufactures cardboard packaging products to achieve $172 million in sales in 21 industries. President Jeff Callion has observed changing customer values during his eight years with Houston. Research during the first year of his presidency indicated that customers were concerned with the strength of cardboard boxes and containers. Houston put its focus on strength and proudly led all competitors in sales of reinforced containers to manufacturers of heavy industrial products.

In recent years, with increased competitive pressures within industries, customer values moved from strength of containers to unit cost. Last year Jeff formed a task force to determine five areas where Houston Paper could reduce its cost of production and resulting customer prices. The task force recommendations included:

▲ utilization of a slightly cheaper bonding product with no compromise to strength;

▲ renegotiation of supplier raw paper prices based on increasing volumes purchased;

▲ elimination of four staff positions;

▲ reduction of product handling procedures; and

▲ creation of an alternative shipping scheduling.

Houston Paper talks to customers every year before annual triage to ensure changes in customer values and expectations are clearly understood. In this way, Jeff continuously improves delivery of customer satisfaction.

BITE 44: IDENTIFY BUSINESS PROCESSES TO BE IMPROVED

Business processes, like those identified by Dresham Dry Cleaners, are a collection of day-to-day tasks, the sum of which becomes a company's ability to meet stakeholder — and most importantly, customer — needs.

Tasks are often grouped along functional lines for organizational reporting purposes. For example, advertising, preparing product promotion materials, and designing packaging are commonly grouped under the marketing function, reporting to its manager or vice president. Production activities, from ordering raw materials to shipping, may report to a vice president of production. A similar organization exists for finance and accounting, human resources, customer service, and general administration functions. Most often displayed in tiered organization charts, functional groupings are commonly referred to as "silos," so named for their vertical reporting lines from front-line workers through middle management to senior leaders.

Vertical reporting motivates managers to demonstrate their performance contributions to the next level of management. This is one important way managers enhance their chances of career advancement. In this kind of exchange, little concern may be paid to the needs of other silos. Coordination is left to a senior vice president or the president. The problem is that customers depend on all silos to function in harmony. Customers buy products or services from the company, not a segregated piece of it. They expect an order placed with sales to be referred to production quickly, produced according to their specifications, and then delivered on time and with an invoice. Value is delivered only through unified and coordinated functions from all silos. In short, customers don't care about a company's internal problems. They want quality products and services delivered in a timely fashion.

This vertical accountability within silos, then, runs counter to the needs of customers. No one person takes complete responsibility for customer satisfaction between the time an order is placed and a product is delivered. No one person determines customer needs, writes an order, ensures production produces to specification, then packages and delivers the product to the customer exactly as requested. Instead, each silo completes tasks according to its leader's demands and then passes products and paperwork on to the next silo. Those operating in one silo have no interest in what happens in the next. It has completed its tasks according to its timetable, available resources, and scheduling — all factors of internal convenience, not customer satisfaction.

To determine whether business processes respect customer values, leaders must look across silo boundaries. Product delivery, for example, touches on order taking, production, and distribution. Similarly, purchasing processes may involve all silos. Identifying each process and then tracing its activities through each functional silo frequently reveals inefficiency and duplication. Each department may have its own administrative costs and support personnel to ensure documents are prepared, filed, and transferred to the next silo. This activity adds to product cost to customers, but does not always add value. What seems to be a justifiable expense in production may be duplicated in other departments.

Preparing business plans by silo will not always clearly identify processes in need of improvement. To ensure plans are based on customer needs, each process must be traced through each silo to determine how well those needs are met, and at what cost and level of efficiency. Only through this process can inefficiency and waste be identified for elimination. The pitfalls of segregated silos is demonstrated well by Green Bay Manufacturing.

Green Bay Manufacturing Ltd., a successful carpet manufacturer worldwide, maintains sales of $820 million. Company leadership is organized by its president, George Apso, along traditional functional lines as illustrated in Figure 71.9.

Recently, internal disputes have increased, particularly between the vice presidents of sales and production. The two frequently argue about production and product-delivery times. Their respective support staffs have increased in number to ensure all matters of dispute are documented, raising overhead expenditures and the company's break-even level of sales in the process. George grew impatient with the squabbling and eventually engaged external advisors to make recommendations.

After a month of study, the advisers were convinced Green Bay's organization was a breeding ground for customer problems. Functional silos operated independent of each other with little knowledge of overall product delivery processes. The vice president of sales knew only his own functional area, while the vice president of production knew nothing of sales. Neither understood the activities in other functional areas.

Orders for carpet manufacturing move horizontally from order taking in the sales department to production scheduling and fulfillment.

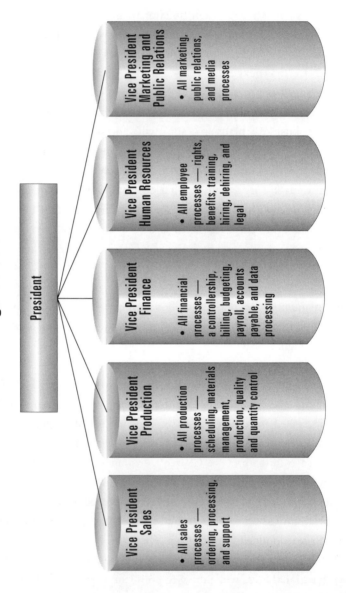

Green Bay Manufacturing
Process Organization Chart

President

Vice President Sales
- All sales processes — ordering, processing, and support

Vice President Production
- All production processes — scheduling, materials management, production, quality and quantity control

Vice President Finance
- All financial processes — a controllership, billing, budgeting, payroll, accounts payable, and data processing

Vice President Human Resources
- All employee processes — rights, benefits, training, hiring, dehiring, and legal

Vice President Marketing and Public Relations
- All marketing, public relations, and media processes

Figure 71.9

Once orders leave sales bound for production, they are forgotten by sales personnel unless customers complain. Production prioritizes orders based on its own scheduling process. No linkage exists between production scheduling and customer values. Each employee is responsible for a small piece of silo activity. No one is responsible for overall customer well-being.

When customers complained about product delays, management increased inventory of popular carpet products for quick availability. Green Bay compensates for fractured silos with duplicate clerk time and increased inventory levels.

Consultants prepared a schematic of existing sales processes from order placement to delivery and presented it to George Apso. As shown in Figure 72.9, responsibility for each process rests with managers noted at the bottom of each silo.

Notice what happens when an order moves through Green Bay's system. Responsibility and control moves from vice president of sales to the vice president of production to the manager of inventory control to the vice president of finance. Each has a limited knowledge of the other's activities and no one has overall responsibility for customer well-being as the order moves through the system.

Also notice the number of times each order is checked and approved. Is value added to the customer each time, or is there a redundant process increasing the cost of each order? George's advisers suggested he eliminate duplicate costs and refocus the organization toward the customer, and away from itself.

In their preliminary report, the advisers recommended the company identify each major business process, make a detailed chart of its tasks, and then plan improvements to refocus the organization.

Each process for improvement would have to have a technical and human resource plan to manage any change — especially where existing processes housed fiefdoms.

George's advisers also offered a new sales process, outlined in Figure 73.9. Responsibility for the entire process would rest with the vice president of operations, to whom all operating personnel would report, including those from sales and accounting. Multiple silos are replaced by a single silo, with the vice president of operations driving all

Green Bay Manufacturing
Existing Sales Process to Customers

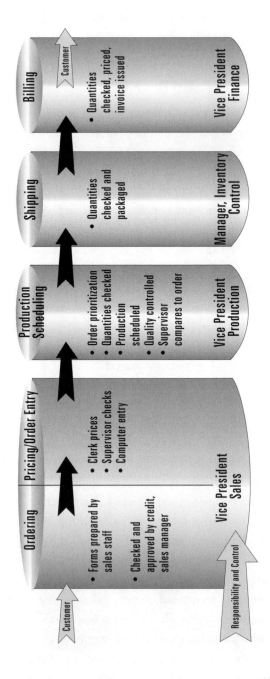

Ordering
- Forms prepared by sales staff
- Checked and approved by credit, sales manager

Pricing/Order Entry
- Clerk prices
- Supervisor checks
- Computer entry

Production Scheduling
- Order prioritization
- Quantities checked
- Production scheduled
- Quality controlled
- Supervisor compares to order

Shipping
- Quantities checked and packaged

Billing
- Quantities checked, priced, invoice issued

Vice President Sales

Vice President Production

Manager, Inventory Control

Vice President Finance

Customer

Customer

Responsibility and Control

Figure 72.9

Green Bay Manufacturing
New Sales Process

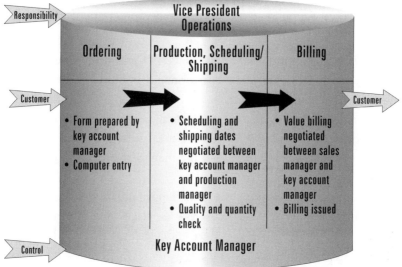

Responsibility		Vice President Operations	
	Ordering	Production, Scheduling/ Shipping	Billing
Customer	• Form prepared by key account manager • Computer entry	• Scheduling and shipping dates negotiated between key account manager and production manager • Quality and quantity check	• Value billing negotiated between sales manager and key account manager • Billing issued	Customer
Control		Key Account Manager	

Figure 73.9

functions from ordering to billing. Customer well-being lies with key account managers assigned to major customers: they have the responsibility to maintain the satisfaction intelligence necessary for triage goals and actions. Account managers are the customer's guardian angels, ensuring orders meet expectations at minimum cost. No longer will orders limp through five silos before product and invoice are delivered to the customer. One leader ensures operations comply, while key account managers guarantee superior customer satisfaction.

Account managers discourage unnecessary product handling, checking, and cost duplication. Ordering enters quantities, delivery requirements, and scheduling codes directly at process commencement. Production marches mechanically toward delivery dates. Quantity and quality checks are completed once, just prior to shipment. As a final step, billed amounts are compared with value received by the customer.

Minimum price guidelines encourage account managers to consider value billing. If an order is unique — in size, dye lot, or delivery cycle time, for example — extra value may be earned. This is decided only at the end of the sales process, when value can be truly determined. Predetermined prices frequently give profit away if average prices are assigned to all products. Not all orders are equal. Products with higher customer value should carry greater reward for the company.

This is process improvement at its best. Customers drive company values, account managers control performance, and processes that do not add value are eliminated. Green Bay is rewarded with value billing when customers experience superior satisfaction, and penalized with lower prices for poor performance. Reward and penalty become linked to customer satisfaction experience — the manageable bites way of maintaining competitive advantage.

Green Bay Manufacturing's story is a happy one. Unfortunately, not all process improvements yield this result — especially if customer values or company competitive advantages are miscalculated. Kirkland Trucking should put the point across quite nicely.

Kirkland Trucking owns a fleet of 620 tractor-trailers, vans, and courier vehicles, providing short- and long-haul service to 154 customers. Vern Kirkland owns and manages the operation with assistance from a number of fleet managers, dispatchers, and full- and part-time drivers.

Last year when Vern noticed a decline in customer demand, he visited key customers to ask why. He discovered that competitors had lobbied customers for a share of the business previously enjoyed by Kirkland. Each customer felt pressure to share the work, not wanting to be economically dependent upon one trucking company. Spreading the risk made sense. Vern himself had more than one fuel supplier for that very reason. He settled on a strategy of superior customer service to win volume back.

During the next 12 months, business continued to decline, forcing Vern to sell five trucks to eliminate excess capacity. Truck prices were low, and losses were sustained on each sale.

Alarmed by declining fortunes, Vern interviewed a number of additional customers. This year's interviews were substantially different.

Competitors had installed new fuel-efficient systems in their trucks and were charging two cents a mile less than Kirkland. They offered reduced rates for customers who placed more weight with them, deliberately setting low cash-refund thresholds so customers could experience volume refunds early.

While Vern thought customers were sharing work to spread risk during the past 12 months, competitors had discovered a process to rebate customers for savings from fuel efficiency. They had created a competitive advantage over Kirkland, entrenching themselves in Vern's customer territory.

Vern's poor customer intelligence caused him to misread customer values. Even today, with a rebate system similar to those of his competitors, Vern can only hope to recover lost ground. He will certainly not achieve a competitive edge. Competitors correctly identified pricing as the primary customer value and improved their costing processes to meet it. Their process improvement took away Vern's competitive advantage. Now, greater incentives are necessary to regain that competitive advantage. In reality, Vern needs the next 12 months to successfully implement what competitors offer today. Twelve months of complacency can mean a lifetime of catch-up. There's no time to blink when managing competitive advantages.

BITE 45: APPOINT A LEADER OF BUSINESS IMPROVEMENT

As with management of core competence and change, business improvement is unlikely to continue unless someone is assigned responsibility for its well-being. Green Bay Manufacturing assigned this responsibility to advisers who were engaged to review sales processes. Although advisers are fine for projects, the temporary nature of an engagement doesn't create a culture of continuous improvement. Processes require ongoing attention to be maintained and improved. By assigning responsibility for continuous improvement, leaders acknowledge its importance and help to spread the culture of continuous improvement through all organization levels.

Process improvement leaders should exist for all businesses, both large and small. The smaller the business, the more likely responsibility will be borne by the owner. But importance is not diminished if the leader performs other duties. Let's look at Johnson Service Centers as a case example.

Joe Silantro owns and manages 26 automobile service stations under Johnson Service Centers Inc. with the organizational structure illustrated in Figure 74.9. Each center's store manager reports to Bill Wallace, vice president of station operations. Cathy Wayne ensures the lowest prices are attained from all vendors and core competence is maintained. Sandy Lucas ensures accounting and finance matters are properly controlled and managed. Joe relies entirely upon Bill to manage station operations, freeing himself to pursue profitable growth and business improvement.

Last month, Joe spent two days reviewing average times for standard grease-and-oil service sales, resulting in the data presented in Figure 75.9. Much to his surprise, the time required for each service, between the most efficient and inefficient stations, ranged from 20 minutes to one hour. Customers were charged $49.95 for service regardless of location. Service personnel were paid $10 per hour and the average cost of materials used for lubrication was $23.

Johnson Service Centers Organization Chart

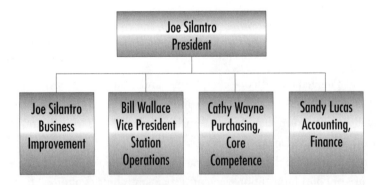

Figure 74.9

The most inefficient station charged $49.95 for an hour's service with a cost for labor and materials of $33. Although earning a margin of $16.95 from inefficient performers, the company was actually losing profit when the results were compared with those requiring only 20 minutes to service. Efficient stations produced net profit of $70.85 per hour compared to $16.95 for the most inefficient.

Joe was determined to move every station to a standard of three automobiles per hour. Staff meetings focused on ways to achieve the new standard. Those having difficulty complying were temporarily assigned to the most efficient stations to improve their productivity.

Johnson Service Centers
Station Efficiency Analysis

	3 Automobiles per Hour	1 Automobile per Hour
Revenue	$149.85	$49.95
Labor	10.00	10.00
Materials	69.00	23.00
Total Expenses	79.00	33.00
Net Profit per Hour	$ 70.85	$16.95

Figure 75.9

Joe delegated operational matters to his vice president so he could concentrate on new ways to improve profit margins. As leader of business improvement, his sole job was to seek out waste and inefficiencies for elimination. Even if you can't afford the luxury of a leader devoted solely to business improvement, someone has to take responsibility for the role. Remember Linda Baker, from Baker Chemical Company? As both leader of change and leader of business improvement, she identified accounting as the process to be improved, then managed the implementation of the change. In larger companies, two different leaders often handle the two tasks. Whatever the arrangement, the two roles work in concert. Leaders of business improvement conduct regular process reviews. They encourage everyone to ferret out every ounce of waste and eliminate non-value-added activities. Leaders of change then eliminate these self-serving functions. Together, these leaders stimulate the culture of continuous improvement so critical to sustained business success.

X

Check Your Leadership Powertrain

"To lead the people, walk behind them."
— *LAO-TZU*

Successful leadership, as we have discovered, means guiding people who are willing to follow. Followers must understand and respect leaders, and leaders must understand and respect followers. It's what William Hazlitt meant when he said, "To get others to come into our ways of thinking, we must go over to theirs; and it is necessary to follow in order to lead." This method of leading is a radical departure from traditional business leadership. Let's examine.

Chapter I warned that *50 Steps to Business Success* would interchange the terms leadership and management without concern for historical differences between the two. This was deliberate because the manageable bites process demands the two operate as one, parallel and in tandem.

The American Heritage Dictionary of the English Language defines management as "the act, manner, or practice of managing, handling, or controlling something." Historically, when it came to day-to-day operations, management emphasis was placed on the word *control*. Control ensured continuous uninterrupted customer delivery and a consistent accounting of business transactions. Managers were police, ensuring employee performance, product quality, and customer service were in line with both the corporate mission and company goals and action plans.

In postwar business, organization leaders offered a vision, while traditional managers controlled processes to realize those visions. Leaders, with their visions, became the church; managers, with their ability to govern, became the state. While churches offered spiritual guidance, the state managed the day-to-day affairs of followers. But even with leaders focused on vision and managers dedicated to goals and actions, the traditional companies that were successful ensured church and state were synchronized with one dream. Figure 76.10 outlines the vision and leadership of both traditional and future organizations.

To meet the leadership challenges of tomorrow, the church and state will merge. Less time and energy will be spent controlling and directing. More time will be spent training, monitoring, and leading. Employees will be empowered to a greater extent, given guidelines of conduct rather than strict rules. Removing the emphasis from control will lead to even further streamlining of traditional management while encouraging leadership cultures throughout organizations. This shift will solidify the need for leaders of core competence, change, and process improvement to act as coaches within leadership cultures. Employees will be measured by their leadership accomplishments, not by adherence to controls established by managers. The result of this shift will be the elimination of positions, and their associated costs, which existed solely to control processes and people. Leadership cultures will reduce the need for control as education, training, and coaching create a generation of self-motivated employees.

The time and expense required to make improvements and changes in traditional organizations was staggering. Because they were hierarchical and directive, successive layers of management expected and waited for direction. This continuous push-down mentality was expensive and time-consuming. It worked competitively only because competitors had similar cultures. Not so anymore. Successful leaders are now aware of the high cost associated with push-down and control cultures and they've learned that these cultures add little, if any, value for customers. Today, leaders strive to create cultures of initiative and participation at all levels, where employees are constantly in search of new ways to deliver products and services better, faster, and more cheaply.

This reinventing of leadership requires leaders to constantly take stock of their own performance, to develop plans for their leadership that are in line with those of the company, and to evaluate their performance through the eyes of those they are leading. Only through this type of honest assessment and renewal can leaders expect to keep the confidence of their employees and lead them to success.

Traditional Versus Future Organizations

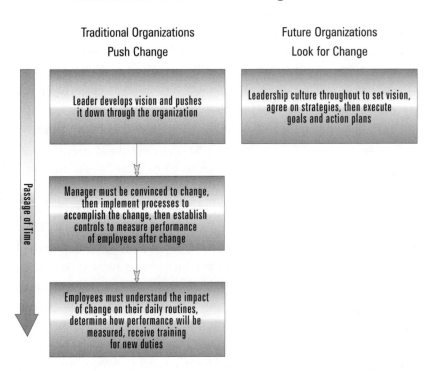

Figure 76.10

BITE 46: PREPARE CONGRUENT LEADERSHIP PLANS

Whether owner-manager, president, or chair of the board, you must develop a leadership plan. In the same way a business plan steers your company, your leadership plan will set out the goals and action plans that will be your personal road map to leadership success. For business success, your plan has to be congruent with the overall business plan of the company. The process of developing a leadership plan requires some soul-searching. What vision is required for success? Are all employees inspired to move annual planning toward the vision? Which employees need coaching? Am I properly rewarding people for results I expect of them? These are just a few of the questions visionaries must ask themselves each year. Your answers will provide insight into your leadership strengths and weaknesses. Let's see how Blue Ridge Manufacturing Company handles the issue.

Blue Ridge Manufacturing Company manufactures bathroom fixtures from six locations. President Jason Small built the company from a small single location that opened 18 years ago. Annual sales approximate $121 million, supporting 83 employees. Jason diligently completes triage and business planning each year.

Until Blue Ridge grew beyond three locations, Jason was a hands-on manager with only a plant manager in each location. When he expanded, annual triage revealed the necessity for additional managers. Jason could then take on a true presidential role.

Before any change, he engaged human-resource consultants to conduct aptitude tests for himself and his managers. Tests would rate leadership skills, managerial abilities, business aptitude, management style, tolerance for risk, and receptiveness to new ideas. Jason scored higher on leadership than managerial skills. Yet, he had managed, rather than led, Blue Ridge from a start-up to a $121-million operation. How could he have scored so low on managerial skills?

Soul mate Bill Fuller always saw Jason as a creative leader and believes his greatest leadership challenge is avoiding day-to-day management detail. Bill felt Jason could be more successful if he learned to stand back from operations and focus on setting the company's direction — its mission. His six managers should take responsibility for day-to-day activities.

Meeting with Bill Fuller and the consultants, Jason was encouraged to conduct a leadership review as an integral part of triage. This review would yield a leadership plan. Jason agreed and, with their help, prepared the goals and action plans shown in Figure 77.10.

His leadership goal is to guide managers toward the long-term vision of the company. His plan has five separate categories, each aimed at cultivating that vision in the company.

Each leadership category is blessed with at least one goal and one action plan to ensure there is a defined road to achievement. Jason realized linking leadership direction with specific actions and milestone completion dates was the only way to measure progress.

Blue Ridge Manufacturing
Leadership Goals and Action Plans

Leadership Category	Goal	Action Plan	Completion Date
Vision	• Communicate and share the vision for the business future with each of six managers.	• Visit one plant each month, by the 15th, meet each general manager to discuss vision and current business plan.	June 15
Inspiration	• Share importance of strategic direction with every employee of the company.	• Hold employee meetings in each warehouse to explain company direction and their importance to the future of the business.	June 15
Stimulating	• Hold monthly management meetings with six general managers to encourage ideas, new ways of looking at business processes.	• Set meeting dates for the 29th day of each month.	As scheduled
Coaching	• Encourage managers to call weekly, to seek help, consult with ideas.	• Call managers individually, be a cheerleader.	Weekly
Rewarding	• Negotiate rewards with each general manager based on achievement of annual goals and completion of action plans.	• Conduct formal review with each manager to negotiate rewards.	January 31

Figure 77.10

> Before lockup, Jason prepared a draft leadership plan. He considered each leadership category to ensure it was congruent first with the company mission, then with each operational goal and action. He finalized the leadership plan after lockup, at the same time that his managers settled on final operational goals. When his plans were finalized, he slipped into a cheerleader role to coach his managers with their goals. By coaching and cheering, he leads. Because he is supportive, managers follow.

Jason Small opted for full integration of leadership and management. As each grew dependent on the other for annual planning, harmony was created, and church and state began to merge. But more and more, competitive pressures are encouraging true synchronization of leadership and management to shorten lead times between visionary ideas and operating results. Blue Ridge's flow of information chart illustrated in Figure 78.10 demonstrates how this synchronization can look.

Arrows pointing in both directions on the chart signify interdependence, first between leadership and creative management, and then between management and competitive analysis, operations, and controllership matters. When Jason communicates his vision and coaches and cheers employee performance, he implements creative management — a strong step toward a leadership culture. Day-to-day customer service, allocation of resources, and management of change is focused on taking the steps necessary to achieve the vision. Managers break vision into manageable bites and adopt smaller action plans to provide a trail to success.

To build leadership vision into action plans, market and competitive analysis are necessary. Dillman Engineering, for example, used its analysis of resource allocation to ensure it selected contracts congruent with its leadership vision. This process strives to avoid competitive strategies that fail the vision.

Once strategies are identified, annual operation plans begin to form. Core competence is assigned to marketing and competitive strategies, while leaders of process improvement and change seek efficient implementation of plans based on the strengths and weaknesses analysis of each operating area. Controllers then translate operating plans into budgeted performance and seek to eliminate weaknesses in financial and operating controls.

Blue Ridge's flow of information schema links generalities of leadership thinking to managing performance. Leadership translates into creative

Blue Ridge Manufacturing
Annual Triage and Business Planning
Flow of Information

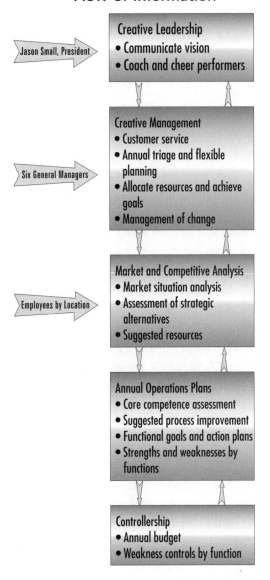

Figure 78.10

management, which translates into competitive analysis, on to operating plans, all the way down to controllership functions, all of which send feedback up the chain for reassessment of leadership.

Sharp changes in competitive analysis affect management's approach to resource allocation, which leads, in turn, to changes in operating plans and budgeting. Results are then communicated back to management and leadership for fine-tuning of corporate plans. We now return to Blue Ridge for a practical application.

> Before lockup, one manager reported that two major competitors had reduced prices. Market intelligence indicated they secured more favorable porcelain prices for bathroom fixtures and research supported this fact.
>
> Jason summoned the purchasing manager to research and negotiate similar pricing with suppliers. Suppliers, afraid of losing Blue Ridge business to their competitors, lowered their prices.

Now, what effect did this have on Blue Ridge's annual planning process? Change began when an employee identified the competitive advantage of a competitor. When the employee alerted Jason Small, the process of change management began. Should the company ignore market information or research it? Would they find process improvement savings elsewhere? Should they reallocate resources or implement action plans to match the competition's advantage? Jason chose renegotiation with suppliers to reduce vendor prices to match those of his competitors. When a new price was secured, operating plans and budgets were readjusted to reflect the change. Blue Ridge's quick reaction to its competitor's price advantage is a testament to the integration of its leadership, management, and business planning. The change affected every level of Blue Ridge business planning. Organizations that are not so finely tuned often find that competitive information stalls for weeks, even months, until competitive disadvantages cause sales decline.

Leadership plans must be prepared and implemented in small businesses as well. More flexibility may be demonstrated with small business leadership plans. Paul's Hobby Shops is the selected case study here.

> Paul's Hobby Shops, owned and managed by Paul Rangler, operates four stores, generating sales of $3.2 million throughout the city. In business since 1964, Paul has managed to develop a loyal clientele of hobbyists at each company-owned, free-standing store.

In the 1960s, retailers normally bought locations as an investment and so Paul bought each property, expecting customers to shop at single locations for hobby needs.

Customer buying habits began to change during the 1970s, moving away from multiple-stop shopping toward the convenience of large shopping centers. Traffic at free-standing stores began to decline in 1973, leading to store failures in traditional downtown shopping areas.

Three large shopping centers were developed with large department stores as anchor tenants, surrounded by boutiques and smaller shops. Paul's retail friends signed leases, hoping to find increased traffic to help them survive. Paul, experiencing only slight declines in store traffic, was reluctant to move. People still identified hobby needs with Paul's Hobby Shops and most drove out of their way to his locations.

During the early 1980s, department stores, hungry for new lines of business, identified hobby products as a potential area for profit. Two shopping center department stores began to carry model kits, railroad sets, and remote-control airplanes and boats. Paul's market share, then estimated at approximately 42 percent, declined steadily over 34 months to 29 percent. Convenience of one-stop shopping was now a major threat to Paul. He requested a meeting with his business adviser and soul mate, Robert Langois.

Robert convinced Paul that the days of customer loyalty were gone. Retailers now have to fight for every market share percentage point, while customers feel free to purchase products anywhere. Paul needed a plan to regain market leadership and drive the chains from the hobby market.

It was difficult for Robert to persuade him to sell his locations and move into shopping centers, preferably next to the chains carrying hobby products. When Paul had his properties valued, he was surprised at how much equity had accumulated. Purchased for a total of $2 million during the 1960s, the four properties were conservatively estimated to realize $4.3 million after selling costs. Being mortgage free, the $4.3 million would be available for discretionary purposes.

Shopping center competition for tenants was strong and Paul received attractive tenant inducement offers. One center offered him $150,000 toward store improvements if he signed a five-year lease. Others offered $100,000 to $125,000.

Paul and Robert concluded the tenant inducements would pay for all store refits, so it would cost Paul little to move. The $4.3 million, proceeds from real estate sales, would eliminate bank debt, run a healthy advertising campaign, and pay a dividend — the first in 10 years!

The leadership plan itself became 10 pages of details but Paul summarized it easily, as outlined in Figure 79.10.

Moving into shopping centers became an excellent financial decision, but Paul didn't forget his primary goal — to regain his market share from the department stores. All traffic seeking hobby products from large stores now walked by Paul's Hobby Shops. Product selection was superior to that of the department stores and shoppers were drawn in.

To increase volume, Paul changed the image of his stores. Dated 1960s decorating styles were replaced with more exciting colors and layout. He also allocated $100,000 of property sale proceeds to major advertising campaigns to create a more exciting image. Taking no chances, he wrote personal letters to loyal customers, asking for continued support. Following this final, important step, the leadership plan was complete.

The hobby shop case study demonstrates that leadership plans can and must be applied to small business. When Paul chose to ignore changing retail environments, he failed to lead. Only eroding sales informed him that his leadership was an issue. If he didn't follow the retail industry, he would be left behind. Even as an excellent store manager, he would fail. Management alone will not survive long-term without leadership.

Paul's Hobby Shops
Leadership Goals and Actions

Goal	Action
• Regain 42 percent market share of hobby retail products	• Sell free-standing stores and lease next to competitors in malls • $100,000 advertising campaign • Direct customer correspondence • Carry a selection of products superior to that of department stores

Figure 79.10

Paul's Hobby Shops
Leadership Goals and Actions

Goal	Action
• Become debt-free as store prominence is regained	• Repay bank loan of $1.3 million when properties sell • Negotiate lease inducements from property managers to refit mall locations
• Create modern store image to attract younger buyers	• Engage architect/designer to create common, fresh theme for all stores

Figure 79.10 (cont.)

Matching leadership and business plans is so important, it warrants a third case.

Hamilton Corporation manufactures and sells electric typewriters in a small secondary niche market. Company president Justin Hamilton has managed his 21-person company for 26 years.

Justin's primary leadership goal is to increase market share at the expense of niche competitors. His strategies have included developing personal customer relationships over the years and strong advertising campaigns. He witnessed his market share grow from 39 percent to 51 percent between 1975 and 1985. Soul mate Allan Froth expressed concern that personal computers would become a threat to the typewriter industry. Justin ignored Allan's concerns because he believed personal computers would achieve a certain level of business sales success, but not home use popularity.

When financial results were completed for 1985, as shown in Figure 80.10, Justin's banker expressed serious concerns. Sales had declined from $4.5 million in 1975 to $2.6 million 10 years later. Similarly, profit had dropped from $463,000 to $39,000. Justin argued profits would return as market share increased. Hamilton's banker remained unconvinced, believing Justin was underestimating the magnitude of the personal-computer threat to the typewriter industry. Profitability analysis later revealed that Justin was actually enjoying a larger share of a shrinking market. Once the banker learned this, he was not prepared to continue lending to Hamilton. The bank demanded repayment of the company's $1.1-million loan. Justin was unable to raise the funds necessary to repay his bank debt and was forced to liquidate in 1986. Justin Hamilton not only lacked leadership vision, but he ignored warnings from those who had some. Having no leadership plan meant he also had no business plan to cope with marketplace threats. Justin's myopic view of market share importance led to corporate failure.

Hamilton Corporation
Profitability Analysis

	# of Units Manufactured and Sold	Sales	Profit	Market Share (%)
1975	13,825	$4,492,125	$463,400	39
1985	4,900	$2,572,500	$ 39,000	51

Figure 80.10

Leadership Influences

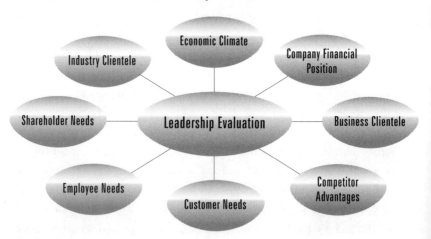

Figure 81.10

BITE 47: EVALUATE LEADERSHIP THROUGH THE EYES OF FOLLOWERS

As shown in Figure 81.10, there are many influences on the style of leadership and implementation of leadership plans. Your company's industry affects leadership evaluation. It's influenced by such factors as whether the industry is growing or declining, the economic environment of your company and marketplaces determining both customer and business confidence to buy. The company's own financial position demonstrates the strength with which it functions in the economic climate within the industry. It's compared to competitor analysis and customer and shareholder needs. Overall business climate is different from those of economic and industry by factors related to specific market locations. Company specific factors include leadership needs of employees. All influences are considered when leadership is evaluated. A strong financial position in a healthy economic climate in a growing industry suggests a leadership strategy different from that required of a company with declining customers, poor local business clientele, and competitors with greater advantages.

Alexandre Ledru-Rollin said, "I've got to follow them — I am their leader." Following the followers means knowing and understanding their needs, then planning your performance to meet those needs. When isolated from followers, leadership lacks its most important aspect: constructive follower input. Jason Small ensured he received input by involving managers in his leadership planning.

When followers are asked for input into leadership plans, they frequently assume the die is already cast. Leaders can be accused of going through the motions of follower involvement, without the intention of taking suggestions seriously. Zempa Corporation provides one positive approach.

In 1982, Zempa Corporation owned and managed three data processing centers, selling computer time to more than 150 clients. Sales sat at $4.8 million, having fallen over the previous five years from a high of $9 million. Company president Fred Zempa attributed revenue decline to trends away from mainframe computers toward lower-priced mini computers. Rapid industry change was slowly forcing Zempa out of business.

Fred enlisted support from soul mate Garth Turnbull and from a strategic planning firm to help develop a new corporate survival direction. Garth insisted employees should be included when developing change ideas. Concluding the advice was sound, Fred agreed and, with the help of strategists, designed a questionnaire for employees to complete, shown in Figure 82.10.

Fred hoped to receive positive, constructive views and suggestions from employees by asking for input in advance of corporate planning. Not only did he receive excellent recommendations, he noticed tremendous improvement in morale when employees felt their opinions counted.

Zempa Corporation
Employee Leadership Questionnaire

1. Name: _____

2. Years of Service: _____

_____

3. Educational Background: _____

_____

_____

4. List five major initiatives you think the company should be pursuing.

_____

_____

5. Which initiative do you think will yield the most profitable result, and why?

_____

_____

6. What resources will the company require to achieve your priority suggestion?

_____

_____

7. What leadership skills are required to be successful?

_____

_____

_____

Figure 82.10

Zempa Corporation
Employee Leadership Questionnaire

---

8. What managerial skills are required?

---

9. How would you propose to phase in the new initiative?

---

10. List the three points you like about working at Zempa.

---

11. List the three dislikes you have about working at Zempa.

---

12. What suggestions do you have for improving your dislikes?

---

13. List three suggestions for improving existing business processes.

---

14. Comments?

Figure 82.10 (cont.)

Fred, through questionnaires, actually checked the quality of his own leadership. From the results, he developed specific goals and action plans to enhance that leadership — more clearly defining his company's direction. Followers wanted him to lead, but also to make direction changes along with industry. Fred's leadership was regenerated. Although Zempa eventually closed its business during the late 1980s, it was for industry and technological reasons, not leadership.

Paul Rangler's hobby shop experienced a leadership crisis after moving into shopping centers.

Two years after Paul's move from free-standing retail stores to shopping centers, employee morale began to decline. Tardiness, apathy, and higher than normal cash errors became Paul's urgent business problems. He returned to Robert Langois for advice.

When neither of them could pinpoint the exact cause of declining morale, Robert suggested Paul issue anonymous employer effectiveness questionnaires to obtain direct employee feedback. Anonymity made the risk of criticism less threatening and encouraged more candid responses from employees. Although Paul was not convinced this was a good idea, he couldn't think of a better way. So, the two put their heads together one evening to prepare the simple six-question questionnaire illustrated in Figure 83.10, for employee response.

Paul's Hobby Shops
Employer Effectiveness Questionnaire

1. Are you satisfied with company working conditions? Please explain.

2. Do you consider our employee benefits to be fair? Why or why not?

3. Are you satisfied with store hours and staff scheduling?

4. How would you describe shopping center management?

Figure 83.10

Paul's Hobby Shops
Employer Effectiveness Questionnaire

---

5. What do you think store priorities should be?

---

6. How do you rate company management? Suggestions?

Figure 83.10 (cont.)

When responses were in, Paul was blamed for poor leadership and poor employee working conditions. Detailed comments told of frustration with the shopping center hours Paul committed to when signing leases. Stores had to be opened when shopping centers were opened, causing substantial shift scheduling changes and additional weekend hours. Cost of vehicle parking was also an issue. It had been free at company-owned stores.

Paul, trying not to take comments personally, called a staff meeting to reassure employees he would study ways to resolve their concerns.

He struck an agreement with the property manager for free parking commencing on the renewal date of each lease. Unfortunately, leases weren't renewable for another 24 months, so Paul decided to subsidize employee parking for that period.

Scheduling of staff hours was a different matter. Shopping center management insisted stores be open as long as the center was open. This was not negotiable. So more creative solutions had to be found. Paul tinkered with fewer hours during weekdays for permanent staff, with an additional weekend part-time staff person to alleviate stress. This could be accomplished without additional staff benefit costs. Paul also discovered that his employees were willing to accept two hours less pay in return for more leisure time with families.

Initially, Paul was offended by the employee comments. But he realized negative comments were just a reflection of frustration with working conditions. He was willing to see his leadership through their eyes. By adjusting staff scheduling, adding part-time help, and providing a parking allowance, he met their expectations and regained their respect.

Results of leadership assessments may not always end as happily as those experienced by Fred Zempa or Paul Rangler. Horlick & Associates demonstrates a different response.

Horlick & Associates, a firm of 30 lawyers, provides legal advice in real estate, criminal, contract, and international law. Managing partner Earl Horlick has chaired the firm's management committee for the past eight years and has sponsored a third of the lawyers to partnership.

For the past year, management committee members urged Earl to return to international law, his self-professed first love, and step aside to allow someone else to lead the firm. But Earl resisted, not feeling the time was right for change. He either wanted to stay in control or had lost confidence in his ability to practice law.

Tension mounted between Earl and the management committee to the point that he sought the opinions of other lawyers in the firm. Confident he would receive unanimous support to remain as managing partner, he circulated a questionnaire, illustrated in Figure 84.10, together with a ballot for each partner to vote for or against his continued leadership.

Horlick & Associates
Firm Leadership Questionnaire

1. Are you satisfied with the direction and financial success of the firm?
   Why or why not?

2. Are there additional areas of law we should be practicing? Please explain.

Figure 84.10

Horlick & Associates
Firm Leadership Questionnaire

3. What strategic priorities do you think the management should pursue?

4. Are you satisfied with the overall strategic direction of the firm?

5. Comments?

Earl Horlick should continue as managing partner for another two-year term. (Please circle one of the choices below)

Agree   Disagree

Name   Signature

Figure 84.10 (cont.)

> Much to Earl's dismay, all questionnaires were returned with criticism of his leadership, principally because of an inability or reluctance to communicate firm direction to partners. Fifty-one percent voted against his leadership renewal. Earl had no choice but to step aside for the election of a new managing partner.

Earl completely misread the acceptance of his leadership. He hadn't realized he'd missed the leadership mark. The management committee was trying to tell him this by urging his return to international law. He assessed his leadership and found it was not fulfilling company needs. When he failed to follow his followers, they refused him permission to lead.

Earl offers us a side lesson: Know when to quit! Many businesses have suffered at the hands of a leader who has overstayed her welcome. Leadership needs to be refreshed once in a while. There is no shame in this.

It is inevitable. Accept it. Leave your leadership post on a high, with dignity, not when there is a knife pointed at you.

Leadership Powertrain

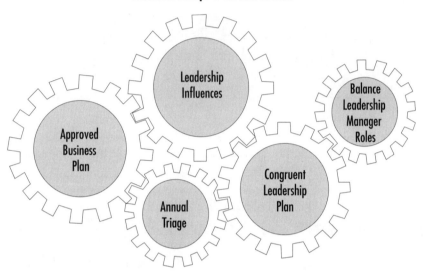

Figure 85.10

As shown in Figure 85.10, leadership can function like a powertrain. It is a series of interconnected process cogs that must be in synch for success to be attained. To balance leadership and management roles, leaders must develop congruent leadership plans for consideration during annual triage. Triage may influence or alter those plans. Business plans reveal changes in resources, market focus, or financial restrictions influencing leadership, managerial balance, and the final leadership plan. Leadership may be altered significantly by business and financial restraints. Like competitive environments, leadership undergoes constant change. It must be checked annually and after major business changes to make sure it is in line with and supports company goals and action plans. Successful leaders are malleable. They look in front to determine necessary leadership for the competitive environment; they look behind to determine employee needs to meet those goals and action plans. Focus must be constantly reviewed for the leadership to be well tuned.

XI

- The Oxen Are Slow,
- but the Earth Is Patient
-

"The recipe for well-being requires neither positive nor negative thinking alone, but a mix of ample optimism to provide hope, a dash of pessimism to prevent complacency, and enough realism to discriminate those things we can control from those we cannot."
— *ANONYMOUS*

50 Steps to Business Success addresses many of the variables that will affect your success as a leader. But of course, the likelihood of optimal performance happening in all areas at all times is remote. One factor or another always taints perfection: consumer spending declines, a key salesperson is lost to the competition, or a production line breaks down. There are always business processes to improve or changes to manage. Successful leaders maintain faith throughout all these ups and downs. To do so, leaders must embrace the soul of manageable bites, as shown in Figure 86.11. By instilling a leadership culture in a company, adopting and holding to a code of ethics, and allowing their leadership spirit to inspire their employees, customers, and suppliers, successful leaders demonstrate their commitment to realizing their vision in manageable bites.

BITE 48: DEVELOP A LEADERSHIP CULTURE

The case of Green Bay Manufacturing demonstrated all too well how businesses organized along traditional, functional lines resist working toward superior customer satisfaction. Locked in vertical silos and focused on departmental allegiance, these companies fail to put customer satisfaction

The Soul of Manageable Bites

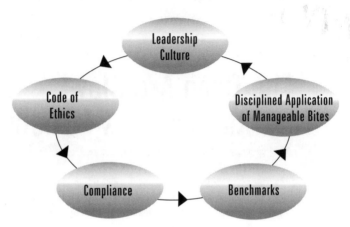

Figure 86.11

ahead of internal politics. As a result, they languish in mediocrity and risk disappearing altogether. But the right leadership, in manageable bites, can turn these situations around. An excellent example comes from Drecher Building Supplies Ltd.

Aldo Drecher opened the doors of Drecher Building Supplies Ltd. 38 years ago. Successfully building manufacturing and retail operations to annual sales of $155 million, the company now employs 250 people.

Last year, Aldo engaged long-time consultant Jim Curran to plan the most appropriate organization structure to meet company vision. Figure 87.11 shows that company organization was very traditional, with vice presidents of marketing and sales, production, finance, research and development, and human resources reporting directly to Aldo.

Jim and Aldo discussed departmental disputes and inefficiencies created by each trying to outperform the other. High-performing departments were identified if products and paper flowed without problems. Unfortunately, high performance in one usually meant poor performance in another.

Orders passed through sales, design, production, quality control, warehousing, and shipping like hot potatoes. Departmental competition was strong, leading to friction and blame when orders or scheduling failed. Aldo's vice presidents seemed more concerned with laying blame than problem solving. Instinctively, Aldo knew time was wasted settling departmental disputes. Inward focus was a problem.

Jim spent three months charting business operations: how decisions were made, annual triage, business planning and, finally, competitive advantage assessment. He proposed quite a different business organization.

Drecher Building Supplies
Original Organization Chart

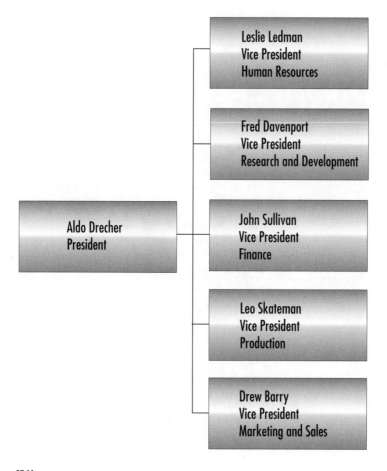

Figure 87.11

Drecher Building Supplies
Organization for Continuous Improvement Culture

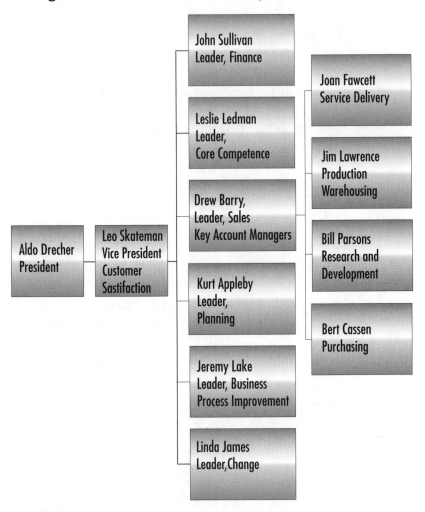

Figure 88.11

Figure 88.11 shows only the vice president of customer satisfaction reporting directly to Aldo, carrying the overall responsibility for meeting customer values. Eliminating the other vice president positions discourages departmental conflicts. Linda James and Jeremy Lake focus on managing change and improved processes. Kurt Appleby is assigned to work as leader of planning, reflecting the importance of annual triage and business planning to Drecher.

Purchasing, production, service delivery, and development departments report to Drew Barry, leader of sales. By funneling these departments through sales, Aldo helps ensure that all operating functions will focus on meeting customer needs. Research and development now also reports to the leader of sales. This ensures future products match customer needs and prevents research from becoming a playground for intellectual stimulation. Considerable savings are expected when future product designs are linked more closely with customers to avoid product rejection.

Leslie Ledman leaves human resources to become leader of core competence. She matches existing competence with what is required to identify needs. She also focuses on maintaining competence through goal achievement rewards and rehabilitation plans.

Drecher's proposed reorganization is indeed a dramatic departure from traditional functional lines. By placing power in a single vice president whose focus is customer satisfaction, Aldo has helped to create a leadership culture. Assessments of customer values begin with key account managers — those responsible for understanding present and future customer needs. These key account managers handle customer orders and make sure they are satisfactorily fulfilled. With production and product delivery also reporting to sales, customer needs are communicated well throughout the organization. Elimination of functional silos gives way to a seamless processing of sales, production, research and development, purchasing, and service delivery. Internal competition is minimized when all functions follow consistent customer values. A leadership culture is forming.

Drecher, with sales of $155 million, approaches the upper end of small business. How does a truly small business bring about a leadership culture? The most impressive example comes from Paul's Hobby Shops.

When Paul Rangler completely changed the image of his four hobby shops, he also reorganized duties and responsibilities between himself and store managers. He struggled with balancing the challenges given his scarce human resources. How could he implement process improvement and product rationalization in all stores while also managing daily operations? At first glance, he didn't have sufficient resources.

To address the dilemma, Paul hosted a Saturday barbecue for managers. At the event, Jill Babcock, manager of the Pinewood Mall outlet, suggested each manager have dual functions — one divisional, one corporate. The divisional role would represent the normal management of individual store operations; the corporate role would be leadership of one company-wide function. No one rejected the idea. The mood was one of cautious optimism. Jason Blaine, manager at the Silverwood Mall store, expressed concern that corporate roles would give one manager implied authority over the others. With each manager considered equal, corporate authority might create friction in an otherwise cohesive team. Paul sketched possible solutions. When the barbecue was over, they had agreed upon the structure depicted in Figure 89.11.

Paul's Hobby Shops
Organization for Improvement Culture

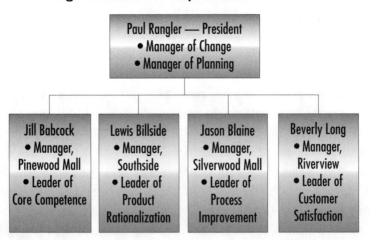

Figure 89.11

Each manager would be responsible for one corporate role, the others giving up authority for that function. This also meant that each manager was accountable to the other three in their performance of that function. If egos could stand aside, Paul could manage all roles with existing resources. When all his managers agreed to the system, Paul was convinced he had found the right organization for improvement culture.

While Paul continues to lead change and planning, Jill ensures core competence is maintained across all stores. Lewis Billside studies product profitability to determine which products to sell or discontinue. Jason concerns himself with ways to improve corporate business processes. Concentrating on customer values, he studies ways to deliver the right product for the least cost, on time. Beverly Long, manager of the Riverview outlet, meets frequently with Jason and Jill to improve customer satisfaction.

Paul's improvement culture encourages managers to continue working together. Even though one has authority over others for one function, each requires the support of the others to fulfill corporate roles.

Whitmore Consulting also experienced the creation of continuous improvement culture.

Harold Whitmore, senior partner, is responsible for the overall direction and financial reporting of the management consulting firm Whitmore Consulting. As depicted in Figure 90.11, in excess of 260 consultants are organized into four service areas — strategic planning, core competence, operations, and financial planning.

Each service area is accountable for its own revenue, professional mentoring, business development, and, of course, profitability. Consultants target clients independently, encouraging an ownership mentality. Harold wanted to create a client ownership culture to ensure clients needs are met.

Clients in each service area are substantially different, making it difficult to target a unified list of clientele. Judy Simpson, senior partner for strategic planning, was concerned with consultants' unwillingness to target common clients. Her calculations indicate current revenues of $32 million could grow organically to $50 million if the four service areas harmonized efforts and targeted common clients. Functioning as four distinct consulting groups had become a barrier to profitable growth.

Whitmore Consulting
Organization

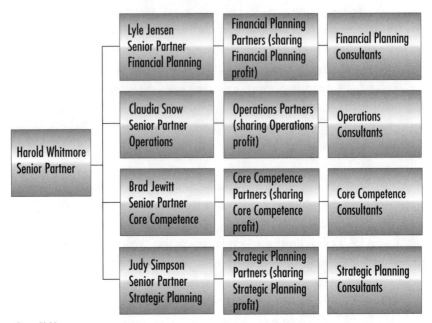

Figure 90.11

Service area rivalry grew to the point where senior partners would not refer potential business to each other. With partners in each area measured by billings volume and sharing resulting profits of their own area only, there was little incentive to act as a unified consulting firm.

Judy offered to apply her strategic planning skills to her own firm. Studying the original organization chart, it was easy to conclude the four organizations within Whitmore Consulting had to change. She analyzed the four separate profit-sharing arrangements that discouraged overall partnership goal alignment. There had to be a better structure.

Studying many partnership models, Judy settled on one she felt would best appeal to the senior partners at Whitmore. She asked to be placed on next week's partnership agenda.

In preparation for the meeting, Judy prepared a number of slides designed to encourage partnership change. Her proposal recommended the creation of one profit pool for all partners, to encourage them to think as one team.

Whitmore Consulting
Judy Simpson's Proposal

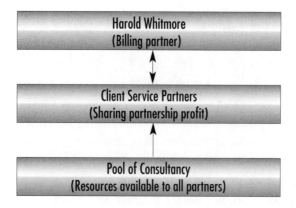

Harold Whitmore
(Billing partner)

↕

Client Service Partners
(Sharing partnership profit)

↑

Pool of Consultancy
(Resources available to all partners)

Figure 91.11

All billings would be issued in the name of Harold Whitmore to eliminate territorial friction. Staff would be organized in one pool from which all partners would draw assignment resources.

The organization for improvement culture placed all senior partners together in one organization box reporting to Harold Whitmore as a team, as illustrated in Figure 91.11. Stripped of individual client billings, profit sharing, and staff fiefdoms, each senior partner would now be measured by his or her contribution to partnership teams and partner income.

Judy's proposal was debated for hours. Partners currently earning the largest share of profits resisted it vigorously. In the end, they decided in favor of what was best for long-term partnership health, what would motivate profitable growth behavior — in other words, Judy Simpson's proposal. Harold, being chairman and the only billing partner, was not regarded by leaders as internal competition. Client service partners included in one team still performed individual practice services to certain clients, but now their own prosperity depended upon how well all partners performed. Pools of consultancy resources exposed junior staff to multiple service areas, mentoring them to become stronger performers with broader experience. Harold eventually took Judy's proposal one step further by creating client service teams, further discouraging internal rivalry.

Let's visit Melrose Plumbing Inc. as a final example of continuous improvement culture.

Bill Melrose, president and chief executive officer of Melrose Plumbing Inc., manages 48 employees to achieve sales of $8.9 million from construction, renovation, retail, and wholesale divisions.

Melrose is organized into three divisions, as depicted in Figure 92.11. Jake Harper manages new house construction, Sam Carrin leads a renovation team, and Sharon Barrett manages both retail and wholesale sales to other plumbing and construction companies. Considerable rivalry exists between Jake and Sam. Jake believes all plumbing contracts are construction, whether they be for new installations or repairs to old systems. Sam, on the other hand, believes plumbing installation to buildings over one year old is renovation of existing structures, not construction.

Each manager receives an annual bonus if sales targets are exceeded, and Bill likes to create a healthy rivalry among the three when he sets those targets.

In recent years, Bill's healthy rivalry grew to unhealthy proportions between Jake and Sam. Each was constantly looking to steal business from the other. Focus, more and more, became individual sales bonuses rather than company profit performance.

Bill's soul mate, John Billman, observed the deterioration of Melrose's internal professional relationships. He believed the Melrose reward system encouraged negative rival behavior. Sales were surely being lost while Jake and Sam treated each other as independent competitors.

John questioned the need for an organizational split between renovation and construction. These terms were used in building construction, not plumbing. All plumbing, regardless of the age of the building, had to be installed or sold. He recommended Melrose Plumbing have only the two divisions, installation and merchandise sales, as shown in Figure 93.11.

John suggested Sam and Jake work as installation division coleaders with sales of approximately $4.9 million. Sharon would continue as manager of merchandise sales. All three would receive divisional net income bonuses not based on sales. Bill took his soul mate's advice. Sam and Jake are now dependent upon each other to earn bonuses. The two are motivated to maximize installations for both old and new buildings.

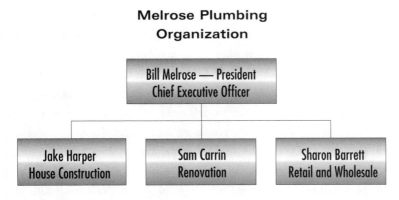

Figure 92.11

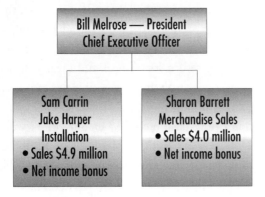

Figure 93.11

Both Whitmore Consulting and Melrose Plumbing had created organizations discouraging continuous improvement and a leadership culture. Measuring employees by individual performance when expecting team success produced dysfunctional behavior in each organization. Changes were needed to create improvement cultures.

BITE 49: ADOPT A CODE OF ETHICS

A code of ethics is a pillar of continuous improvement. Principles guiding interaction with customers, employees, and stakeholders become the social fabric and culture of a business. Open discussions, truthful advertising, quality of products, and frankness in career counseling with employees are examples of business ethics in action. Ethics develop conscience. Conscience encourages appropriate behavior. Appropriate behavior brings stakeholder respect. Stakeholder respect supports profitable growth.

Companies without ethics cannot sustain continuous improvement. They have no way to determine what's right, wrong, and fair when dealing with customers, employees, creditors, and shareholders. In successful companies, these ethical rules become benchmarks of success. They help leaders motivate and measure success.

Ethics are often overlooked in favor of profit pressures. Although business may sustain greater profits in the short term without a code, long-term financial performance demands an ethical image for the well-being of customers, employees, lenders, shareholders, and the public. Quick profit businesses come and go. Successful businesses concern themselves with the welfare of their constituents and the respect it earns from them. Codes of ethics are engines of respect. Tired of liberal advertising, poor product quality, inadequate warranty, and product misrepresentation, customers today demand ethics in return for respect and loyalty. Customer respect is a premise for account growth. Where there is no respect, there is no growth.

Ethics attract not only customers but employees as well. Productive, hard-working, honest employees are drawn to ethical leadership. An employee with pride in the company he works for is more likely to do an excellent job.

Suppliers are also comforted by having reputable companies for customers. They are proud of those they attract and retain. And let's not forget shareholders who feel proud holding shares in admirable companies. Not many would brag about holdings in companies indicted for tax fraud or misleading advertising — even if the companies generate high rates of return.

If ethics are so attractive, why don't we hear more about them? The answer is that there is a presumption of their existence. Stakeholders quietly assume ethics widely exist and are not considered a competitive advantage. Competition hasn't chosen to make ethics a marketplace issue — yet. This may not continue.

More and more, customers are gravitating toward companies with sustained corporate respect. And codes of ethics are critical for this respect. Ethics are renewed through the drafting of leadership plans that address customer values in an ethical manner. Our first case is Edinburgh Drugs Inc.

Edinburgh Drugs Inc. manufactures pharmaceutical products under the leadership of David Edinburgh. Boasting worldwide markets, David believes Edinburgh's corporate image is a key business success factor. Customers trust pharmaceuticals manufactured by the company. Shareholders trust the company to ensure its products are safe.

David believes well-defined and clearly communicated codes of ethics, followed by employees, are the foundation of trust. He personally signs each employee copy, encouraging them to live the code inscribed in Figure 94.11.

Critics argue Edinburgh has a code of ethics because of the industry it belongs to. Not so. More relevant here is customer expectation of trust. The marketplace expects and demands ethical suppliers regardless of industry.

Leaders need to encourage employees to truly adhere to ethical codes. For this to happen, employees must believe the code is their code. Living the contents of the code must take place daily and adherence questions must become part of annual employee performance evaluations. Employees should be rewarded for compliance, while noncomplying employees need to be given rehabilitation plans.

Goal conflict may arise between short-term profitability and the code of ethics. Testing pharmaceuticals 20 percent longer than required by law consumes profit at Edinburgh Drugs. Many will argue against spending funds beyond legal requirements. Edinburgh believes the extra cost creates greater public comfort — a competitive advantage. Consumers buy Edinburgh products knowing they are tested longer and more rigorously than any competitor. Although this particular ethic is not required for

Edinburgh Drugs
Summary Code of Ethics

1. Each employee will complete his or her daily tasks in the highest possible professional manner.
2. All advertising, written, video, or audio must be prepared truthfully and without exaggeration of pharmaceutical testing — false hope never suggested.
3. Packaging instructions shall list every warning identified during testing.
4. Pharmaceuticals, in the development stage, shall be tested 20 percent longer and more rigorously than required by existing drug laws.
5. Employees shall not hold themselves to have greater than actual skills.
6. Edinburgh Drugs' business affairs remain confidential, not discussed outside business hours.
7. Employees comply with all patent and drug laws.
8. Employees contribute generously to the community, whether with time or funds.

Figure 94.11

other industries, it illustrates the struggle between long- and short-term profit considerations. Paul's Hobby Shops refers to its code of ethics as customer policy.

> Customer policy was revised by Beverly Long, leader of customer satis-faction, shortly after she assumed the role. Beverly, by persuading her peers to adopt the new code in Figure 95.11, assured customers of consistent treatment.

Paul's customer policy is a process improvement suggested by Jason Blaine. Beverly implements it across store lines, and then Jill Babcock uses it to reinforce core competence behavior. Everyone benefits from the code when the company meets customer values.

Paul's Hobby Shops
Customer Policy

1. Prices guaranteed to be $1 less than competitors.
2. Money is refunded at any time if hobby kit is unsatisfactory.
3. Every customer is greeted in a courteous and helpful manner.
4. If we don't have the kit you want, our staff will tell you where you can buy it.
5. We invite helpful customer suggestions, which may be desposited in suggestion boxes located in each store.

Figure 95.11

Capolano Golf Accessories Ltd. offers another example of commercial ethics.

Jerry Spritz is chief executive officer of Capolano Golf Accessories Ltd., a manufacturer of balls, gloves, clubs, tees, and other accessories, with sales approaching $78 million. A successful company, Capolano takes pride in its manufacturing quality.

Enjoying steady growth during its 30 years in business, Capolano earned approximately 10 percent profit after income tax, for every year except one — the year of quality problems with golf balls. Eight years ago, Jerry began receiving complaints that golf balls were disintegrating into powder. By season end, defective balls approached 10 percent of production, causing panic in senior leaders. The Capolano name became the joke of the fairways.

In September, Jerry engaged a research and manufacturing team to solve the problem. Early indications suggested defective supplier materials together with poor adhesive mix were to blame. The poor image of the balls caused all Capolano product sales to decline. The research team spent $1.8 million changing manufacturing processes and procurement standards to prevent reoccurrence. Jerry then rebuilt his competitive edge.

Without a second thought, he ordered his management team to prepare advertising and letters to golf clubs informing them of Capolano's new quality policy, outlined in Figure 96.11. All communication apologized for inconvenience created by defective raw materials and manufacturing processes.

Capolano Golf Accessories
Quality Code

Capolano Golf Accessories Ltd. will:
1. Provide two new balls for each defective old one, regardless of condition;
2. Buy any future dissatisfied customers a competitor's ball of their choice if not 100% satisfied with Capolano's new product; and
3. Offer all those who have been inconvenienced a 10 percent discount on the purchase of any other Capolano product.

Figure 96.11

Jerry's code is designed to overcompensate inconvenienced customers. By offering two balls for each defective one, customers perceive greater value. Then, guaranteeing the purchase of competitor balls if customers are not 100 percent satisfied is not only good ethical practice, but brilliant marketing for customer satisfaction. Jerry probably could have gotten by with exchanging one new ball for each defective one. But that wasn't ethical to him, and not powerful enough for Capolano to regain its competitive advantage.

Whitmore Consulting also offers an example for us.

Harold Whitmore guarantees client satisfaction with Whitmore Consulting's advice. For projects that are in trouble, he will assign additional staff to save assignments from failure. It costs substantial time, but in most cases, the investment secures client satisfaction. But there was one case where Whitmore's policy didn't work.

Three years ago, Marian Blaze was leading an assignment to replace human resources at Sandford Chemical. The $1.2-million contract was to reorganize senior management and to search for three senior vice presidents. Searches identified five potential candidates. Marian supervised standard testing to ensure proposed candidates met the personality, educational, and intellectual requirements of Sandford. All went well until a month after the executives commenced work.

Police investigators arrived at Sandford to arrest a senior vice president for fraud. In a previous position, he had allegedly embezzled $1.3 million of company funds. Sandford Chemical believed Whitmore should have known about the allegations through reference checking. Legal threats against Whitmore followed. Harold stepped in to negotiate a resolution, offering a second search free of charge. He felt this offer was more than generous under the rules of professional conduct. Sandford was not satisfied with Harold's proposal. Threatening letters were exchanged during the following three months, leading to a lawsuit from Sandford Chemical. Eight months later, Whitmore Consulting refunded $750,000 of its original fee as full and complete settlement of the dispute.

Harold's code of ethics suggested a free second search to compensate for failure. Although commendable, the offer was not sufficient for the magnitude of the situation. Sandford lost time and money and suffered public disgrace by hiring an alleged criminal. Offering to conduct a free search with the same procedures was of little value to Sandford. In the end, legalities forced Whitmore to write a check to Sandford. With his experience, Harold should have sensed a more appropriate ethical response earlier in the dispute rather than fight, presumably on principle. Perhaps then Whitmore could have maintained Sandford as a client.

Melrose Plumbing Inc. also has an ethics story.

Sam Carrin completed a plumbing renovation contract for Burrows Place, a high-rise apartment building. Contract obligations called for installing new plumbing in four apartments, at a cost of $28,000.

When soldering new copper piping between walls, Sam's crew didn't notice one of their torches dangerously close to dry 20-year-old studding. The crew went to lunch and when they returned, they found the apartment ablaze. Emergency fire crews successfully contained the fire to one apartment area, limiting damage to $47,000.

Bill Melrose wasted no time. That afternoon, he engaged a construction company to estimate and plan rebuilding the apartment. He offered a 10 percent premium to have the job start the next morning. With construction successfully negotiated, Bill met with the building owner and tenant with restoration plans. He laid out steps for restoration at his expense and guaranteed the work would be completed before the weekend. Owner and tenant didn't know what shocked them more, the fire damage or the swiftness of Bill's restitution.

Bill didn't wait for complaints and legal letters. His ethics demanded that he eliminate his customer's anxiety immediately. By treating owner and tenant loss as his own, Bill acted quickly and in good faith to repair damage caused by the carelessness of his work crew. Ethics sustained his reputation and may have guaranteed future plumbing business from the owner of Burrows Place.

BITE 50: LEAD WITH SPIRIT

Spirit, as an element of leadership, plays two important roles at once. It is the source of the vision, the desire, and the belief that drive a leader to follow his dreams. In short, spirit is what separates a leader from a follower. But more than that, leadership spirit is the confidence and strength that leaders experience when they apply manageable bites with patience, consistency, discipline, and ethics, the four pillars of leadership spirit shown in Figure 97.11. Before delving into the heart of leadership spirit, let's examine these pillars.

Patience is the lifeblood of manageable bites. Patience allows time for logic and objectivity. Implementing revenue and profit improvement goals demands patience. Calculating risk of decisions demands patience. Managing demands patience. No other personal trait is more pervasive among successful leaders. Without patience, a person is anxious, prone to costly and hasty decisions. Without patience, luck becomes the leadership style, and it's just a matter of time before it runs out.

Personal Pillars Supporting the Spirit of Successful Leaders

Figure 97.11

Discipline is the second pillar for successful leadership spirit. Unfortunately, it is the one most often forgotten. Everyone says they have it but few demonstrate it by their actions. Discipline is absolutely crucial for the successful application of manageable bites. Without it, occasional successes may occur, but continued and consistent success will not. As building blocks, each bite depends upon the others in the construction of sound leadership processes. Only disciplined application of all bites yields the desired results.

Leaders who have discipline also know the importance of consistency. Leading one successful year's business activity requires discipline, but leading every year successfully — the goal of any good leader — demands consistency.

Last but certainly not least is ethics. As discussed, ethical behavior is critical to cultivating customer and employee respect. Ethical leaders reap their rewards in the form of esteem, reputation, trust, and, as a result, sustainable business success. Spirit, then, is the culmination of leadership in manageable bites. Trusting that they are on the proven road to success, and supported by the patience, discipline, consistency, and ethics to stay on it, leaders have the confidence to bring about their success. But, as mentioned, true leaders have a spirit that goes beyond this formula. They have something inside themselves that will not be silenced.

When leaders embark upon change, they are alone. Followers tend to resist change because they are comfortable with what they know and afraid of what they don't know. Leaders face enormous challenges just trying to convince others that change is necessary. They then have to align resources to implement the change and manage it through to completion. They are salmon swimming upstream and they always face a setback of some magnitude along the way. Yet, successful leaders swim on — often against all odds — often alone. So there is something quite magnificent about leadership spirit that can manifest itself as Herculean behavior.

Spirit requires belief both in yourself and in the dreams you hold. It is the passion to visualize those dreams. It's the conviction to convince others that those dreams are worth fighting for. It's the intense belief that giving up is far worse a fate than carrying on, no matter what obstacle stands in the way. Spirit is excitement for the vision when others are cynical. It's optimism when others are pessimistic. As a leader, you must have the will and energy to persevere, the courage to get up every time you're knocked down, and the imagination to find ways around every obstacle. And, when you've gotten around those obstacles, you must have an insatiable appetite for new challenges. You must have the strength to motivate, console, and coach those who follow, and the wisdom and generosity to give them all the credit for success. This is the heart of leadership spirit.

If you have it, the world is yours. With it, you'll find the patience, the discipline, the consistency, and the ethics to execute manageable bites, the proven path to business success. As you face the continual challenges and setbacks of business leadership, remember the proverb, "The oxen are slow, but the earth is patient." This is *50 Steps to Business Success: Entrepreneurial Leadership in Manageable Bites*.

Appendix:
Manageable Bites Cases